Ireland's Exiled Children

Ireland's Exiled Children

America and the Easter Rising

ROBERT SCHMUHL

OXFORD
UNIVERSITY PRESS

OXFORD
UNIVERSITY PRESS

Oxford University Press is a department of the University of Oxford. It furthers
the University's objective of excellence in research, scholarship, and education
by publishing worldwide. Oxford is a registered trade mark of Oxford University
Press in the UK and certain other countries.

Published in the United States of America by Oxford University Press
198 Madison Avenue, New York, NY 10016, United States of America.

Library of Congress Cataloging-in-Publication Data
Schmuhl, Robert, author.
Ireland's exiled children : America and the easter rising / Robert Schmuhl.
pages cm
Includes bibliographical references and index.
ISBN 978–0–19–022428–8
1. Ireland—History—Easter Rising, 1916. 2. Exiles—United States—History—20th
century. 3. United States—Relations—Ireland. 4. Ireland—Relations—United States.
5. Irish question. I. Title.
DA962.S36 2016
941.5082'1—dc23
2015032224

3 5 7 9 8 6 4 2
Printed by Sheridan, USA

For Judy,
who never could have predicted how
history would determine our future

Contents

Note on the Text

The rendering of names throughout this book follows a specific style: For the seven signatories of the Proclamation, the spelling reflects how they actually signed the document. "P. H. Pearse" appears that way rather than Pádraig Pearse or Pádraig Anraí Mac Piarais, and "Sean Mac Diarmada" is written as he wanted it instead of Sean MacDermott. Elsewhere, I try to use the most common or popularly accepted spelling of a name. For example, Seán T. O'Kelly, a close associate of de Valera and his predecessor as president of Ireland, is mentioned in place of Seán T. Ó Ceallaigh. Direct quotations, however, reproduce how a name appears in the quotation cited.

Easter Rising Chronology, American Involvement, and Aftermath

1842   *September 3*—John Devoy is born near Kill, County Kildare, Ireland.

1856   *December 28*—(Thomas) Woodrow Wilson is born in Staunton, VA. After an academic career, including eight years as president of Princeton University, he's elected governor of New Jersey before winning two terms as U.S. president—in 1912 and 1916.

1858   *March 17*—The Irish Revolutionary Brotherhood (later called the Irish Republican Brotherhood or IRB) is founded in Dublin by James Stephens, and this secret organization is dedicated to establishing an independent republic in Ireland. A likeminded American organization, the Fenian Brotherhood, is founded in New York by John O'Mahony shortly thereafter.

1866   *February 22*—Devoy is arrested by British authorities in Dublin for his involvement in the Fenian cause and remains in prison until he's exiled to America early in 1871.

1867   *June 20*—Clan na Gael, a secret revolutionary organization based in America and with objectives similar to the Fenian Brotherhood, is founded in New York City by Jerome J. Collins.

1871   *January 19*—Devoy arrives in New York after being exiled to America following incarceration in England for his involvement in Fenian activities.

1882   *October 14*—Éamon de Valera is born in New York City, the only child of Juan Vivion de Valera and Catherine Coll.

1883   *May 15*—Devoy becomes a naturalized U.S. citizen. (On July 7, 1924, he applies for his first American passport to "visit relatives" in the Irish Free State.)

1900   *July*—At an Atlantic City, N.J., convention, the Clan na Gael reunites following more than a decade of division and feuding. Devoy is elected as secretary of the reorganized brotherhood.

1901   *December 4*—United Irish League of America, U.S. arm of the Irish Parliamentary Party, is formed in New York.

1902–1903 *September to January*—James Connolly conducts a U.S. speaking tour for the Socialist Labor Party of America. He returns to the United States in September 1903 and remains active on behalf of workers before returning to Ireland on July 26, 1910.

1903   *September 19*—First issue of the weekly newspaper *The Gaelic American* is published in New York City, with Devoy as editor and Thomas Clarke as assistant editor.

1905   *November 2*—Clarke becomes a naturalized U.S. citizen following his second immigration to America. (He had previously lived in the States during a portion of the 1880s.) He returns to Ireland in 1907 to become actively involved in the work of the IRB.

1905   *November 28*—Sinn Féin, with its objective of independence from Great Britain for all of Ireland, is founded in Dublin by Irish nationalist Arthur Griffith.

1912   *September 23*—Seán Mac Diarmada serves as the IRB delegate to the Clan na Gael convention in Atlantic City, N.J., and stays in America into November.

1913   *January 13*—The Ulster Volunteer Force is established by the Ulster Unionist Council.

1913   *November 19*—The Irish Citizen Army is founded by Connolly.

1913   *November 25*—The Irish Volunteers are founded. In September 1914, the Redmondite National Volunteers (an estimated 150,000) leave the Irish Volunteers. Approximately 10,000 continue as Irish Volunteers and serve under Eoin MacNeill.

1914   *February 18 until May 7*—P. H. Pearse visits America to raise funds for his Dublin school, St. Enda's, using revolutionary rhetoric to appeal to Irish-American donors.

1914   *April 2*—A women's auxiliary volunteer force, Cumann na mBan, is established in Dublin.

1914   *July 20*—Roger Casement arrives in New York City in search of financial assistance for the Irish Volunteers to participate in a rebellion in Ireland. On October 15, 1914, with support from U.S. funds, he leaves for Germany in the hope of gaining arms and raising an "Irish Brigade" of captured prisoners. He spends eighteen months in Germany before returning to Ireland in a submarine just prior to the Rising and is captured on April 21, 1916, near Tralee.

1914   *July 21–24*—The Buckingham Palace Conference on Ireland, called by King George V, concludes without agreement between Irish nationalists and unionists over home rule for Ireland.

1914   *July 26*—The delivery of rifles at Howth for Irish Volunteers leads to the killing of four civilians and injuries to over three dozen people by the British military at Bachelors Walk, Dublin.

1914   *August 4*—Great Britain declares war on Germany.

1914   *August 8*—The Defence of the Realm Act (DORA) passes the House of Commons without debate, establishing executive authority to suppress criticism of the government in wartime.

1914   *September 9*—At a meeting of IRB leaders and other physical-force separatists, the decision is made to mount an uprising while Great Britain is engaged in the Great War in Europe.

1915   *May 7*—The RMS *Lusitania* is attacked and sunk by a German U-boat off the southern coast of Ireland, killing 1,198, including 128 Americans.

1915   *August 1*—Pearse delivers an inspirational funeral oration for Jeremiah O'Donovan Rossa at Glasnevin Cemetery in Dublin. Rossa died in New York on June 29, 1915.

1915   *August 23*—Joseph Mary Plunkett, director of military operations for the IRB, arrives in New York to talk with Devoy about the plans for the Easter Rising. Plunkett is the last of the Rising leaders and Proclamation signatories to visit the United States.

1916   *January 19–22*—Connolly, the leader of the Irish Citizen Army, meets in secret with the IRB Military Council, which was formed the previous May. Connolly and the council decide to stage a rising no later than on Easter 1916.

1916   *March 4*—The first Irish Race Convention begins in New York City, with over two thousand delegates attending. A new organization, the Friends of Irish Freedom (FOIF), is created during the convention.

1916   *April 24*—The Easter Rising begins and the General Post Office (GPO) in Dublin is occupied. The GPO becomes the rebels' headquarters, and Pearse reads the Proclamation of the Provisional Government of the Irish Republic there.

1916 *April 25*—Martial law is declared in Dublin, and it continues until November 4, 1916.

1916 *April 29*—Pearse orders unconditional surrender by the rebels, leading to mass arrests of the Rising's participants and others.

1916 *May 3*—Pearse, Clarke, and Thomas MacDonagh—all signatories of the Proclamation and Rising leaders—are executed by firing squad at Kilmainham Jail. Eleven more executions take place at Kilmainham, before concluding on May 12.

1916 *May 7*—The *New York Times Sunday Magazine* features Joyce Kilmer's article, "Poets March in the Van of Irish Revolt," while the executions continue to take place in Dublin.

1916 *June 1*—General Sir John Maxwell, commander-in-chief of the British military forces in Ireland after the Rising, establishes a Press Censor's office in Dublin, and on June 5 a detailed directive circulates among editors of Irish newspapers that warns against publication of articles from U.S. newspapers or letters from the United States.

1916 *June 28*—A memorial poetry reading takes place in New York City's Central Park. Called a "Tribute of American Poets to the Poet Patriots of Ireland," the event draws approximately two hundred attendees.

1916 *August 3*—Casement is hanged at Pentonville Prison in London, following his June trial in the Old Bailey for treason and the rejection of his appeal in July.

1916 *August 20*—Kilmer publishes a lengthy interview with a participant in the Rising ("Irish Girl Rebel Tells of Dublin Fighting") that appears in the *New York Times Sunday Magazine*, and the article is subsequently reprinted in Ireland in violation of the Press Censor's orders.

1916 *November 7*—Wilson is re-elected president of the United States by defeating former Supreme Court Justice Charles Evans Hughes by a margin of 49.2 percent to 46.1 percent. (Wilson didn't receive the majority of the popular vote either time he sought the White House.)

1916 *December 7*—David Lloyd George replaces Herbert Henry Asquith as prime minister of the British government.

1917   *April 6*—The U.S. Congress formally declares war on Germany four
        days after President Wilson requests the declaration.

1918   *January 8*—Wilson delivers his "Fourteen Points" speech to a joint ses-
        sion of Congress, proposing an "association of nations ... for the
        purpose of affording mutual guarantees of political independence
        and territorial integrity to great and small states alike."

1918   *July 30*—Sergeant Joyce Kilmer is killed while serving in the intelli-
        gence unit of the U.S. 69th Infantry Regiment, the Fighting Irish,
        near the French village Seringes-et-Nesles.

1918   *November 11*—The Armistice of World War I is signed in France.

1918   *December 13*—Wilson arrives in Europe for the Paris Peace Conference,
        which formally opens on January 18, 1919, and continues through
        June—with the signing of the Treaty of Versailles on June 28. The
        first incumbent U.S. president to visit Europe, Wilson returns to
        New York on July 8, 1919.

1919   *January 21*—Dáil Éireann, the parliamentary assembly formed on
        behalf of a separate and independent Ireland, is established in Dublin
        by Sinn Féin representatives who refuse to serve in Westminster. On
        September 12, 1919, the British government declares Dáil Éireann a
        dangerous association and illegal organization, forcing Dáil mem-
        bers to meet in secret.

1919   *June 11*—Éamon de Valera, who was elected president of Dáil Eireann
        on April 1, arrives in New York as a stowaway, seeking U.S. support
        for the Republic of Ireland and financial support for Irish indepen-
        dence. He tours the United States until December 10, 1920, on his
        campaign, arriving back in Dublin on December 23.

1919   *June 28*—The Treaty of Versailles is formally signed in France, ending
        the state of war between Germany and the Allied Powers.

1919   *October 2*—Wilson suffers a crippling stroke after becoming ill dur-
        ing a hectic cross-country trip by railroad to seek public support
        for the approval of the Treaty and for formation of the League of
        Nations.

1919   *November 19*—The U.S. Senate rejects the Treaty of Versailles when it
        is brought up for a vote.

1920   *January 17*—De Valera begins the promotion of a bond drive in the
        United States to create an Irish republic.

1920 *February 6*—De Valera causes controversy within Irish America over an interview he granted to the *Westminster Gazette*, suggesting Ireland's dependence on Britain.

1920 *March 19*—The Senate fails for a second time to ratify the Treaty of Versailles, ending Wilson's dream of U.S. involvement in the League of Nations, which he had championed.

1920 *October 24*—As feuding between factions of Irish America and de Valera continues, Devoy receives a letter saying that Clan na Gael is no longer affiliated with the Irish Republican Brotherhood, breaking the long-established ties between the two secretive, physical-force organizations.

1920 *November 16*—De Valera announces the establishment of the American Association for the Recognition of the Irish Republic (AARIR) in Washington, D.C. The AARIR is intended to compete with the Friends of Irish Freedom (FOIF), exacerbating the U.S. "civil war" among Irish Americans.

1920 *November 18 and 19*—The American Commission on Conditions in Ireland holds its first hearings in Washington, D.C. Ultimately, this blue-ribbon commission releases an extensive report detailing political and social problems of concern to the U.S. people.

1920 *December 16*—The American Committee for Relief in Ireland is established in New York City and starts raising contributions for humanitarian assistance.

1921 *April 18–20*—The de Valera–backed AARIR holds its first convention in Chicago.

1921 *August 26*—De Valera wins election to the newly created position of president of the Irish Republic in the Dáil and serves until January 9, 1922. From April 1, 1919, until August 26, 1921, his title was President of Dáil Éireann.

1921 *October 15*—The second drive to sell bonds that will help Ireland begins in the United States.

1922 *December 6*—The Irish Free State is declared, bringing an end to the post–Easter Rising struggle for independence from Britain.

1923 *September 10*—The Irish Free State is admitted to the League of Nations.

1924 *February 3*—Woodrow Wilson dies in Washington, D.C.

1924 *July 26*—Devoy arrives in Ireland for a six-week visit as (in the words of W. T. Cosgrave, the first president of the Executive Council of the Irish Free State) "the guest of the State" to recognize a long life "spent in the country's service."

1928 *September 29*—Devoy dies in Atlantic City, N.J., at age 86, and on June 16, 1929, following a state funeral in Ireland, he is buried in the Patriots Plot of Glasnevin Cemetery in Dublin. Devoy's memoir, *Recollections of an Irish Rebel*, is also published in 1929.

1932 *March 9*—Éamon de Valera becomes the second president of the Executive Council, and in 1937, the position's title is changed to the Taoiseach. He serves as the head of the Irish government from 1932 to 1948, 1951 to 1954, and 1957 to 1959. From June 25, 1959, until June 24, 1973, he is head of state as president of Ireland. He dies on August 29, 1975, six weeks before his 93rd birthday.

Prologue

IN HER SONNET "THE NEW Colossus," Emma Lazarus gives voice to the "mighty woman with a torch" in New York Harbor and formally named "Liberty Enlightening the World." Simultaneously commanding and comforting, the statue's declarations extend a "world-wide welcome" to those from distant shores seeking a new life in the unnamed land at the end of their voyage:

> "Keep, ancient lands, your storied pomp!" cries she
> With silent lips. "Give me your tired, your poor,
> Your huddled masses yearning to breathe free,
> The wretched refuse of your teeming shore.
> Send these, the homeless, tempest-tost to me,
> I lift my lamp beside the golden door!"[1]

From the misery of the Great Hunger in the middle of the nineteenth century until Lazarus composed her poem in 1883, "huddled masses" from Ireland exceeded 2 million immigrants, and by 1916 the number jumped to over 3.5 million. Extrapolating from the 1910 U.S. census, with the waves of prior immigration and then the settling down to raise often-sizable families, an estimated one-fifth of the total U.S. population of nearly 92 million possessed Irish heritage to one degree or another.[2] Lazarus never calls her subject by her more popular title, the Statue of Liberty. Instead the poet christens the woman as "Mother of Exiles," a name that conveys special meaning for Irish Americans. The "Mother of Exiles" symbolized for these "poor banished children of Eve" (in the phrase of the Catholic prayer) and their heirs hope for a future much different from the past.

The Proclamation announcing armed insurrection to attain "freedom" and "the Irish Republic," which was read and circulated on Easter Monday (April 24, 1916), the first day of the Rising, mentions only one country other than Ireland. The rebels battling the British to establish their own "Sovereign Independent State" acknowledged the Ireland they envisioned was "supported by her exiled children in America." Nurtured by values the "Mother of Exiles"

1

represented, the "exiled children" received explicit recognition for their role in a revolutionary cause across the Atlantic.

Early news reports about the Rising in the United States drew parallels to American history, and these became recurring reference points for the public. Dublin combat was likened to the Boston Tea Party or the first skirmishes at Lexington and Concord, which began the Revolutionary War. P. H. Pearse, president of the "Provisional Government," was portrayed as George Washington, and Roger Casement, with all his international maneuvering on behalf of Irish independence, was compared first to Benjamin Franklin, and later to the executed abolitionist John Brown. To devout republicans, Irish Parliamentary Party leader John Redmond was viewed as a traitor: the Benedict Arnold of the moment. Moving beyond personal references, some observers wondered whether Easter Monday would in time become Ireland's Fourth of July.

As with the American Revolution, independence from Great Britain in Ireland took several years to achieve, required bloody warfare, and tested people's allegiances. The Fourth of July and the Rising mark moments of no return, historical tipping points that created new realities, as well as defining departures from the past. In his poem "Easter, 1916," W. B. Yeats writes "All changed, changed utterly." Yeats wrote "Easter, 1916" immediately following the Rising and the subsequent executions. Though he divined much of the significance of what had just happened, Yeats and many of his contemporaries could not realize then what we now understand in retrospect: that to a large extent, the roots of the Rising grew in U.S. soil and that the American reaction proved critical to determining its consequences.

While many echoes of America's founding can be heard in 1916 Ireland, an event sixty years after 1776 also has historical resonance. Like the Rising, the Battle of the Alamo was a decisive military defeat that subsequently metamorphosed into the inspiration for future fighting and eventual victory. In 1836 and later, the rallying cry of "Remember the Alamo" echoed along the U.S.-Mexico border, and in no time the Alamo was well known for its nickname: "the Cradle of Texas Liberty." For the Irish, the General Post Office has the same totemic value as the birthplace of the modern movement for independence. As time passed, a monument to loss became the cornerstone of memory. Remembering the GPO is akin to remembering the Alamo.

The burden of both history and remembrance influenced the lives of the "exiled children." For many Irish in America, the famine years and their dislocating consequences made them hungry for all the freedoms—of association, religion, activity, speech, press—enjoyed by citizens in the New World. Indeed, John Mitchel, an Irish journalist and nationalist who advocated sedition and was convicted of treason felony in 1848, escaped in 1853 from incarceration in what is now Tasmania and came to the United States. Upon arrival, at a banquet in New York City that was given in his honor, he concluded his speech by saying that he was "a professed revolutionist now, an adventurer, a seditious propagandist. I mean to make use of the freedom guaranteed to me as a citizen or inchoate citizen of America, to help and to stimulate the movement of the European democracy, and especially of Irish independence." For his fellow revolutionary refugees, "America shall be to them the very standing ground prayed for by Archimedes, whereon they may plant a lever that shall move the world."[3] The Land of Liberty was not only a refuge but also a place that could serve as a model for ending an empire's rule—the same empire from which it had freed itself.

Although the Proclamation's statement of support from the "exiled children in America" is somewhat vague, the United States functioned as more than a distant historical model. Many members of the American Irish community nursed grudges and grievances, if not ancient enmities, against the British, plotting their overthrow among themselves and contributing money to advance the cause of Irish independence. Indeed, the financial resources that came from America, especially as a result of John Devoy's fundraising, paid the costs of the arms and matériel used by the rebels.

In *The Irish Issue in Its American Aspect* (1917), Shane Leslie, the writer and diplomat from a prominent Anglo-Irish family (as well as Winston Churchill's first cousin), points out that some Irish Americans favored Germany during the early years of World War I for the simple reason that "they would have declared themselves pro-Hell had they sufficient proof that the devil was anti-British."[4] The European war created confusion in the minds of the American Irish, with many reluctant to take sides. Others, most notably Devoy and some of his colleagues in Clan na Gael, viewed an alliance with the Germans as beneficial to the Irish cause. As Leslie, a constitutional home-rule nationalist, insightfully notes, Roger Casement, the knighted British foreign service officer who became a fervent Irish nationalist and toured the United States to raise money for the looming fight, "went into Germany [in 1914] as the ambassador of the Irish-American extremists. From Ireland he carried no commission."[5]

Despite involvement to varying degrees from relatives and friends thousands of miles away, it would stretch historical accuracy to paint 1916 too brightly in red, white, and blue. The Easter Rising was planned and executed in Ireland, with supporting assistance from some Irish Americans and (though a key shipment of guns and ammunition was, ultimately, scuttled) the German government. Explaining the prelude to mounting the insurrection, the historian Kevin B. Nowlan notes that "the real decisions were made in Dublin and not in New York or Berlin."[6] As Nowlan also notes, "confidential emissaries" in America who were helping make the Rising a reality worked in secret. A handful of people knew details of the actual plot, though the objective of Irish independence enjoyed approval (at different levels of intensity) within the United States. Fiery Fenian-style republicanism received regular stoking in the open-air environment of free speech that American rights guaranteed, though more mainstream supporters of home rule and the Irish Parliamentary Party favored a methodical approach over armed conflict. Others among the American Irish (usually, those with close relatives across the Atlantic) were less inclined to make a definite commitment to any organization with an avowed agenda, but saw merit in a greater degree of freedom for Ireland.

Regardless of someone's location on this broad spectrum of opinion, the Rising and its aftermath forced Irish Americans (and Americans in general) to think about Ireland and its future in new ways. Nonetheless, those involved from a distance couldn't have predicted the many turns the events would take or how their consequences would shape the years ahead. John Reed called his classic reportage on the Russian Revolution *Ten Days That Shook the World* (1919). The title of Charles Duff's 1966 account of the Rising is shorter in time and smaller in scope, yet an echo of Reed in its significance: *Six Days to Shake an Empire*. Though the United Kingdom's declaration of war in 1914 helped prevent a civil war between Irish nationalists and unionists,[7] republicans two years later sought to use the cover of British wartime preoccupation to strike for independence. Internal insurrection amid the throes of the Great War was not welcomed, and Whitehall responded as a wounded lion might. In *Ireland*

and the Great War, Keith Jeffery puts the Rising in the context of contemporary events:

> The Battle of Verdun was raging on the Western Front. On the day the Easter Rising began there was a Zeppelin raid on East Anglia and five days later General [Charles Vere Ferrers] Townshend surrendered at Kut in Mesopotamia where 9,000 British and Indian troops were taken prisoner. The pressures of wartime policymaking in general undoubtedly contributed to the somewhat haphazard approach to Irish matters taken by the government.[8]

During the first battles of the Rising, an estimated one thousand rebels took on a British force of about four hundred to occupy Dublin's General Post Office and other locations around the city. Intense fighting, complete with building-leveling carnage, continued throughout the week, as rebel strength grew to sixteen hundred or so. Stories circulated widely in city streets that large numbers of Irish Americans (as well as Germans) had landed in Ireland, spoiling for combat on the republican side. However, according to James Stephens's *The Insurrection in Dublin*, published a few months after the revolt and executions, the stories were just rumors. The British rushed as many as twenty thousand troops and advanced equipment to Dublin to quell the rebellion. After Pearse surrendered on Saturday and the smoke cleared, some 450 people were dead, including 254 civilians, 116 military personnel, 64 rebels, and 16 police officers. Over 2,600 others suffered injuries, and the cost in property damage, especially in downtown Dublin, was estimated to be over £2.5 million (or almost $12 million at the time). That amounts to nearly £165,000,000 (or $255,000,000) in today's currency, according to one calculation by an economist.[9]

The Irish intellectual and essayist Conor Cruise O'Brien once observed that the Rising "seemed to almost everybody except the participants a bolt from the blue."[10] While the Irish struggled to make sense of what happened, Americans (with or without Irish blood) were also perplexed, wondering whether a new front—within a combatant's borders—was opening up in the European war. Though many initial judgments on both sides of the Atlantic accused the rebels of undertaking a foolhardy adventure that was costly in terms of casualties and the destruction of property, public thinking about the

Rising was unsettled. References to what happened exhausted the thesauruses of journalists at U.S. newspapers, leading to extensive coverage of a "revolt," "rebellion," "rising," "uprising," "insurrection," "outbreak," "filibuster," "disturbance," or "trouble" (in the singular). For those outside Ireland, especially those with relatives back in Dublin, events of consequence had definitely occurred; however, their precise meaning was difficult to gauge. Wartime censorship of both news accounts and letters coming from Ireland compounded the problem of arriving at a clear picture or comprehensive understanding, and charges of possible German involvement perturbed many.

Early on, British officials recognized the gravity of the insurrection and its potential to influence U.S. public opinion. On Wednesday of that Easter Week, Augustine Birrell, chief secretary for Ireland from 1907 until his resignation shortly after the Rising, told the House of Commons: "We were very anxious, indeed, during these last few days that news should not reach the neutral countries, and particularly our friends in America, which would be calculated to give them an entirely false impression as to the importance of what has taken place, important as that is." Birrell went on to explain that that was why news was temporarily being censored and filtered through the Press Bureau.[11] British censorship and worry over what Americans might think persisted long after the last shots were fired. The so-called Irish Question remained an evergreen topic in the pages of the U.S. press because of either newsworthy events or opinion pieces that challenged the status quo of British rule.

However, what most dramatically changed the public's perspective was the British retaliatory crackdown in Ireland. Between May 3 and May 12, 1916, a period of over a week, fourteen rebel leaders in Dublin's Kilmainham Jail were executed. In all, more than thirty-five hundred men and women either involved or suspected as sympathizers were arrested. Nearly two thousand people were summarily shipped to prisons or internment camps across the Irish Sea. The aftershocks spread out from Dublin to encompass much of the entire island.[12]

The period of reprisal made the British look cold-blooded and motivated by revenge rather than justice. To a certain extent, the British were caught off-guard twice: with the Rising itself and with the revulsion to their response to it. They were trying to put down (in the words of A. J. P. Taylor) "the only national rebellion which occurred anywhere at any time in the war."[13] An insurrection, even one mounted by a relatively small number, was perceived as an internal and incendiary imperial threat at a time when the projection of strength meant nearly as much as the exertion of military power.

At the time, brute force was standard operating procedure. Capital punishment served as a default response by U.K. military officials during World War I. The British executed 306 of their own soldiers for desertion or cowardice as the war ground on, many of whom were clearly suffering from shellshock (now known as posttraumatic stress disorder) or some other psychological maladies. That number included 28 Irishmen. (All 306 men were officially pardoned with the passage of the 2006 Armed Forces Act in 2006.[14])

Nonetheless, the reprisal reflected a tension in the British command. On the one hand, it wanted to project resolve and on the other hand encourage a perception of justice. In the court of public opinion, the latter was lost. By May 9, even moderate nationalist opinion in Ireland was against the policy of execution, and the *Freeman's Journal* noted that "sympathy" for the executed was already "being aroused ... where nothing but indignant condemnation of their criminal enterprise previously existed." The pro-British *Irish Independent* seems to have misread the public mood by publishing articles on May 10 and 12 that advocated additional executions.[15] Most subsequent assessments have emphasized the excessive nature of the British response. It was a response some have argued the Irish radicals consciously sought. In *The Age of Empire 1875–1914* (1987), Eric Hobsbawn observed that "support for the Irish insurrectionaries remained so narrow and shaky that their strategy for broadening it was essentially to court martyrdom by a foredoomed rebellion, whose suppression would win the people to their cause."[16]

The Rising did more than just create heroes and martyrs, though that proved significant. It also shifted the political ground, opening up perilous chasms for certain figures. John Redmond, the chief proponent of constitutional Irish nationalism in the House of Commons, was sent two separate messages from the United States on May 15, three days after the last executions in Dublin. Shane Leslie, who was living in the States at the time, wrote in a letter to Redmond: "The present wave of fury sweeping through Irish America originated with the executions and not with the rising. The rising only called out sympathy for you, except in a small circle. The executions enabled that circle to spread their ripple further than they had hoped or dreamed."[17] Michael J. Ryan, former president of the United Irish League of America and a strong supporter of Redmond's approach before the European war, dispatched a telegram, complete with bulletin-style capital letters, typo-graphical mistakes, and no punctuation:

> IRISH EXECUTION[s] HAVE ALIENATED EVERY
> AMERICAN FRIEND AND/CAUSED RESURGANCE
> OF ANCIENT ENMITIES[.] YOUR LIFE WORK/
> DESTROYED BY ENGLISH BRUTALITY[.] OPINION
> WIDESPREAD THAT PROMISE OR[f] HOME RULE
> WAS MOCKERY[.][18]

Redmond's objective of conciliation and a governmental path to home rule no longer gathered a following. By 1918, less than two years later, he was dead at the age of sixty-two. Among his last words to a priest at his bedside were: "Father, I am a broken-hearted man."[19]

Ryan's telegram signaled a sea change. In America, the conviction that the British had gone too far after the Rising was widespread, with much of the media attention devoted to Roger Casement. Fascination with "Sir Roger" framed U.S. press coverage of rebellious Ireland. From reports on April 25, describing his capture near Tralee after he arrived on a German submarine, until he was hanged for treason in London on August 3, a steady series of stories about Casement's previous adventures and his ensuing courtroom dramatics kept the Rising newsworthy and in the public's mind. That he had been returning to Ireland from Germany with the supposed objective of trying to halt the insurrection added a sense of mystery to his involve-ment. Casement's mental state was vigorously debated in several profiles—the *Washington Post* on June 4, for example, published "Madmen Make History: Sir Roger Casement Would Have Been Immortal If He Had Succeeded"—which raised serious concern that the British government's use of the death penalty constituted cruel and unusual punishment. Casement played on the attention he was getting in the United States. Following his sentencing, he delivered a detailed statement in his defense in which he thanked Americans for their "generous expressions of sympathy." "In that country," he continued, "as in my own, I am sure my motives are understood, for the achievement of their liberties has been an abiding inspiration to Irishmen and to all elsewhere rightly struggling to be free."[20]

America's ability to stir the imagination, especially for people enduring what they considered political repression, is a thematic refrain in contem-porary journalistic accounts of the Easter Rising. But it's elsewhere as well.

The British Library includes in its holdings a volume with the simple descriptive phrase "Irish Tracts" stamped on its spine. The more formal catalogue description reads "A collection of leaflets, pamphlets and miscellaneous matter relating to Irish history and politics, 1916–1921." One of the nine poems in the booklet *Songs of the Irish Republic* is called "Three Thousand Miles Away," which is the distance between Ireland and the U.S. mainland. The second stanza is a tribute to those who sacrificed their lives to achieve the liberty that America had already won:

> We'll sing of the great departed
> And the valleys where they lie,
> The brave, the noble-hearted
> Who showed men how to die;
> And every man, of every clan,
> We'll guard his memory,
> Who died in Ireland, fighting
> For Ireland's liberty.

Among the "Irish Tracts" is an eight-page pamphlet defending "The Authority of Dáil Éireann," which reprints a quotation from America's Declaration of Independence on its cover. The text makes several comparisons between the formation of the Continental Congress during the American Revolution and the establishment of the Dáil (in effect, the parliament) in 1919: "The American people were not unanimous in this declaration of their Republic. The majority made the national decision and none has said that that decision is not binding upon the whole American people. The majority of the Irish people have also this power to create an independent state—monarchy or republic, according to their will." The pamphlet goes on to argue "the establishment of the Irish Republic of 1916 was as binding an act upon the Nation as the America Declaration of Independence was upon the American people." The United States, and particularly the Declaration of Independence, which the Second Continental Congress unanimously passed, provided a historical model for the Irish to follow, and expressions of these efforts brought material and moral support from three thousand (or so) miles away.[21]

The Easter Rising serves as a textbook example of an event that deserves consideration beyond the immediate to its longer-term implications and effects. Indeed, even before the end of 1916, several authors on both sides of the Atlantic sought to provide comprehensive accounts with context, including

James Stephens in *The Insurrection in Dublin* and Maurice Joy in his edited volume, *The Irish Rebellion of 1916 and Its Martyrs: Erin's Tragic Easter*. Many other accounts and assessments appeared the following year.

The shift in American public opinion offers just one dimension to evaluate. Change in thinking also happened individual by individual. No less a figure than Michael Collins, who fought at the GPO and later served as president of the Irish Republican Brotherhood and chairman of the Provisional Government (among other posts) before being killed during the Irish Civil War, wrestled with the Rising's impact a few months after the combat and executions. In a letter written in early October 1916 from the Frongoch Internment Camp in Wales, Collins, who earlier toyed with immigrating to America, wrote that while he admired those who were involved and who "died nobly at the hands of the firing squads" he did not think the Rising week "was an appropriate time for the issue of memoranda couched in poetic phrases, nor of actions worked out in a similar fashion." "Looking at it from the inside (I was in the GPO) it had the air of a Greek tragedy about it, the illusion being more or less completed with the issue of the before-mentioned memoranda."[22] In Collins's view the Rising was "bungled terribly."[23] Yet in *The Path to Freedom*, a volume of his writings and speeches published shortly after his death in 1922, it was clear that passage of a few years had tempered his criticism of the Rising, which

> carried into the hearts of the people the flame which had been burning in those who had the vision to see the pit into which we were sinking deeper and deeper and who believed that a conflagration was necessary to reveal to their countrymen the road to national death upon which we were blindly treading. The banner of Ireland's freedom had been raised and was carried forward. During the Rising the leaders of Easter Week "declared a Republic." But not as a fact. We knew it was not a fact. It was a wonderful gesture—throwing down the gauntlet of defiance to the enemy, expressing to ourselves the complete freedom we aimed at, and for that reason was an inspiration to us.[24]

Collins wasn't alone in noting the ambiguity of the Rising. W. B. Yeats wrote in "Easter, 1916" with its famous lines, "All changed, changed utterly: / A terrible beauty is born." As noted earlier, Yeats composed his poem immediately after Easter Week—but he waited four years to publish it. Although the phrase "terrible beauty" is the most often invoked description of the Rising, during the past century less poetic ones summarize it as "a brilliant disaster," "a heroic fiasco," and even "the most successful failure in history."

Playwright George Bernard Shaw, who was born in Dublin but was a long-time resident of Britain, frequently commented on Irish affairs in New York (and London) periodicals during the tumultuous months of 1916. Even before the last executions on May 12, Shaw wrote a detailed letter to the *Daily News* in London, which the *New York Times* republished on May 11. His viewpoint is not in doubt, and he acknowledges how "American Gaels" reacted to his earlier opinions. Noting the inhumanity of shooting "in cold blood … prisoners of war," Shaw argues: "It is absolutely impossible to slaughter a man in this position without making him a martyr and a hero, even though the day before the rising he may have been only a minor poet." Shaw went on to argue that he was not a "Sinn Feiner" and had tried to discredit its efforts, but even he couldn't pretend to neutrality about what had happened in Dublin. "But I remain an Irishman and am bound to contradict any implication that I can regard as a traitor any Irishman taken in a fight for Irish independence against the British Government, which was a fair fight in everything except the enormous odds my countrymen had to face."[25]

More than a decade later, in the 1934 preface to *John Bull's Other Island*, Shaw looked back with an unblinking eye: "If all Ireland had risen at this gesture it would have been a serious matter for England, then up to her neck in the war against the Central Empires. But there was no response: the gesture was a complete failure."[26] Though relatively few Irish answered the call of revolution, the British—in Shaw's sage estimation—certainly did, going well beyond the realm of reason in reacting militarily to "the gesture." His earlier judgment does not change, and he even admits "Clan na Gael, which in America had steadfastly maintained that the constitutional movement was useless, as England would in the last resort repudiate the constitution and hold Ireland against the Irish by physical force … was justified."[27] The executions had been a catastrophic miscalculation. "Nothing more blindly savage, stupid, and terror-mad could have been devised by England's worst enemies."[28]

As with other participants and observers, Shaw recognized that the British reprisals proved more consequential than the initial actions of a relatively few rebels. In the United States, the Rising represented a major turning point, with growing numbers of Irish Americans and others supporting independence for Ireland moving decidedly away from the rocky, slow path toward home rule to a more decisive break from the British empire. Two days after the last executions in Dublin on May 12, some two thousand people gathered in Washington, D.C., to launch (in the words of the *Washington Post* on its front page for May 15) "what is expected to become a nation-wide movement in sympathy with the Irish revolutionists." The main speaker at this meeting, Jeremiah O'Leary, a prominent supporter of Irish independence and president of the anti-British American Truth Society, according to the report, "constantly drew similes between America's fight for liberty in 1776 and the Dublin uprising of April, 1916." At one point, O'Leary is quoted as saying, the "Dublin martyrs faced the firing squad with American principles in their hearts."[29]

As this book took shape, an insight J. J. Lee makes in his classic work, *Ireland 1912–1985: Politics and Society* kept coming to mind. Writing about the reaction to the Rising in Ireland and the relative lack of real-time sources for analysis, Lee notes that the "real historical challenge is to reconstruct reactions *in the light of the information actually available to the public at the time.* This is not as simple as it sounds. It is in fact extraordinarily difficult to reconstruct the public response."[30]

In America, by contrast, information of all kinds proved readily available and evaluating it helps "to reconstruct the public response." That is why throughout this study I focus on the actual documents and journalistic coverage directly related to the Rising and its aftermath. Contemporary commentary will help readers put primary sources in context and also (one hopes) help them to become more immersed in events of a century ago.

Surveying the entire territory brought into bold relief specific figures, all with strong ties to the United States, and all central characters in either the Rising itself or in responses to it—or both. That is why each chapter uses an individual to tell the larger story of what happened in each phase: the preparation, the fighting, and the aftermath. Thus, each chapter is principally a biographical essay, combining personal details and fitting them within the context of the Rising and the greater Irish-American connection. However, from time to time I stray from a tight focus on the central figure to take up related people or points. For instance, in the chapter involving Joyce Kilmer, which concentrates primarily on contemporary accounts of American reactions to the Rising, I give some attention to Kilmer's prose and poetry, as well as responses to it. As with the 1916 reflections of Cecil Spring Rice, Britain's ambassador to the United States, in the chapter about Woodrow Wilson, the point is to show what Americans were learning about the events in Ireland and how public opinion was being shaped after the Rising and the executions.

The stories of John Devoy and Éamon de Valera serve as bookends for this volume. Each lived a long life—Devoy to eighty-six and de Valera to nearly ninety-three—and each was animated by the dream of an independent Ireland. For Devoy, a naturalized American living in New York, the Rising, which he helped to plan and to fund, was the culmination of a half-century struggle to free the place of his birth from British rule. The Rising established de Valera, who was born in New York, as an Irish leader, one who somehow escaped execution to launch a political and governmental career that spanned nearly six decades. Devoy's life provides necessary background to describe the Fenian passion for freedom that fired so many Irish exiles in America from the mid-nineteenth century onward. In its way, de Valera's subsequent service to Ireland and his ties to the United States reflect the extended and continuing hold the Rising exerts. Though both were involved during Easter Week and afterward, Devoy and de Valera represent "before" and "after" figures whose singular lives illuminate the larger, transatlantic narrative.

The roles Kilmer and Wilson played in the uprising come between Devoy and de Valera, and they are critical in responding to it. A journalist and poet, Kilmer was quick to put into words for American readers what the rebels had done. By contrast, Wilson did his best to avoid committing to a stand on an international and domestic situation loaded with what he viewed as political dynamite. While Kilmer's reactions to the Rising left no doubt as to his sympathies, Wilson tried to keep his precise views within the walls of the White House, despite pressure from Congress and Irish-American organizations to make his position clear.

For Americans concerned about Ireland and its fate, the New World's revolutionary past and its own struggle to break from Britain provided a mental yardstick for comparison. That historical reality, though, also danced with the romance and mystique of a land across the Atlantic that still exercised a claim on people's imagination. Tellingly, one of the most popular songs in the United States during 1916 was recorded that summer and carried the title "Ireland Must Be Heaven, For My Mother Came from There."[31] The confluence of popular culture appeal and the public's fascination with the Rising was far more than coincidental. The "exiled children" and their descendants looked to an island many hungered to see free of British rule—and to the prospect of an independent Ireland they wanted to lend a hand in founding.

John Devoy
(Courtesy of the John Devoy Memorial Committee)

1

John Devoy: The Intrigue of Exile

WITH THE FIRST BATTLES OF insurrection waged that April 24 and the General Post Office (GPO) in downtown Dublin now occupied by rebel forces, P. H. Pearse stood under the portico of the GPO to tell passersby—and the world—the reasons for the earlier gunfire and combat. Reading a formal proclamation declaring "The Provisional Government of the Irish Republic," Pearse, the president of the just-named Republic, used present-tense verbs and bold language to make his case: "Ireland, through us, summons her children to her flag and strikes for her freedom." The second sentence he read that Easter Monday in 1916 notes that his kindred fighters, assembled from members of the Irish Republican Brotherhood, the Irish Volunteers, and the Irish Citizen Army, were "supported by her exiled children in America" and, somewhat more vaguely, "by gallant allies in Europe."

In the Proclamation, Ireland's "children" and the "exiled children in America" join forces as the Easter Rising begins. Aside from "the Irish nation," America is the only other country he specifically names. Great Britain, the ancient enemy of an independent Ireland, is dismissed as "an alien government" and "a foreign people and government" without more explicit identification.[1]

For Pearse and his followers, the journey to the GPO on April 24 depended on plotting and planning that had taken place in both Ireland and America over the course of several years. In the United States, John Devoy saw the Rising as his life's crowning achievement. Born in 1842 in County Kildare, Devoy was exiled by the British government to America in 1871. A member of the secretive Irish Republican Brotherhood (IRB) before he was twenty, he worked to recruit to the Republican side Irish soldiers serving in the British army, and in 1865 he helped IRB founder James Stephens escape from prison—before being arrested himself on February 22, 1866. At his trial a year later, he pleaded guilty to the charge of treason felony and was sentenced to imprisonment of fifteen years at hard labor. After nearly five years of incarceration, including the pre-trial period, he received amnesty, banishing him from the territory of Great Britain until the end of his sentence.

In the opinion of one commentator, Devoy kept himself on a war footing for over half a century, and his wait wasn't in vain.[2] As much as anyone, he embodied the American "exile" referred to in the Proclamation. Although Devoy became a naturalized U.S. citizen in 1883, for nearly six decades in his adopted country he never stopped dreaming about independence for Ireland. He headed up Clan na Gael (the American counterpart to the IRB and also a secret organization); raised money for republicanism (contributions from the United States proved critical in financing the Rising); and engaged in journalism (besides working on newspapers in New York and Chicago, he launched the *Irish Nation* in 1880 and *The Gaelic American,* a weekly newspaper based in New York City and foursquare republican in its viewpoint, in 1903). In short, Devoy kept freedom for Ireland the animating principle of his life. For the Rising, and though three thousand miles away, he was simultaneously planner, paymaster, and propagandist.

While Devoy played different yet intersecting roles, he also balanced his approach. The ideologue was also a pragmatist. The consummate insider who whispered conspiratorial schemes to other Clan members was also a well-known journalist and public speaker. The proud Irishman was an equally staunch defender of American ideals. Historical assessments of Devoy often compare him to Lenin for what he contributed to the cause of Irish independence, and someone once observed that "only the pen of Balzac could do him justice."[3] Just five feet six and solidly built like a fighter, his thick beard complemented his intense gaze.

Devoy built on a foundation earlier exiles and immigrants had established. Particularly during the famine years (1845–1852) and their aftermath, the numbers of the American Irish community swelled with remarkable speed. According to statistics compiled by the Commission on Emigration and Other Population Problems in Dublin, 740,216 Irish emigrants departed for America between 1851 and 1855, with a total of 989,834 through 1861. During the next decade (1861–1870), another 690,845 followed. In the seventy-year period between 1851 and 1921, some 3,794,852 people left Ireland for the United States—out of a total of 4,514,017 who emigrated from there. Counting second-generation Irish in America, more Irishmen and -women resided in the United States by 1900 than lived in Ireland.[4]

Many arrived carrying little more than a grudge for the British. For some, the great hunger produced even greater hatred—and a longing to see their native land as a miniature America, independent and free from England. In

1848, Henry Grattan Jr., a member of the House of Commons from County Meath, told a session of Parliament at Westminster about a conversation he had the year before at an Irish seaport with a man preparing to sail to the United States. In Grattan's telling, "I advised him to remain at home. 'No, Sir,' said he, 'I will go to the Land of Liberty.' 'But consider your sons' was my reply. 'Oh! They will come back,' was the response, *and when they do come back it will be with rifles on their shoulders.'*"[5]

The United States offered religious freedom, political maneuverability, and economic opportunity. It was also the place to plot and to fantasize about an Ireland that at some point might offer the same. In his 1882 book *The American Irish and Their Influence on Irish Politics*, Philip H. Bagenal provides an account of the significance that emigration had on the homeland, particularly following the Young Irelander Rebellion that took place in 1848, an "abortive insurrection" that shifted "the base of Irish revolution from Ireland to America." Bagenal observes that as many as a million and a half emigrants left the shores of Ireland. "Thus a new nation was formed, whose principal literature was hostile to England, whose heroes and martyrs were either political prisoners or executed felons, and whose every aspiration and hope was at variance with the established order of things in the land which they had left."[6]

The burgeoning community across the Atlantic could provide not just financial assistance to relatives and friends still living in Ireland but also religious and political inspiration. These exports, tangible and intangible, created a dynamic unlike any that had existed previously, one that influenced how the Irish on both sides of the ocean thought and acted. Sir William Harcourt, who served as Britain's Home Secretary from 1880 until 1885, openly complained and adopted the same word—*nation*—as Bagenal, "Now there is an Irish nation in the United States ... absolutely beyond our reach and yet within ten days sail of our shores. ..."[7] The Irish who endured the famine and immigrated to the United States discovered that they now enjoyed freedom to seek revenge, if they desired, and many were willing to contribute money from their new American jobs to the cause.[8]

Most of the Irish who came to the United States after the famine years stayed together in urban neighborhoods with their own Catholic churches, schools, hospitals, orphanages, clubs, and other institutions. The parish, the precinct, and the pub became native grounds to these immigrants, serving as refuges from religious and ethnic prejudice. Close association invigorated their sense of ancestral heritage and incubated schemes for achieving independence for Ireland. The Land of Liberty, as the United States was called during the nineteenth century, provided fertile soil for a transplanted variety of Irish nationalism to grow and flourish. For many Murphys, Kellys, and O'Briens, this nationalistic spirit became stronger in Chicago than it had been in Cork. In the opinion of Conor Cruise O'Brien, in his *States of Ireland*, "The beginnings of the Irish revolution—that is, the revolution of the Catholic Irish—are as much in America as in Ireland."[9]

Devoy's dual work in popular journalism and organizing for his homeland's independence naturally complemented each other. In Thomas N. Brown's path-breaking study *Irish-American Nationalism 1870–1890*, he observes that Irish-American newspapers played a vital role in delivering news about Ireland and planting seeds about nationhood in the old home country. "It was to the newspaper," Brown wrote, "that the immigrants turned when in their newly awakened consciousness they sought knowledge of Ireland and the Irish."[10] In the 1880s, five weekly newspapers circulated among New York Irish Americans, and as Brown notes, the *New York Herald* was preeminent as a daily.[11] Devoy wrote constantly throughout his long life in the United States, including as a reporter and foreign editor for the *Herald*. There, and particularly in the newspapers he founded and edited, he pushed his agenda at the same time that he provided the latest news for his Irish-American readership. The impartial approach was alien to his larger and abiding objective.

From the famine years on, talk of "insurrection" and "revolution" occurred with greater regularity. The Proclamation on Easter Monday 1916 noted, "In every generation the Irish people have asserted their right to national freedom and sovereignty: six times during the past three hundred years they have asserted it in arms."[12] Early on it was assumed—at least among the more extreme, IRB-oriented thinking—that for the Irish to end English rule, violence would be unavoidable. Devoy, who enlisted in the French Foreign Legion in 1861 and served in North Africa to gain military experience, personified that assumption and, more broadly, Fenianism as a movement. The Fenians had started to organize in America shortly before Devoy joined the IRB in 1861. The term "Fenianism" was coined by John O'Mahony, a Gaelic scholar—the word *fianna* in Gaelic refers to legendary Irish warriors—who was born in Ireland, participated in the 1848 rebellion, and went into exile, first to France and then, in

1854, to America. In 1858, O'Mahony and Michael Doheny established the Fenian Brotherhood with the objective of creating an independent Ireland by the violent overthrow of English rule. Given the surging number of Irish immigrants now living in the United States, the Fenians received moral and financial support that Devoy would later build on and develop. American Fenians, including Devoy, created the base of support that culminated in 1916.

Devoy came early to the conclusion that the Fenian approach—violent overthrow—was the only way. A decade after his arrival in America, he wrote in the second edition of the *Irish Nation*, "There is no use ignoring facts. If Ireland wins her freedom, she must wade to it through blood and suffering and sacrifice. Independence means revolution, red-handed and remorseless."[13] Always as pragmatic as he was strategic, he kept one eye on Ireland and the other on the United States. The Irish in each place shoulder responsibility for what lay ahead were Ireland "to be freed in this generation." To his way of thinking, "The people at home must be prepared—*they must be armed*. They must not be left at the mercy of flying columns and squads of police, and their spirit broken before the time to strike can come. We in America must do more than make speeches and subscribe money 'to keep the agitation alive.'" What he meant by "more" was obvious enough, but he became explicit: "*Let us get arms*. Without them no program is possible."[14]

To Devoy, "home" always meant one place—Ireland—and "agitation" meant more than a war of words. Irish independence would not happen without a bloody fight. In strategy and tactics, Devoy was clear-eyed and able to adapt, when a situation called for change. Before launching the *Irish Nation* in November 1881, he made a speech in Holyoke, Massachusetts. Chastised for being too moderate by supporters of a more bellicose, terrorism-now approach, Devoy by this point had sharpened his rhetoric: "Ireland's opportunity will come when England is engaged in a desperate struggle with some great European power or European combination," he announced with eerie prescience, "or when the flame of insurrection has spread through her Indian Empire, and her strength and resources are strained."[15]

Ultimately, World War I provided "opportunity." Devoy's life was defined by his unbending commitment to "bloody sacrifice." From his youthful days in the French Foreign Legion, he was a hardheaded realist who understood the struggle ahead was more than a symbolic exercise. Preparing for the revolution was, as one historian described it, a "grubby business."[16]

Before he began to set in motion the support of the "exiled children in America," Devoy devoted himself to other activities to help Ireland, including associations with Irish Parliamentary leader Charles Stewart Parnell and Irish National Land League founder Michael Davitt. Those efforts, however, ended with him falling out with them both. Devoy's life was marked by ruptured relationships. Never married, he remained single and single-minded, breaking with anyone not inclined to pursue his agenda in his way. "He could dismiss all personal romance from his record in the simple and final phrase that he was an old bachelor of eighty-six," notes one historian.[17]

The "old bachelor" was never shy in letting someone know where he stood. But he didn't engage in feuds with everyone. Thomas J. Clarke, the first signatory of the 1916 Proclamation, affectionately called Devoy "the Old Man," and worked closely with him for many years on the Clan na Gael/IRB agenda of a republican Ireland. A devout Fenian and proponent of physical force—he spent the spring of 1883 through the fall of 1898 in English prisons for treason after being captured carrying explosives for use in a bombing in London— Clarke immigrated to America twice: in 1880 (until early 1883) and then in 1900 (until late 1907). When he returned in 1900, Clarke worked directly with Devoy on Clan business and in 1903 was named assistant editor of Devoy's newly launched *The Gaelic American*.[18] Like Devoy, Clarke became a naturalized U.S. citizen. Unlike Devoy, he went back to Ireland, setting up a couple tobacconist-newsagent shops that became unofficial meeting places for younger though no less militant IRB members.

For Clarke, America was not only a refuge but also a country where he could speak freely with people who shared his heritage. Clarke was alone among the Rising's leaders in gaining U.S. citizenship, but five of the seven signatories of the 1916 Proclamation spent time in America (and the other two also had connections). All five of the Proclamation signatories who came to America fought in the GPO during the Rising. Devoy knew each of them personally. In his posthumously published memoir, *Recollections of an Irish Rebel*, Devoy mentions James Connolly's involvement in Easter Week and his eventual execution as the last of the seven leaders to face a British firing squad in Dublin's Kilmainham Jail. Although Devoy avoids mentioning it, Connolly spent nearly eight years in the United States (1902–1910), dedicating most of his time to developing a labor movement. A gifted speaker and writer with special appeal to Irish-American workers, Connolly toured the United States on behalf of the Socialist Labor Party and later the Socialist Party of America.

At the time, the Industrial Workers of the World (the "Wobblies") were trying to organize the labor force into a union with muscle, and Connolly championed economic and social justice in worker pay and rights. Though respected in labor circles, Connolly never felt at home in America. The land that inspired so many had an opposite effect on him. Reluctance to embrace democratic socialism within the dominant capitalist culture played a part, with Connolly at one point referring to the United States as "this cursed country."[19] One reason Devoy and Connolly found common ground was that both viewed a large percentage of Irish-American politicians as "descendants of the serpents St. Patrick banished from Ireland."[20] To be of Irish heritage went just so far for the "exiled children" who had republican nationalism as their animating principle.

In a 1908 issue of *The Harp*, Connolly ruminated on the Statue of Liberty with a withering scorn: "It is placed upon a pedestal out of the reach of the multitudes; it can only be approached by those who have money enough to pay the expense; it has a lamp to enlighten the world, but the lamp is never lit, and it smiles upon us as we approach America, but when we are once in the country we never see anything but its back."[21] His reservations about the United States even extended to its weather. In a letter he sent back to Ireland in 1902, he complained about the summer heat in New York: "It is obvious to me that hell will be a greater punishment to us than to the Americans."[22]

Upon his return to Ireland in 1910, Connolly continued to devote his attention to the labor movement, becoming active in the Socialist Party of Ireland and related organizations. When the Irish Citizen Army was established in late 1913 as a defense force for workers, nationalist militancy assumed more meaningful significance for Connolly, and he quickly became one of its leaders. Later, as plans for the Rising began to take shape, he saw socialism advancing only after independence had been gained.[23] Connolly and about two hundred members of the Irish Citizen Army fought during Easter Week. He suffered a compound fracture of his left shinbone from a ricocheting bullet, forcing him to direct his troops from a stretcher in the GPO. After the surrender and his court-martial on May 9, the news circulated that Connolly had been shot sitting down.

Both Clarke and Connolly lived and worked in America several years before returning to Ireland. Seán Mac Diarmada, P. H. Pearse, and Joseph Mary Plunkett, the three other Proclamation signatories to visit the United States, spent less time in the New World. Mac Diarmada, for example, came over to attend the 1912 Clan na Gael convention, held in Atlantic City, New Jersey, as the delegate of the IRB. A close associate of Clarke's in Dublin, Mac Diarmada spent several weeks on the East Coast, getting to know many republican sympathizers among the American Irish. Still, the 1912 visit was an important step in creating stronger links between key organizations that would later be involved in the Rising.[24] For many years, internal feuding and divided opinions had undercut Clan na Gael's purpose, weakening Devoy's leadership of the ostensibly secret organization. The 1912 convention helped Devoy consolidate its clout.

During the years before Britain entered World War I in August 1914, the American Irish (by then close to one-fifth of the U.S. population) were anything but unified in how they viewed the future of their ancestral homeland. Some were reluctant to look back and concentrated instead on rebuilding their lives. Others embraced the Clan's militancy and its weekly sermonizing in the pages of *The Gaelic American*. Still others—and for a long time the largest group—supported the moderate, constitutionalist approach of John Redmond, Parnell's successor as the leader of the Irish Parliamentary Party in the House of Commons. Focused more on creating home rule for Ireland than on independence, Redmondite followers had their own U.S. organization— the United Irish League of America—and a weekly publication, the *Irish World*, to compete with *The Gaelic American*.

When P. H. Pearse arrived in the United States on a speaking tour in February 1914 to raise money for the school, St. Enda's, he had started in Dublin in 1908, it didn't take him long to figure out which group would be more receptive to his message and appeal. Some historians have seen this three-month visit as seminal.[25] While getting to know Devoy and using the offices of *The Gaelic American* as his headquarters, Pearse discovered a strong correlation between the passion of his oratory and the level of contributions to his school. Three thousand miles from Ireland, he kept to himself an opinion he had expressed in 1907: "If our American exiles—our 'deserters,' as a prominent Gaelic Leaguer once called them—would let us alone, the matter [of abandoning Ireland] would not be so bad; but their interest in Ireland is chiefly manifested in their efforts to induce the remnant of the population that remain in the country to leave it."[26]

Pearse devoted two of his major addresses in America to commemorations of Irish nationalist Robert Emmet, who was hanged and then beheaded for leading a failed insurrection against the English in 1803. Emmet was well known in Irish-American circles, as was his brother, Thomas Addis Emmet, who immigrated to New York in 1804 and became a prominent lawyer involved in his adopted country's political life. Speaking at the Academy of Music in Brooklyn on March 2, 1914, Pearse said of Emmet's execution: "Be assured that such a death always means a redemption. Emmet redeemed Ireland from acquiescence in the Union. His attempt was not a failure, but a triumph for that deathless thing we call Irish Nationality."[27] Later, Pearse observes that in Ireland "the new generation is reaffirming the Fenian faith, the faith of Emmet" and moving beyond the Redmondite approach: "What one may call the Westminster phase is passing: the National movement is swinging back again into its proper channel."[28]

Just a week afterward, at the Aeolian Hall in New York City, Pearse concentrated more directly on opposing the British to gain independence for Ireland: "England is right in suspecting Irish loyalty, and those Irishmen who promise Irish loyalty to England are wrong."[29] Pearse concluded his oration by linking the Fenian past to his vision for the future: "To the grey-haired men whom I see on this platform, to John Devoy and Richard Burke, I bring, then, this message from Ireland: that their seed-sowing of forty years ago has not been without its harvest, that there are young men and little boys in Ireland to-day who remember what they taught and who, with God's blessing, will one day take—or make—an opportunity of putting their teaching into practice."[30] With Devoy's support and Pearse's leadership, the "one day" arrived two years later, on Easter Monday of 1916.

Before then, however, Pearse learned more about the American-Irish commitment. Devoy, in particular, impressed him, and the two talked at length about both the past and their common goal. Devoy's life, with its decades of fighting the British and supporting the republican cause, was, in Pearse's mind, the history of the Fenian movement distilled.[31] At the meetings and lectures arranged for Pearse, the "exiled children" of all ages appreciated the fervor animating his rhetoric, and he felt at liberty to express himself in more openly rebellious terms.

Pearse arguably found his voice in America, and that voice would assume greater importance in the months leading up to the Rising, giving him what one historian has called a "sense of destiny."[32] He also discovered that many of the authentic revolutionaries resided in the States rather than in Ireland, with the aging Devoy foremost among them. A significant public moment in that "sense of destiny" came on August 1, 1915, when Pearse delivered

the "graveside panegyric" for Jeremiah O'Donovan Rossa at the Glasnevin
Cemetery in Dublin. Along with Devoy, Rossa had been one of the five men
who had accepted release from imprisonment in 1871 and traveled to the
States on a ship called the *Cuba*. Though at odds for many years, the two
elderly Fenians renewed their friendship as Rossa's health failed.

When Rossa died on June 29, 1915, Tom Clarke and other IRB members in
Dublin saw political potential in honoring the old Fenian on his native soil.[33]
Once Rossa's casket arrived in Ireland, it lay in state at the City Hall before
removal to the cemetery. Devoy described the funeral as "the most significant
demonstration against English Rule that had taken place before Easter Week,
1916, and it had considerable effect in preparing the way for it."[34] What the
Irish on both sides of the Atlantic remembered most was Pearse's oration at
the grave. Vowing in explicit terms that "we pledge to Ireland our love, and
we pledge to English rule in Ireland our hate," his last sentences were among
his most inspired rhetoric:

> Life springs from death; and from the graves of patriot men and women
> spring living nations. The Defenders of this Realm have worked well in
> secret and in the open. They think that they have pacified Ireland. They
> think that they have purchased half of us and intimidated the other half.
> They think that they have foreseen everything, think that they have pro-
> vided against everything; but the fools, the fools, the fools!—they have
> left us our Fenian dead, and while Ireland holds these graves, Ireland
> unfree shall never be at peace.[35]

Looking back in his memoir, Devoy called Pearse's "a historic speech."[36]
Now included in nearly every collection of great Irish speeches, it placed Pearse
at the center of the republican movement. With the war in Europe preoccupy-
ing the British, he, along with other IRB members and Irish Volunteers, could
prepare more seriously than before for a time to translate inspirational words
into action.

Indeed, less than a month after Rossa's funeral, Joseph Mary Plunkett
arrived in New York to discuss with Devoy the Irish plans for the upcoming
Rising. Plunkett, a poet who would later carry the title of Director of Military
Operations for the IRB, was the fifth and last signatory of the Proclamation
with whom Devoy had direct contact. Plunkett's visit, though, wasn't without its difficulties. Suffering from tuberculosis, he was initially denied entry
into the United States when he arrived at Ellis Island. Both suspicious and

circumspect in using the U.S. mail to communicate information of a potentially sensitive nature, Devoy avoided using any names to inform Joseph
McGarrity, a Clan na Gael stalwart in Philadelphia, about Plunkett in a letter
dated August 24, 1915, and signed "Hudson": "There is no hope of getting
that man ashore. The doctor's examination settles it, but the formal examination has not taken place."[37] Despite Devoy's reservations, he kept working
on Plunkett's behalf, even coming up with $1,000 for a bond and contact-
ing New York Senator James O'Gorman to intervene. Because of O'Gorman's
help, Plunkett was allowed to spend two weeks on the East Coast. Besides
reporting to Devoy that the Rising would take place in the near future and
enjoy cooperation from Germany—Plunkett had recently been in Berlin
to talk about specific arrangements—he had an opportunity to spend time
with some American literary figures, including the poet and essayist Joyce
Kilmer.[38]

Devoy never had the chance to meet Thomas MacDonagh. Another Irish
poet and Proclamation signatory, MacDonagh published a collection of his
verse in 1910 with the title *Songs of Myself*, echoing Walt Whitman's classic
poem, "Song of Myself." The promising Irish literary figure and teacher kept
looking to America as the place where he needed to go to advance his career
as a poet. Several of MacDonagh's letters to Dominick Hackett, who had
immigrated to the United States in the early 1900s, raised the possibility of an
American lecture tour to become better known. One letter, dated March 15,
1909, and among other typescript copies in the National Library of Ireland,
asserted that he hoped to get his material placed in American papers "without
selling my soul."[39] MacDonagh never made it across the Atlantic, though his
poetry was widely reprinted in the United States after his execution in 1916.

Éamonn Ceannt is the only other signatory aside from MacDonagh never
to visit the United States or to meet Devoy. Considered the least renowned of
the seven men whose names are printed on the Proclamation—Ceannt and
MacDonagh commanded forces elsewhere in Dublin while the other signatories were, as noted earlier, stationed at the GPO—Ceannt worked with Pearse
and Plunkett on the IRB council responsible for planning the Rising, and during Easter Week, he commanded a battalion of rebels at the South Dublin
Union. Though he was executed on May 8, a news article, published by the *Los
Angeles Times* on May 13, reported that Mac Diarmada and Connolly were the
last of the signatories to face the firing squad the day before. The article also
notes that a cablegram was sent from Los Angeles to the *Freeman's Journal*

reading as follows: "Inform family of Eamonn Ceannt they will be cared for."[40] Even today the cablegram provokes puzzlement. A search of several issues of the *Freeman's Journal* does not substantiate that the Dublin-based newspaper ever printed this item. One possibility is that the correspondent for the Associated Press responsible for the dispatch read the cable at the offices of the *Freeman's Journal* and included it in the dispatch being written for an American audience. But why an unnamed person in Los Angeles wanted to help Ceannt's family remains a mystery.

What is no mystery or in doubt is that Devoy's personal relationships with so many leaders of the Rising provide a strong human connection to his involvement, with his long-time link to Clarke of critical importance. From afar and despite over four decades in exile, Devoy kept stoking Fenian fires. He actively participated in planning insurrection and, more significantly, collected money through Clan na Gael to help bankroll the Rising and the activities preceding it.[41] With the arrival of Roger Casement in New York on July 20, 1914, and Britain's declaration of war against Germany fifteen days later (on August 4), Devoy, then seventy-one, started to devote more of his attention to the then-undefined republican action in Ireland. For Devoy and others, the outbreak of the Great War provided an opening—the "opportunity" he had predicted more than thirty years earlier in the Holyoke speech—and the occasion for exploitation, if practical arrangements could be made.

The seventh and concluding part of Devoy's *Recollections of an Irish Rebel* includes thirteen chapters about the Rising: the people who participated, the preparations, and the aftermath. Five of the chapters focus specifically on Casement, with the first beginning: "Roger Casement is one of the most tragic figures in Irish history."[42]

Heroic yet self-centered, as Devoy described him, Casement presents a compelling and contradictory figure. Although he wrote in 1910, "The more I see of Americans, the less I believe in them,"[43] four years later he arrived in the States to raise money to buy arms for the Irish Volunteers. The Irish Volunteers was founded in late 1913 in response to the creation earlier that year of the Ulster Volunteer Force, which pledged to fight for the continuation of British rule. The Irish Volunteers subsequently splintered into two branches in September of 1914: the Irish Volunteers (heavily infiltrated by IRB members) and the National Volunteers (largely controlled by John Redmond, a strong supporter of home rule who urged Irish enlistment in the British military for World War I, which dedicated nationalists and republicans protested). By the time Casement came to New York to start discussions about what Devoy referred to as "the Cause of Irish Freedom" (each major word set off with a capital letter), he had been knighted in 1911 by King George V for his part in helping Amazonian Indians in Peru. Following his retirement from the Foreign Service just a year before his trip to the United States, "Sir Roger" (as Devoy invariably calls him) had become an outspoken nationalist for Ireland, where he had been born and raised.

Like Devoy, Casement viewed Germany as a potential ally in gaining Irish independence. Indeed, while Casement was making the rounds within the Irish-American community to spread his message, Devoy initiated talks in New York with the German ambassador to the United States, Count Johann Heinrich von Bernstorff, and other embassy representatives. The point of the meetings, in Devoy's phrase, was "military help only" without the exchange of any money. "The point was stressed that a rebellion in Ireland would necessarily divert a large part of the British army from the fighting front on the Continent and that therefore it would be to Germany's interest to help Ireland in her fight for freedom."[44] When the war began, American public opinion was very much divided. The principle of "neutrality" guided the Wilson administration's approach and was the basis of his campaign in 1916. In the more militant Irish-American enclaves, however, hatred of the British king far exceeded any sympathy for the German Kaiser, and an overture like Devoy's—a case of the enemy of my enemy becoming my friend—made sense. Casement shared Devoy's thinking and began planning a mission to Germany to secure arms and to make a direct appeal for additional assistance on behalf of the Irish cause.

An abiding principle of the republican movement was aptly encapsulated in a five-word phrase: "England's difficulty is Ireland's opportunity." Devoy, Casement, and others considered Britain's preoccupation with the war in Europe as the moment to launch a rebellion. And there was another factor: America's neutrality contributed to Ireland's opportunity. Without formal national support for any combatants across the Atlantic, there was greater flexibility to engage in intrigue and scheming from the summer of 1914 until the spring of 1916. The Clan na Gael coffers subsidized Casement's trip to Germany, which began in October 1914 and kept him there until his return to Ireland right before the Rising. In a lengthy remembrance, "Some Facts about Easter Week, 1916," that Devoy published in *The Gaelic American* six years later, Casement receives almost obsessive attention. Was the Clan leader trying to justify his involvement in a dubious misadventure? After explaining the financing provided to Casement ($16,000 for his time in Germany and another $5,000 for his defense after his arrest), Devoy maintained that Casement had lost touch with reality. The envoy "evidently believed he was above us all, both in Ireland and here, and that he was *directing the whole movement from Germany.*"[45] The italics emphasize Casement's healthy sense of self-importance. Later in his memoir, while more deliberately assessing Casement's mission—of obtaining military help, influencing German opinion on Ireland's plight, and organizing a brigade of German-held Irish prisoners to fight against the English—Devoy is more judicious and provides this evaluation: "Casement did his best in all these things, but did the first ineffectively, succeeded admirably in the second, and failed badly in the third."[46]

Ultimately, Casement was captured on Good Friday 1916, after a German U-boat brought him to a landing point near Banna Strand in County Kerry. The next day (as touched on in this book's prologue), a ship carrying arms for the Rising, the *Aud*, was stopped by the British near the Irish coast and scuttled by the captain, bringing an inglorious end to the German participation in the rebel cause.

Casement's trial for high treason during the summer of 1916 became a cause célèbre in America, provoking widespread public interest and attempts at governmental intervention, including from the White House. Casement had conspired with the Germans, yet had been returning to Ireland to try to stop the Rising. His mental state was a matter of debate. His hanging in London nearly three months after the Dublin executions made the British look vindictive in the extreme.[47]

Devoy's involvement with the Germans—principally his meetings with the military attaché, Franz von Papen—came at a high price, too. Always suspicious that the secret work of Clan na Gael could be compromised, Devoy knew that approaching the Germans for arms would at some point bring down the wrath of the Wilson administration, which he believed sided with Britain and opposed Germany from the war's beginning. When *The Gaelic American*, with a circulation of some 30,000, was barred from the U.S. mail by the postmaster general on January 21, 1918, Devoy understood the "personal enmity" involved.

All the effort by Devoy, Casement, and others to secure German weaponry for the Rising didn't produce the twenty thousand rifles, ten machine guns, and five million cartridges they had hoped for. Nor did it a produce a definite day to launch the insurrection. Nonetheless, Devoy was able to funnel $100,000 (nearly $2.5 million in today's money) to help provide the republicans with "the means of striking their historic blow" and resulted in the largest "sum ever previously received by an Irish insurrectionary movement."[48] Devoy gave the lion's share of credit to the leaders of the IRB and Irish Volunteers in Dublin, but also scrupulously detailed all of the contributions from Clan na Gael to underwrite Casement and the broader Irish cause. Devoy's papers in the National Library of Ireland include precise accounting records of the money he received, with offerings as small as a dollar duly noted. The old Fenian, who dreamed of a new Ireland, also devoted himself to the most mundane details.

Devoy was not only meticulous but also ingenious in making sure financial support arrived safely and secretly over in Ireland. The Royal Commission of Inquiry, which began investigating "the rebellion in Ireland" on May 18, 1916, at Westminster, probed connections between the men and women involved and other people who might have furnished aid of one kind or another. Early in the official report, a section entitled "Funds from America" outlined the way the money flowed into Ireland before the split between the National and Irish Volunteers. Eoin MacNeill, chairman of the council involved in the formation of the Irish Volunteers and subsequently the chief of staff, was the key figure involved. In the words of the investigative document:

> Sums roughly amounting to £16,000 continued to be sent into the account up to September, 1914. After that it was not possible to trace the method of receipt in Ireland of funds from America. It was believed that a large part of the funds available for anti-British organisation were expended in the maintenance of seditious newspapers, and the circulation of seditious leaflets, and the employment of organisers to travel the country to win people to join the Irish Volunteers, and become in their turn organisers in this direction.[49]

Throughout the nearly six decades he spent in America, Devoy maneuvered between clandestine activity to advance independence "at home" and public work to inform and organize Irish America. Whispered plotting for Clan na Gael took place simultaneously with the journalism he wrote and the speeches he delivered across the country. On February 5, 1916, for example, Devoy received a coded message from Dublin with the date the Rising was set to begin. A month later, what was called the first "Irish Race Convention" took place in New York. For two days, March 4 and 5, some twenty-three hundred delegates, the largest such gathering ever assembled, brought American members of the "race" together under the banner of a new organization, the Friends of Irish Freedom, with Devoy open about his involvement with this more mainstream, publicity-seeking group. At a key moment—with the Rising but a few weeks away—the Friends of Irish Freedom applauded American ideals and criticized English imperialism before unequivocally advocating freedom for Ireland. In his memoirs, Devoy reprints the nearly seven-page "Declaration of Principles and Policy" adopted at the convention, and he adds this editorial comment: "It was an opportune Declaration of Irish Independence which the stifled voice of Ireland itself could not then utter to the world, and a reassertion of the principles on which the American Republic was founded. It exerted a powerful influence on the people of the United States."[50] Away from the speaker's stage and cheering camaraderie, however, Devoy worried that plans for the insurrection and his own key role would be exposed by spies for Britain or the United States. Indeed, in "Documents Relative to the Sinn Fein Movement," released in 1921 by the British Parliamentary Archive, Devoy receives attention in the context of Casement's 1914 visit to America before Casement departed for Germany. Devoy was "the chief agent in America for communication between Germany and Sinn Fein, and was described by Von Skal, one of Count Von Bernstorff's staff in Washington, as their 'Confidential Agent' in a despatch from the German Embassy in America to Berlin in February 1916." The document notes that Devoy "was known as 'Sean Fear' (The Old Man) among the Irish revolutionaries."[51]

Just six days before the Rising began, the U.S. Secret Service raided Germany's New York consulate. With guns drawn, several agents seized papers from the desk of a military attaché, Wolf von Igel. Some of the documents were specifically related to preparations for the Rising, implicating Devoy by name. For reasons unknown, possibly because he didn't want to interfere in the imminent insurrection, Devoy downplayed the raid and the revelations contained in the papers now in the U.S. government's possession. The next day, April 19, in writing to Joseph McGarrity in Philadelphia and hiding his identity by signing the letter "David Jones," Devoy converted the raid into a fire, worried that his message might be intercepted in the mail:

> I know you will be anxious after hearing of the fire in our home to learn
> if we all came off safe. I am glad to be able to inform you that all the

papers relating to the property were saved except one little scrap, and that will not be much of a loss. The sale will come off on time and everything looks all right. We were very anxious for a whole day, but when the firemen got through with their work of salvage we found we had no cause for worry.[52]

Several such messages, now in the New York Public Library and the National Library of Ireland, show the lengths to which Devoy went in keeping his Clan na Gael/IRB work secretive. On March 1, 1916, just before the Irish Race Convention, Devoy (writing as "William Johnson") sent McGarrity a note reading, "Another very dangerous man has turned up and results have begun to come, of which I will tell you when I see you. I was going to go tonight to the place I used to see him, but I have decided instead to go where you, John and I were last time and stay there till after Sunday."[53] Later letters in 1916 deal explicitly with the Rising and Casement's actions. Writing to McGarrity on July 18, weeks after the Rising, Devoy reported that he had received "[t]wo new arrivals with a mass of authentic news"—meaning he now has in his possession dispatches from Ireland with more complete, uncensored information about what happened. "It is a very full and most interesting story," Devoy writes. "It confirms previous stories and surmises about R [Roger Casement] going over to stop the thing [the Rising]. The Captain is expected here soon and will tell all."[54] The identity of the "Captain" is not revealed; however, it is clear Devoy wanted to learn every detail about the insurrection: not only for his journalistic purposes at *The Gaelic American* but also for his own knowledge as a planner and provider of funds. The plotter and paymaster was also a principal proponent who wanted to publicize his side of the story in the most positive way.

As early as April 25, with the first news reports of the Rising starting to appear, speculation about Devoy's possible involvement surfaced, though he wasn't specifically named. On page 2 of the *Chicago Tribune* that day, a bold headline with every word in capital letters—"REVOLT IN DUBLIN, RUMOR"—sits atop a dispatch with a New York dateline:

> NEW YORK. April 24.—[Special]—A rumor circulated around town today that the Irish in Dublin had revolted and seized Dublin castle. The story had it that the revolt had quickly spread over a considerable portion of the country and that the British authorities had been overwhelmed.

While a great many prominent Irishmen in town had heard this report, it was impossible to discover how it had started or on what authority it rested.

One version was to the effect that the news had first come to the publisher of an Irish periodical in a code message from the other side. This did not seem probable, however, as code messages are not permitted by the British censors.

These three paragraphs illustrate what became a pattern of American press coverage of the Rising and its aftermath. British censorship and difficulties in reporting directly from Ireland led to the publication of erroneous information (such as the seizing of Dublin castle) and to a reliance on rumor—a word that recurs in the reporting—or hearsay statements from people without the usual journalistic means for verification. In this story, however, suggesting that "the publisher of an Irish periodical" first learned of the possible revolt indirectly draws Devoy into the story. Another pattern also emerged in the first wave of articles. Whatever is happening in Ireland created reverberations within Irish America, and those local responses to the Rising make news of their own, far removed from the approval or disapproval of British censors in either London or Dublin.

By April 28, Devoy was being identified by name in American press coverage as a central figure in the uprising in Ireland. While the rebels continued to fight, Devoy was doing verbal battle with the Wilson administration. A front-page story in the *New York Times* captured the conflict in the first sentence of a dispatch from Washington: "Secretary [of State Robert] Lansing today flatly denied the statement made in New York yesterday by John Devoy, editor of *The Gaelic American*, that the information which enabled the British Government to frustrate a German landing in Ireland and capture Sir Roger Casement was furnished to Great Britain by the Wilson Administration." Two paragraphs later, a more ominous chord is struck: "Officials would not say today whether the government would take any action on Editor Devoy's reported admission that he had been a party to the uprising in Ireland, which in his case would constitute a violation of the neutrality laws."[55] The *Times* quoted the most vituperative passages of Devoy's *Gaelic American* editorial, "Wilson's Base Act of Treachery," calling into question the president's avowed neutrality about the war. Claiming that the U.S. government gave the British advance warning of the Rising,

Devoy judged the alleged deed the "most disgraceful and dishonorable act ever committed by an American President." The editorial then pits the Irish against the English, with Wilson squarely on the wrong side, calling him a "petty Czar who is now King George's Viceroy in the White House." "Come on, Mr. Wilson, start your prosecutions of Irishmen for 'breaches of neutrality,' and between now and election day you will wish that you had never been born."[56] As reported in the *Times*, Devoy's America was becoming another front in the fight for Irish independence, and sharply worded phrases would serve as the principal weapons.

Although Pearse formally surrendered on Saturday, April 29, Irish-American reaction to what had happened grew in intensity in the days following the actual hostilities. Once again, Devoy was the most visible and vocal proponent of the rebels' cause. On April 30, he was a main speaker at a hastily arranged gathering of what was called "the United Irish Societies of America" that brought several thousand people to the George M. Cohan Theatre in New York City. Devoy directed his fire not at the White House but at John Redmond and the New York newspapers for supporting the British. According to one news account of his remarks, Devoy said he had received several death threats from "cowardly Englishmen posing as Irishmen" and that "John Redmond is himself responsible for this revolution."[57]

Devoy's criticism of Redmond did not go unanswered. The day after the first executions on May 3, the *New York Times* published two stories focusing on Irish-American reaction. One appeared under the headline "Call Executed Men Martyrs to Cause," introducing a religious connotation to the narrative of events,[58] and the other was an interview with Patrick Egan about Devoy's role. Active in the IRB back in his native Ireland, Egan had taken a completely different road from Devoy. After immigrating to the United States, he rejected the violent approach to Irish independence and became involved in traditional politics, first in the Republican Party and then with the Democrats. From 1889 until 1893, he served as the U.S. Minister to Chile, and while active in Irish politics, he had backed Parnell and then Redmond. "My heart goes out to those men who had to face the firing squad in London today," Egan told a reporter. "They were brave boys, sincere in their love for Ireland, but they had been deceived into backing an impossible cause." Egan made clear who was responsible. "If any one were shot it should have been John Devoy, who hatched the whole nefarious scheme here in New York and was personally responsible for it."[59]

Egan's tirade against Devoy continues for four more paragraphs of direct quotation. From his viewpoint American involvement had been central not only to the Rising but also to Casement's overtures to Germany and whatever German assistance Ireland could receive. Poisonously pointed, this article (complete with the erroneous information about the executions taking place in London) amplifies the criticism of Devoy that existed within more moderate quarters of Irish America and emphasizes his importance to the insurrection itself. A few days later, Egan received additional attention when a meeting of the Redmondite United Irish League of America got broken up by pro-Rising raiders. Devoy remained the chief culprit ("it is he who should pay the penalty"), but opinion of the American Irish was beginning to crystallize. Egan introduced a resolution deploring "the insane attempt at rebellion in Ireland" and "the heartrending executions of the last few days." It was adopted unanimously.[60] Within Irish America of whatever shade of green, the executions were wrong from beginning to end, while the Rising itself was a subject of considerable debate and controversy.

On May 7, in the Roxbury neighborhood of Boston, Devoy spoke at a public Clan na Gael meeting that drew some eight hundred people. Introduced as "the revolutionary apostle of Irish freedom," according to the *Boston Globe*, Devoy castigated the British for rushing through the court-martials and sentences. "The martyrs put to death by the British firing squad will go down in history with Emmet and the others who died on the scaffolding or on the battlefield."[61] Devoy didn't merely dwell on what was unfolding across the Atlantic but looked ahead. "It is only a question of transportation that prevents 200,000 trained Irishmen here from going over to help."[62]

In addition to the speeches he made to evoke sympathy for the rebels and their cause, Devoy turned his newspaper into a weekly commemoration of the Rising and what it meant to the republican movement. The coverage in *The Gaelic American* is distinctive for the breadth of its treatment, despite its limited reporting resources. As late as July 29, 1916, the third paragraph in a detailed, eyewitness report entitled "Inside History of the Easter Week Rebellion," complete with what is called an "Insurrection Map of the City of Dublin," begins: "The whole inside story cannot be published at present, but enough can be made public to clear up the situation for the benefit of Nationalists in America."[63] Succeeding issues provide amplification with great specificity: "James Connolly Butchered While Wounded" (August 12), "Graphic Story of the Battle of Ashbourne" (September 23), and "Widow's Own Story of Skeffington's Murder"

(December 30). Within the pages of *The Gaelic American*, the Rising became a news story without a conclusion. The newspaper turned a military defeat into a symbolic victory—with martyrs to mourn and a cause to champion.

Besides chronicling the heroism of the rebels and their cause, *The Gaelic American* directed criticism at the coverage by large U.S. dailies. In the May 20 issue, along with a lengthy article, "Facts of the Rebellion Begin to Arrive" (as though whatever facts previously reported in other outlets might not have been reliable), appeared a story about Casement's preliminary hearing on the charge of high treason. The writer—clearly Devoy—accuses the cabled reports and the headlines as "hostile to the prisoner except those of the *American*, the *Evening Journal*, and the *Evening Mail*." But the *Sun's* correspondent was the "meanest liar among them." "He confessed himself a pimp, described how he looked over Sir Roger's shoulder to spy on the notes he was taking, and lied like a cur about his 'nervousness' and 'perturbation,' which the other correspondents denied. Of course this fellow is an Englishman. But, whatever his nationality, he is a dirty skunk."[64]

Devoy rarely missed the chance to take a punch at other journalistic organizations, with the *New York Times* a favorite target. One article, published August 5, carried the headline, "Lying for England," and began: "The New York *Times*, which, in its European news, is an echo of its London namesake and loses no opportunity of presenting the English side of every case."[65] *The Gaelic American* then reprinted a dispatch from the *London Times* that the *New York Times* had also published—with the sole purpose of showing the gross inaccuracies and biases on display for less like-minded readers.

In his memoir, Devoy returned to the role as press critic. In one of the five chapters about Casement, he wrote:

> As in the case of the men who joined Casement's "brigade," every man in Ireland and America who took Ireland's side, was charged by the press with being in receipt of "German gold." The real fact in the situation was that English money had purchased the support of a large part of the American press, and the reptile editors in this country vied with their English contemporaries in vilification of Irishmen who had spent their lives in efforts to prepare the Irish people for just such an opportunity as the war presented.[66]

American coverage had clearly gotten under Devoy's skin in ways he couldn't forget—or let go. Gone is any sense of professional propriety—the ethical conflict between his central involvement in the Rising and his championing or celebrating it in the pages of *The Gaelic American*. Viewed another way, a leading actor in the drama was also an applauding reviewer of the performance. Editors of major newspapers might be "reptilian," but Devoy had no moral qualms whatever about his own role or journalistic approach.

The most revealing document Devoy composed about the Rising was neither in his journalism nor in his memoir, but delivered by hand to Laurence de Lacy, an Irishman then living in San Francisco. In a letter dated July 20, 1916, Devoy remarked he was dispatching it through a courier for a definite reason: "Nothing is safe in the mails in this free country."[67] Encompassing several pages—the complete text is published in the second volume of *Devoy's Post Bag: 1871–1928*—the epistle presents Devoy as less restrained in assigning blame and offering criticism than he was in his memoirs, and, unlike some other letters that summer, his meaning was not obscured with coded language or double meanings. For Devoy, Casement was the chief culprit for the disarray that marked the Rising's beginning and prevented it from being a coordinated insurrection throughout Ireland. Casement had sent a message to Eoin MacNeill, the chief of staff of the Irish Volunteers who argued against launching military activity, and MacNeill did, indeed, countermand the order to initiate the revolt on Easter Sunday. So, in effect, just before the Rising, two boats from Germany were sailing to Ireland—one with arms for the fight and the other carrying someone hell-bent on stopping the use of those same arms. Given all the circumstances, J. J. Lee's memorable assessment—"The Easter Rising went off at half-cock"—almost seems like an understatement.[68]

According to Devoy, appeals to Casement to stay in Germany went unheeded, and MacNeill "issued the fatal order." Arguing that Casement "was obsessed with the idea that he was a wonderful leader," Devoy went on: "We knew he would meddle in his honest but visionary way to such an extent as to spoil things, but we did not dream that he would ruin everything as he has done."[69] Always more practical and results oriented, Devoy continued to castigate Casement and to compliment the Germans for trying to supply the arms. Near the end of the letter, he echoed the poem of Yeats that "whatever comes, the old Ireland is gone."[70]

Though Devoy feared disclosure by spies intercepting communication through the U.S. mail, this letter was seized in a government raid of de Lacy's home and was published in American newspapers in late February 1918. By then, *The Gaelic American* had been barred from distribution outside

New York City by the U.S. postmaster general, and Devoy's earlier collusion with Germany struck a discordant note in wartime America. Much of the text was even reprinted in Dublin by the United Irish League as a special publication under the bold headline: "Easter Week: John Devoy Tells How the Rising Was Arranged." The explanatory subhead notes: "The following Letter was seized by the American Government and published in the American Newspapers, February 26, 1918." The man who craved secrecy for his republican activity was now, nearly two years after the Rising, completely unmasked—and, in some quarters, had become a political pariah.

As Devoy grew older, he never wavered in his commitment to transform "the old Ireland" into an independent nation. Obstinacy also remained a defining trait. In March 1861, more than a half-century before the Rising, when Devoy first met James Stephens, the founder of the IRB in Dublin three years earlier, Stephens was heard to remark: "That is the most stubborn young fellow that I have ever met."[71] His single-mindedness continued to affect personal relationships, some of which created post-Rising divisions within Irish America. When Joe McGarrity, his long-time Clan ally, brought up the possibility of working with Woodrow Wilson on resolving Ireland's status at the 1919 Paris Peace Conference, Devoy balked, rejecting any overture to the administration that stopped the postal delivery of his newspaper and tarnished his name by releasing the letter about German involvement in the Rising. He never forgave Wilson, writing in his memoir, "Woodrow Wilson was the meanest and most malignant man who ever filled the office of President of the United States. His enmities were implacable and they grew with time. He pursued with unrelenting hatred every man who incurred his dislike, and resorted to the meanest methods in wreaking vengeance."[72] This late-in-life assessment extended an antipathy he expressed in an editorial for *The Gaelic American* just before Election Day of 1916: "That President Wilson hates the Irish with the implacable hatred of the Ulster Orangeman—the stock he comes of—has been shown so many times since he became President that there can be no successful attempt at denial." A few sentences later, Devoy took on Wilson's Southern roots and the president's own father, a Presbyterian minister, and his mother:

> Mr. Wilson has never missed an opportunity of repeating his false accusations of disloyalty against a race that proved its loyalty on the bloody battlefields of the Civil War, fighting for the Union, while his relatives

were fighting to destroy it and his father was desecrating a Christian pulpit by ranting in favor of human slavery. The "monumental gall" of a man of such antecedents and environment in accusing of disloyalty the kindred of the men who contributed a glorious part to the defeat of an attempt backed by England, his mother's country, to destroy the Republic cannot be matched in American history.[73]

Devoy's hatred of Britain extended to U.S. domestic politics and poisoned alliances. Abraham Lincoln's Republican Party fought to save the Union during the Civil War, while Britain provided support to the Confederate side with its strong allegiance from members of the Democratic Party. Unlike so many Irish Americans who kept Democratic political machines like Tammany Hall in power by voting a straight party ticket, Devoy made political judgments based on a candidate's or office holder's approach to Ireland—or Great Britain. The republican in Irish terms could also be Republican in American ones. In 1884, he went so far as to make a series of campaign speeches for GOP presidential candidate James G. Blaine in his contest against Grover Cleveland.[74]

McGarrity's suggestion of possibly working with Wilson raised Devoy's suspicion about his former comrade-in-arms. Then, when McGarrity, a prosperous Philadelphia wine merchant, started the *Irish Press* as a competitor to *The Gaelic American*, Devoy became suspicious about McGarrity's motives. A rival republican faction now vied for attention and a following among the American Irish, but the undeterred Devoy pursued what he considered the more sensible and realistic agenda. Longstanding friendships came to an end without a second thought if major differences of opinion or of policy took place.

When Éamon de Valera, by then the president of Dáil Éireann, arrived in the United States on June 11, 1919, to raise funds and support for Ireland, Devoy at first joined in heralding the homecoming of the surviving senior commandant of the Rising and his new role in Irish politics.[75] Later, however, in what Devoy's biographer Terry Golway classifies as "Irish America's civil war,"[76] de Valera and Devoy battled over who would be in charge of whatever the American Irish wanted to do on behalf of Ireland. De Valera advocated control from Ireland (with him, of course, in charge), while Devoy argued that U.S. support, especially money, should be managed by Americans.[77]

Supported by McGarrity and other prominent Irish Americans, de Valera defended what he considered his turf and toured the United States, rallying

crowds and raising money during the course of a year and a half. Devoy, however, remained unimpressed, calling de Valera (later echoed in his description of Wilson) "the most malignant man in all Irish history."[78] De Valera's
encroachment on what Devoy viewed as internal Irish-American business was
just one reason for their friction. More substantively, while on American soil,
de Valera talked about Ireland having a relationship to Great Britain similar
to the one the United States then had with Cuba. During an interview with
the *Westminster Gazette*, de Valera drew an analogy to the Monroe Doctrine
and said, "Why doesn't Britain declare a Monroe Doctrine for the two neigh-
boring islands? The people of Ireland so far from objecting would co-operate
with their whole soul."[79]

Devoy and others on both sides of the Atlantic saw this proposal as tan-
tamount to surrender of the goal of Irish independence, because they knew
the United States frequently intervened in Cuban affairs and retained rights
to keep a military base on the island (which remains in existence). De Valera's
efforts to talk his way out of what he said on the record in (of all places) a
British newspaper never satisfied Devoy. The parallel had no relevance to a
proponent of republicanism—and in the February 14, 1920, edition of *The
Gaelic American*, Devoy fumed: "It opens the way for the discussion of a compromise, or a change in objective, while England has her hands on Ireland's
throat."[80] Thus did the gulf between the young Irish politician and the old
Fenian grow even wider and more personal. Devoy placed his reaction on the
front page of his weekly under the headline "John Devoy's Objections." For
good measure, he also added the byline "By John Devoy." Four years earlier,
he had vigorously challenged Woodrow Wilson in print. Now it was another
president's turn.[81]

Congenitally disputatious when challenged, Devoy took on anyone, regardless of position or reputation, if that person tried to maneuver around Devoy
or question the approach he was taking. In Tim Pat Coogan's biography *De
Valera: Long Fellow, Long Shadow*, the author comments, "Devoy might well
be described as a 'difficult man,' but he could not be regarded as less of a
republican than de Valera."[82] As it turned out, while the War of Independence
was being waged in Ireland, Devoy and de Valera engaged in a different kind
of hand-to-hand combat in the United States. Devoy's romantic attachment
to the cause of his life was always tempered by tough-minded realism about
a given situation. De Valera's American agenda was decidedly not Devoy's,

and Devoy fought to maintain his ground—and position. Near the end of de Valera's stay in America, Devoy was informed that the Clan na Gael organization that he had shaped and guided for so many years would no longer be affiliated with the IRB. His new rival, McGarrity, was taking over a reconstituted Clan in the United States. Moreover, and with the intention of crippling the Friends of Irish Freedom, which Devoy was instrumental in starting, de Valera created the American Association for the Recognition of the Irish Republic. Wherever Devoy turned, someone was taking him on. With more regret than defiance, he wrote Harry Boland, the IRB representative in the States: "After sixty years of the best that was in me, instead of dying by an English bullet or the hangman's rope, I am driven out by the chief officers of the Irish Republic."[83]

In the years that followed the Rising, Devoy kept producing *The Gaelic American* and speaking his mind about Ireland's course. De Valera and his U.S. supporters received his enduring enmity. He labeled the treaty that ended hostilities and established the Irish Free State "a surrender." Not long afterward, however, when de Valera's opposition to the treaty became known, Devoy changed his mind, siding with Michael Collins and pro-treaty proponents. When Collins and his followers prevailed in a close vote of 64 to 57, de Valera resigned as president of the Dáil, the Irish parliament.

Ireland wasn't a republic as yet—that wouldn't formally occur until Easter Monday of 1949—but the compromise of the treaty and the defeat of de Valera provided Devoy with a sense of both vindication and satisfaction. The Rising had set in motion a chain of events to transform "the old Ireland" in enduring ways. Devoy could look back on his own role and see the consequences of his involvement, which overshadowed all the internal strife and vying for power in Irish America that occurred after 1916. Feuds and splits notwithstanding, he prevailed, and at that point de Valera had been defeated and lost his power. When de Valera resigned in early 1922, Devoy saw an opening for himself to take a final trip to the country that occupied so much of his mind and life for over sixty years. He set sail from Hoboken on July 19, 1924, and arrived in Ireland a week later. It was a hero's return, complete with applause-filled occasions hosted by President W. T. Cosgrave and other officials of the Free State government. For six weeks, the only Fenian to be honored by the new Ireland traveled around the island, receiving awards and cheers at every stop. The *Freeman's Journal* in Dublin took note of his unflagging commitment: "Never have his labors relaxed, never have his fires dimmed, never has he ceased to cherish the larger hope."[84] In Devoy's case, the word *never* goes together with *always* and the abiding dream to achieve independence for the country of his birth.

At a farewell banquet in Dublin, at which President Cosgrave once again offered the nation's gratitude, Devoy had a chance to reminisce—and to speak his mind. He regretted not being in Ireland for the Easter Rising: "I have often since then regretted that I failed and was not shot with Tom Clarke." Even at this celebratory good-bye, the old Fenian was not above referring to the treatment he received from de Valera, though the object of his scorn is never named, telling his audience he had been "called a traitor for standing by the Irish Republic by the man who first lowered its flag and who sent men bribed with money which I had helped to collect to repeat the lie all over the United States and to make the worst split in all Irish history, which he later brought to Ireland to bring ruin and disaster upon her."[85] With wounds still healing from the recent Irish Civil War between forces loyal to de Valera and to Collins— Collins was gunned down and killed on August 22, 1922—Devoy's attack[86] wasn't the message his audience expected to hear, but a lifetime of political machinations and maneuvers hadn't softened the edges.

When Devoy died on September 29, 1928, in Atlantic City, the *London Times* marked his passing on October 1 with an obituary combining fact and opinion. The first sentence referred to him as "the oldest of Irish revolutionaries and the most bitter and persistent, as well as the most dangerous, enemy of this country which Ireland has produced since Wolfe Tone, the organizer of the United Irish Movement at the end of the eighteenth century." Before reciting specific details of his life, the unsigned article noted: "For sixty years Devoy was unremittingly engaged in conspiracies, both in Ireland and in America, for the establishment of an Irish Republic."[87] Many years after Devoy's death one historian observed: "His political longevity and his influence on both sides of the Atlantic meant that Devoy had personal contact with just about every figure of note in Nationalist Ireland and in the Irish-American communities of cities such as New York, Boston and Chicago from the early 1860s to the late 1920s."[88] No matter the figure involved, the republican cause, as he envisioned it for six decades, was unwavering.

Although most of his plotting was clandestine and done from a distance, Devoy's intentions were never in doubt. Peadar O Cearnaigh, who composed the lyrics for "The Soldier's Song," Ireland's national anthem, set down his remembrances in a manuscript that his nephew, Seamus de Burca, subsequently published as part of the book *The Soldier's Song: The Story of Peader O Cearnaigh*. Devoting considerable attention to Easter Week and the IRB, O Cearnaigh, who died in 1942 and fought during the Rising and the War of Independence, observed: "The future historian of a free Ireland, when dealing with the modern Fenians, will undoubtedly give pride of place to John Devoy as the most potent force in that movement, from the collapse of '67 to our own day. . . ."[89] Nothing bearing "on the vital phases of the revolutionary movement passed between this country and America except through Tom Clarke and John Devoy."[90]

In June of 1929, Devoy was buried in the section for patriots in Dublin's Glasnevin Cemetery. Under his name on the headstone was chiseled "Fenian." Another side of the headstone reads "Rebel." The third simply says "Patriot." The exile had come "home" to an elaborate military ceremony attended by a Who's Who of Irish governmental and civic life, as well as to the public at large. Philip J. O'Donnell, a Boston priest who officiated at Devoy's funeral in New York City on October 2, 1928, one that was attended by more than a thousand people, delivered the graveside oration in Dublin before interment. According to an account in the *Irish Times*, Father O'Donnell went beyond the three descriptive words that would be carved on the headstone to take Devoy's full measure: rebel, soldier, political prisoner, writer, editor, orator, statesman, plotter, revolutionist, physical force man, dreamer, man of action, and economist. To conclude, he said: "We give to you for burial here in this cemetery of the great the mortal remains of one of Ireland's greatest sons and liberty's foremost champion—John Devoy."[91]

Long before the final voyage back to Ireland, P. H. Pearse had offered his own opinion about John Devoy and his commitment to the republican cause. In what is titled "A Character Study" of Jeremiah O'Donovan Rossa and included in his *Collected Works*, Pearse took note of other figures in the movement that ultimately led to Easter 1916. He mentions James Stephens ("cold and enigmatic"), Charles Joseph Kickham ("shy and sensitive"), John O'Leary ("scholarly and chivalrous"), and Thomas Clarke Luby ("able and urbane") before saying of Rossa that he was "older and more prominent than the man who, when the time comes to write his biography will be recognized as the greatest of the Fenians—John Devoy."[92] Devoy's contribution to the Rising's planning and to the eventual independence the insurrection helped establish contributed substantially more evidence to support Pearse's enduring and historic judgment. His delight in battle never flagged, and, at long last, he could claim victory for the cause that was also his life.

Joyce Kilmer

(© Bettmann/Corbis / AP Images)

2

Joyce Kilmer: The Romance of Exile

A T 2:30 ON THE AFTERNOON of Saturday, April 29, 1916, P. H. Pearse
offered the rebel force's unconditional surrender, and at 3:45 he signed
a general order to put down all weapons "to prevent the further slaughter of
Dublin citizens, and in the hope of saving the lives of our followers now surrounded and hopelessly outnumbered."[1] After five and a half days of intense
fighting, the dead and wounded totaled more than three thousand people,
while over two hundred buildings in Dublin were destroyed or damaged.

The news dominated the American newspapers. That same day, the
New York Times published eight front-page stories about the Rising (out of a
total of eighteen of varying lengths) and eight more covering it on the second
page (where four articles from the front page were continued). The situation
in Ireland was also the subject of an editorial and a column of commentary.
The Rising received voluminous journalistic attention in America, with the
Times alone devoting page 1 coverage to it for fourteen straight days, from
April 25 through May 8. It was as though the war being waged in Europe
had opened another front—and this one came out of the blue as a manifes-
tation of rebelliousness within what was then called "the United Kingdom
of Great Britain and Ireland." The short-lived militaristic adventurism in
Ireland intersected with other war news, including reports about the Battle
of Verdun in France, then in its third of ten bloody months—resulting, ultimately, in almost 700,000 deaths. That spring of 1916 Britain was on edge and
under attack from German zeppelins and U-boats, so an internal insurrection spelled unprecedented trouble that conflict-centric journalists sought to
describe and explain. Not knowing how events might play out—could additional acts of violence break out beyond the general vicinity of Dublin after
the formal surrender?—news organizations in the United States tried to keep
up with information from abroad, which was subject to British wartime censorship and often delayed.

The Rising also had an irresistible local angle, particularly for big-city
newspapers. The American Irish wanted to know what was happening and

how they might respond. With domestic interest piqued, much of the coverage had a dual perspective. Accounts with London or Dublin datelines appeared together with reaction stories about first- or second-generation Irish Americans and their concerns, or reports about the policy implications of the rebels' cause. Though censorial press restrictions hampered the flow of information originating overseas, what was covered in the United States took full advantage of the First Amendment, and all viewpoints—pro-Rising, anti-Rising, support for Britain, criticism of Britain—received amplification as the events unfolded. Throughout the nineteen days encompassing the Rising and the executions, April 24 through May 12, news about Ireland made the front page of the *New York Times* seventeen times, the *Boston Globe* sixteen, the *Washington Post* thirteen, and the *Chicago Tribune* and the *New York World* eleven. The "exiled children" were kept fully informed, and they used what they learned to form their opinions about what to think and how (or whether) to act.

Journalists, however, weren't the only ones to take up the Rising and its aftermath as a topic worthy of consideration and comment. Poets, playwrights, and novelists reflected on what had happened and contributed to the responsorial chorus. On May 4, the *New York World* included in its package of stories, under the headline "Shoot Four Irish Uprising Leaders in London Tower" (actually, three leaders—P. H. Pearse, Tom Clarke, and Thomas MacDonagh—were executed in Dublin on May 3), a prominent text box with George Bernard Shaw's reaction. Then living in England and writing his opinion for an American audience, Shaw, who was described as "the distinguished Irish playwright," was both witty and Solomonic: "Silly, ignorant, wrongheaded—but honorable, brave and republican."[2] The statement was widely quoted throughout the American press, and it suggested the complexity of arriving at a final judgment at this stage.

From an American perspective, the works of Joyce Kilmer in addressing the Rising stand out from other responses for their breadth, variety, and consequence. In addition, Kilmer's life bears witness not only to the U.S. reaction to events in Ireland but also to what was happening throughout Europe. His character and deliberate self-invention shaped what he believed, wrote, and did. Kilmer made studied and deliberate choices of who he would be and how he would be perceived. In his mind, as well as in his heart, he, too, was one of the "exiled children."

By the time of the Rising, Kilmer, only twenty-nine years old (and considerably more youthful in appearance), with a stocky build and medium height, was well known as a poet, journalist, literary critic, editor, and lecturer. His popularity in 1916 derived principally from one twelve-line poem that he had published three years earlier in *Poetry: A Magazine of Verse*, the modernist, groundbreaking journal edited by Harriet Monroe that featured the work of (among others) W. B. Yeats, Ezra Pound, T. S. Eliot, and William Carlos Williams. Kilmer's poem "Trees" begins with thirteen words countless schoolchildren would later memorize:

> I think that I shall never see
> A poem lovely as a tree.

The short, final stanza contrasts two acts of creation:

> Poems are made by fools like me,
> But only God can make a tree.[3]

Few poems have enjoyed both fame and familiarity, but "Trees" kept Kilmer in the public's mind for generations. The association resulted in the designation (in 1936) of the Joyce Kilmer Memorial Forest, in North Carolina, by the United States Forest Service, while several elementary and middle schools were also named for him. In 1938, however, Cleanth Brooks and Robert Penn Warren published the first of several editions of *Understanding Poetry*, which later the *New York Times* in 1979 called "very likely the single most influential text in the teaching of poetry in this generation and a foundation stone of the New Criticism."[4] Brooks and Warren begin their exegesis of "Trees" by saying: "This poem has been very greatly admired by a large number of people. The fact that it has been popular does not necessarily condemn it as a bad poem. But it is a bad poem."[5] Their New Critical analysis left not a single branch or leaf to admire. The *Irish Times* (in a 1961 editorial comment) took a less academic and more balanced approach to what it refers to, without giving the title, as "Joyce Kilmer's poem": "It is not a good poem, yet it obviously expressed something that a lot of people felt; for it has been learned by schoolchildren in many parts of the world, it used to be a favourite party recitation, and it was even set to music."[6] By the time Ogden Nash's equally famous parody appeared in 1932—"I think I shall never see" / "a billboard lovely as a tree"—the original was set in the public imagination.

Over a century after "Trees" first appeared, the poem seems anachronistic to the point of satire or even ridicule. Indeed, since 1986, the Philolexian Society of Kilmer's alma mater, Columbia University, has sponsored what is called the "Alfred Joyce Kilmer Memorial Bad Poetry Contest," complete with a dramatic reading of "Trees" to conclude an evening of competitive parody. Though still anthologized in collections of American poetry—the poem, for example, appears in the Library of America's volume of early twentieth-century verse[7]—"Trees" tends to obscure the sturdy stand of poems, essays, and feature articles Kilmer produced from 1913 until his death in 1918, works that brought him international recognition during his lifetime. To a certain extent, the enormous attention "Trees" received ultimately became a literary albatross, preventing people today from seeing him as a significant Catholic writer, an early champion of the poetic achievement of Gerard Manley Hopkins, and an astute commentator on the Easter Rising.

Despite his productivity as a poet (three book-length collections between 1911 and 1917), Kilmer primarily earned his living, from 1913 until 1917, writing for the *New York Times Magazine*. What he called his "Sunday stories" appeared with almost weekly regularity, and from time to time he even responded to the news through poetry. For instance, after the Germans torpedoed the RMS *Lusitania* off the coast of Ireland, killing 1,198 of the 1,959 on board (including 128 Americans), he composed "The White Ships and the Red," which was widely republished at the time and frequently included in anthologies of the early twentieth century and the Great War. The sinking occurred on May 7, 1915. The *Times Magazine* devoted its first page nine days later to the eleven-stanza poem, with an original drawing surrounding it. Strikingly, the *Lusitania* is never named. A contemporary reader would have known the identity of the red ship of the title and the news-chasing verse, which concludes with this memorable image:

> When God's great voice assembles
> The fleet on Judgment Day,
> The ghosts of ruined ships will rise
> In sea and strait and bay.
> Though they have lain for ages
> Beneath the changeless flood,
> They shall be white as silver,
> But one—shall be like blood.[8]

A year later, on May 7, 1916—during the first executions—Kilmer published a *New York Times Magazine* article with the title "Poets Marched in the Van of Irish Revolt." He conveyed the sense that the insurrection was a word-inspired adventure. "A poetic revolution—indeed, a poets' revolution—that is what has been happening in Ireland during the last two weeks, says Padraic Colum, himself an Irish poet now in New York," Kilmer began his lengthy article before arguing that the Rising was "closely related to the work of the Gaelic League, to the Irish Theatre Movement, and to that phase of literary activity which is termed the Celtic Renascence or the Neo-Celtic Movement. The leaders of the movement were, for the most part, men of letters."[9] Kilmer established the Rising's place in contemporary Irish culture. Though he was pursuing a breaking news story, he was putting it into a perspective far different from the deadline-driven reports for his own and other newspapers, playing off those reports but then circling back to advance his theme: "The leaders of the revolutionary forces were almost without exception men of literary tastes and training, who went into battle, as one of the dispatches phrased it, 'with a revolver in one hand and a copy of Sophocles in the other.' "[10]

In addition to Colum, the article took up the work of P. H. Pearse, Thomas MacDonagh, Joseph Mary Plunkett, James Connolly, Robert Casement, Eoin MacNeill, and Constance Markievicz. There was even consideration given to the play *Cathleen Houlihan* by W. B. Yeats, which Colum remarked "had more to do than any other purely literary writing in inflaming the young Irishmen with love of country and passionate desire for freedom."[11] Colum—who later in 1916 co-edited with Edward J. O'Brien two editions of the collection *Poems of the Irish Revolutionary Brotherhood*, featuring Pearse, MacDonagh, Plunkett, and Casement—linked Yeats to the Rising early on, an association Yeats himself waited a long time to make. In one of his last poems before his death in 1939 ("Man and the Echo"), Yeats expressed his anxiety about the connection between violence and his work:

> I lie awake night after night
> And never get the answers right.
> Did that play of mine send out
> Certain men the English shot?[12]

Kilmer reprinted poems by MacDonagh and Casement in his text, which included photos of Pearse, Clarke, MacDonagh, Colum, and Markievicz.

By dealing with key figures as serious thinkers and writers, Kilmer put a human face on the Rising's participants—and elevated their efforts to express nationalistic longing. The article concluded with a statement from Colum that revealed why the alienation of the rebel-minded erupted in the actions of Easter Week. Colum argued that the Irish read and admired English literature and liked the English people. "What we cannot endure is simply the English Government—simply the imposition upon us of a Government from the outside with which we have no sympathy, and which has no sympathy with us. And the greatest sensitivity is to be found on the highest level—it is the intellectuals among us who feel the agony the most, and are the first to revolt against it."[13]

Kilmer's article is noteworthy for its approach and depth. Despite all the U.S. journalistic attention to the Rising, the coverage suffered from factual mistakes (from which Kilmer wasn't exempt, reporting that the executions occurred in London), a reliance on unverified rumors, and, most important, lack of direct access to information. Journalists were forced to peer through a fog of war and were hampered by institutional restraints, making any objective perspective nearly impossible. One wire-service dispatch that appeared on April 28 in the *New York Times*, the *Washington Post*, and several other newspapers described the basic problem: "Dublin is further from London today than Peking is from New York, so far as communication for the general public is concerned. No Irish newspapers have reached here [London] since the rising, and passenger traffic has been for the most part suspended. The only information comes through official channels."[14]

In a news vacuum and reliance on "official channels," with censorship and martial law in effect, publishing what was available became the only alternative. Except for local stories capturing Irish-American reaction, the early coverage drew extensively from British sources, with their biases. Roger Casement figured prominently at the beginning; it was not until Sunday, April 30 (the day after the surrender), that the name of the leader of the Provisional Government surfaced—and even then it was spelled "Pearce" rather than "Pearse," and he was called "Peter" or "J. H." That same day, a page 1 story in the *New York Times* reported, "Leader Connolly Killed," an erroneous report also printed in the *Washington Post*.

Citing inaccuracies in the coverage is less an attempt at criticism than at transparency. In this case, the chestnut that journalism provides "a rough first draft of history" applied, with *rough* connoting "partial" and "sometimes suspect" information. Kilmer's lengthy article, though, deserves consideration for its comprehensiveness and for identifying the centrality of poets and writers in the Irish cause. The romance of intellectuals being in the vanguard of political action—especially in Ireland, with its reverence for literati—took root early on and helped make the rebels more sympathetic and memorable. In an essay about the fifty-year commemoration of the Rising, Mary E. Daly quoted the American columnist Mary McGrory that 1916 "was the only revolution which was fomented and fought by poets."[15]

Kilmer's articles for the *New York Times Magazine* stood out from other coverage by emphasizing the involvement of poets. Indeed, on the editorial and the commentary pages of the daily *New York Times*, there was no ambiguity about the newspaper's viewpoint on the Rising and its meaning. A day after the first reports of the revolt, a three-paragraph item in the "Topics of the Times" opinion column focused on Casement. "Charity, seeking, as charity must, an explanation that will serve as an excuse for a crime as abhorrent to all the world as treason, finds first and only the possibility that Sir Roger Casement was a victim of the neurasthenia that so often diminishes or destroys the moral responsibility of men who stay too long and work too hard in the tropics." After additional speculation and criticism of the Germans, the comment concluded that Casement's actions were "a sort of suicide, for the plea of insanity, the only plea his friends can make, is unlikely to save him."[16]

The next day Casement was again one of the "Topics of the Times," but his actions were now evaluated in the wider context of Irish history. He was compared unfavorably to Wolfe Tone, one of the leaders of the Rebellion of 1798, and his part in a more encompassing movement was not so clear-cut: "Discretion will probably decide against giving a cause as bad as his its martyr."[17] Both of these anti-Casement outbursts appeared as commentary on the editorial page. However, beginning April 29, the *New York Times* started a campaign of vehement opposition to the rebel cause. Sarcasm and stereotyping provided the principal elements of an editorial simply titled "Ireland." Casement, "that treasonable Irishman," was ridiculed (as he was in another "Topics of the Times" item on the same page, called "A Familiar Form of Insanity"), and this editorial suggested that "the whole expedition was planned by the Germans as a means to get rid of a tall, deep-bearded conspirator whose efforts to explain Irish politics had begun to menace their reason."

The editorial was then broadened in scope to survey Irish history from the time of "clan against clan, King against King" to the present. British rule had led to "a narrative in rebellion," which, in the newspaper's opinion, was anything but admirable: "Rebellion has been the chronic, almost to say the natural, condition of Ireland, being now and then only a little more acute than usual. Never has she been able to rebel unanimously or by a very large majority." The last paragraph solidified the anti-Irish stance of the *Times* editorial policy: "Never has Ireland been free, and yet she has all the more passion for freedom. What these present rebels want is not to be free of England. They pursue an ideal of freedom. England is the symbol of restraint. If it were not England, it might be a King. If it were not a King, it might be the fairies that go about in Ireland, assuming fantastic shapes, to frighten people and make them do all the things they do not want to do."[18]

On May 2, under the heading "The Irish Folly," the *Times* argued that the revolt "had only evil fruits." This time fairies do not frolic at the conclusion. The editorial took on Irish-American supporters, such as John Devoy and his followers in Clan na Gael, in a 108-word tirade:

> The leaders of the movement cannot be acquitted of responsibility, they are altogether blameworthy, but a sterner censure even may justly be visited upon those in this country who have encouraged them and now commend their acts of incredible folly and rashness, for when any man of the Irish race in America speaks in praise of the deplorable Sinn Fein escapade it is hard to shut out the belief that a seeking for popularity here and a political motive purely domestic, rather than sincere sympathy with the Irish "cause" or hope for its success, have been the real prompting to such aid and comfort as has been given.[19]

Two days later another editorial, entitled "Fate of the Irish Rebels," endorsed the first executions, noting "war is a stern business and the subject who sets himself against his King or the citizen who rises against his Government when the nation is straining every resource to overcome enemies in the field can hardly expect mercy."[20] When Kilmer's *Times Magazine* article appeared on May 7, readers of the *Times* found a detailed enunciation of a different, more compassionate perspective on the Rising from what they had received elsewhere in the newspaper up to that point. Kilmer took no cues or directions from the paper's management, nor would he subsequently.

What he wrote served as an explicit counterpoint to the editorial policy of his employer.

However, the extended and seemingly cold-blooded continuity of the punishment of the Rising's leaders did not escape the attention of the *Times*. On page 1 for the edition of May 12, a dispatch with a London dateline began: "The most dangerous factor in Ireland's situation which had been recognized since the brief rising flashed in the pan was that the punishment of the rebels would cause a reaction of sympathy among the warm-hearted and emotional people. This threatening danger appears to be fast materializing."[21] Already there was the suggestion that the public's mood could prove volatile because of the circumstances involved. A modest shifting of opinion is even detectable on the paper's editorial page that same day:

> Fourteen persons have been executed, two or three apparently sacrificed to official stupidity. But the whole proceeding is incredibly stupid . . . unworthy of England. Leave that sort of thing to Germany. No matter if these misguided rebels, intellectuals, visionaries, and miscellaneous poor devils and scalawags were suborned and abetted by Germany. Only an Irish madman would look for help to the Prussian drill sergeants.

In the last paragraph, however, the *Times* regained its traditional moorings by complimenting "the noble, generous British" and the "Irish patriotism of John Redmond."[22]

How the *New York Times* handled the Rising and what followed is a case study of a serious American newspaper trying to provide a full accounting. News reports and feature articles, notably those by Kilmer, presented facts and context, while the editorials and commentary columns articulated opinions and leveled criticism. Interestingly, the *Times* itself had been on the receiving end of criticism one year earlier for taking what was perceived as an anti-German and pro-British bias. In his official, *Times*-published *History of the New York Times: 1851–1921*, Elmer Davis reported that at a U.S. Senate committee meeting in March of 1915 some senators accused the newspaper of advocating certain viewpoints in exchange for money.[23] Among specific charges leveled at the top editors of the *Times* was one they considered especially libelous—that the newspaper had received financial support from England, which directly influenced the content of what appeared in the paper. The "legend of British gold" and the rumor of foreign control of the paper directed the line of questioning of Senator Thomas J. Walsh of Montana, the chairman of the committee.[24] To what extent Walsh's Irish-American heritage might have motivated his concern is unknown, though his biographer, J. Leonard Bates, notes sympathy for Irish-American causes as part of Walsh's service, and on the opening page of his life of Walsh, he wrote, "Learning politics from his father, he functioned at times with the skills of an Irish politico."[25] Besides inquiring about the ownership of the *Times*, Walsh and other members of the committee asked about certain stories. One particular pool report about war news from Europe, which was jointly sent to the *Times* and two other newspapers, differed in its conclusion from those of the other two. Carr Van Anda, managing editor of the *Times*, apparently tutored the Senate committee on his newspaper's strict division between news and commentary: "That was done for the very good and sufficient reason that it was an expression of opinion by the writer."[26]

While other American newspapers at that time blurred the lines between facts and opinions, the *Times* tried to maintain a wall dividing distinct types of journalism. This approach reflected the philosophy of publisher Adolph S. Ochs, who purchased the paper in 1896 and introduced the slogan "All the News That's Fit to Print" the same year. Ochs's commitment to news rather than taking a stand was so serious that he even considered ending the publication of the editorial page.[27]

As events in Ireland continued to receive news attention, Kilmer's *New York Times Magazine* article in early May and his later one in August offered contextual background and elicited sympathy for participants in the Rising. He wasn't alone. Opinion pages and Sunday feature newspaper sections in Boston, Chicago, Washington, and elsewhere probed behind surface facts to explain the larger story. Although, editorially, the *Times* stood four-square against the rebels, other major papers were less inclined to hew to a black-or-white opinion of the situation. As early as April 26, one day after news of the Rising broke, the *Washington Post* opined on "The Outbreak in Ireland" by focusing on Casement and how he "placed his head in the lion's mouth, with dashing intrepidity bordering upon madness." The editorial concluded by arguing that executing him would be a mistake. "Casement executed in the Tower would become a martyr, enshrined in Irish hearts, his faults forgotten, his mad exploit idealized and his example emulated."[28] The possibility that Casement might become a martyr foreshadowed much of the future coverage.

On May 2, a day before the first executions, both the *Washington Post* and the *Chicago Tribune* published editorials proposing the possibility of the British punishment becoming excessive. In its opening sentences, the *Washington Post* found fault with the Rising and Casement, "a harebrained if not insane agitator whose only successful stroke was the enlisting of German assistance. Why the German government or people lent any aid to Sir Roger is not apparent, since the Germans are not usually addicted to wild-goose chases." Still, the editorial cautioned readers, the uprising was "a reminder that the Irish question remains to be settled. Ireland must have a greater measure of home rule. If the British government has not entirely lost its balance, it will not make fierce reprisals in Ireland, but will deal tolerantly even with the ringleaders of the insurrection."[29] The *Chicago Tribune* followed a similar course in its editorial: "There is a hint that this now subdued Irish rebellion will not be followed by many executions to give a new set of memories to the Irish. It would be a wise England that saw the Irish revolt compassionately."[30]

Three days later—after Pearse, Clarke, and MacDonagh had been executed—the *Chicago Tribune*, in an editorial with the heading "Unnecessary and Inexpedient," asserted that the executions had been a mistake. "It might have been far more effective to turn the three men loose in Dublin. Their heroism would have oozed away a little every time a citizen looked at the wrecked post office. The practical result of their fury would have established them in the minds of the comfortable, practical citizens as wild dreamers."[31] The *Washington Post* also published an editorial that denounced the first executions in no uncertain terms: "This hasty, ill-considered and unstatesmanlike act of political vengeance is bound to make still more bitter the relations between England and Ireland, and to be a fruitful source of trouble in the years to come." Contrasting the leniency of the English in handling opposing combatants in the Boer War that took place from late 1899 until mid-1902, with the almost immediate assembling of firing squads in Dublin, the *Washington Post* asked: "How can any man have respect for law thus inequitably, unfairly and one-sidedly administered?"[32]

These editorials and Kilmer's long feature show how competing viewpoints were taking shape in American newspapers. The Rising might have been brief, disorganized, and ultimately unsuccessful, but the British response merited stern criticism. In other words, the action and reaction were judged almost simultaneously, with the evaluation of the reaction proving more influential. The "wild dreamers" did, indeed, become "martyrs," and during that transformation American public opinion changed to the benefit of the rebels and their cause. Whatever people's feelings about the rebellion itself, the aftermath turned public opinion against the British.[33] Meetings and rallies supporting the rebels and their cause took place across the United States. By mid-summer of 1916, what was called the "Irish Relief Fund" had collected humanitarian assistance of between $100,000 and $150,000—an amount slightly higher than Clan na Gael's contribution to help mount the Rising.

In late June, Kilmer participated in a large memorial gathering in New York City to honor victims of the insurrection, especially the poets. As the *New York Tribune* noted, "Tears flowed plentifully at Central Park yesterday afternoon when the Irish poets of New York met to mourn their brothers who died in the Sinn Fein uprising." Pearse, MacDonagh, and Plunkett were referred to as "the martyr poets" by the *Tribune*, and selections from their verse, along with poems and statements written for the occasion by several noted figures in American literary life (such as William Dean Howells, Louis Untermeyer, Harriet Monroe, and Edwin Markham), were read to the crowd. The *Tribune* account focused on Kilmer and the theme he had developed earlier in the *Times Magazine*. "The world used to despise the poet, calling him a long-haired, effeminate creature who shunned a man's work," he was quoted as saying. "It is no longer necessary to defend the poet against this calumny. It was the poets in Ireland who inspired this fight for freedom and it was the poets who fought."[34] Possibly to avoid suggesting the ethical conflict of a staff member taking a definite stand on a current issue in public, the *New York Times* merely mentioned that Kilmer was among those who "read original poems," devoting most of its coverage to the work "A Song for Ireland's Martyred Poets" that Eleanor Rogers Cox composed for the occasion.[35]

In his poetic contribution, "Easter Week," Kilmer proved that he was not afraid to take on Yeats through direct address or to celebrate Ireland's Catholicism (Kilmer had converted to Catholicism in 1913). The nine quatrains, with their intricate internal and end-line rhyme schemes, demonstrate Kilmer's craftsmanship and his ability to imitate the rhythms of popular ballads. He dedicated the poem to the one rebel leader and poet he'd met in New York the summer before.

Easter Week

(In memory of Joseph Mary Plunkett)
(*"Romantic Ireland's dead and gone,*
It's with O'Leary in the grave.")
—William Butler Yeats.

"Romantic Ireland's dead and gone,
    It's with O'Leary in the grave."
Then, Yeats, what gave that Easter dawn
    A hue so radiantly brave?

There was a rain of blood that day,
    Red rain in gay blue April weather.
It blessed the earth till it gave birth
    To valour thick as blooms of heather.

Romantic Ireland never dies!
    O'Leary lies in fertile ground,
    And songs and spears throughout the years
    Rise up where patriot graves are found.

Immortal patriots newly dead
    And ye that bled in bygone years,
What banners rise before your eyes?
    What is the tune that greets your ears?

The young Republic's banners smile
    For many a mile where troops convene.
O'Connell Street is loudly sweet
    With strains of Wearing of the Green.

The soil of Ireland throbs and glows
    With life that knows the hour is here
To strike again like Irishmen
    For that which Irishmen hold dear.

Lord Edward leaves his resting place
    And Sarsfield's face is glad and fierce.
See Emmet leap from troubled sleep
    To grasp the hand of Padraic Pearse!

There is no rope can strangle song
    And not for long death takes his toll.
No prison bars can dim the stars
    Nor quicklime eat the living soul.

Romantic Ireland is not old.
    For years untold her youth shall shine.
Her heart is fed on Heavenly bread,
    The blood of martyrs is her wine.[36]

"Easter Week" was a finalist in the Poetry Society of America's competition for the best poem of 1916, and Kilmer included it in his collection *Main Street and Other Poems* (1917). *Nineteen-Sixteen: An Anthology* was compiled by Edna C. FitzHenry and appeared in 1935. Kilmer's "Easter Week" is the only contribution from an American of the sixty-two poems published in one of three categories: Prelude, Battle, and Requiem. Other contributors to the volume included W. B. Yeats, A. E. (George William Russell), P. H. Pearse, Joseph Mary Plunkett, Thomas MacDonagh, Roger Casement, Eva Gore-Booth, and Dora Sigerson Shorter. In 1951, *Poetry Ireland* published an "Easter Rising Memorial Issue" in honor of the thirty-fifth anniversary. Kilmer's poem appeared in it as well. Over the years, Kilmer has become the U.S. poet most associated with the Rising on both sides of the Atlantic. In a 1966 survey of the poetry about 1916 for an Irish journal, Augustine Martin quoted three entire stanzas and then remarked: "Though an American, Kilmer was familiar enough with both Irish history and poetry to fasten, with the poet's intuition, to the more evocative symbols of revolt."[37]

The poem struck chords that reverberated for readers in Irish America. Among Kilmer's papers in the Georgetown University Library's Special Collections Research Center is a letter from a New York attorney, John Jerome Rooney, dated March 31, 1917, almost a year after the poem was written. Complimenting Kilmer on addressing "the Irish struggles for liberty," Rooney praised the poet's "fine spirit and work in this matter," but then used it as an excuse to mourn the loss of the "old American spirit." He wrote: "People seem to divide now along lines of pro-German or pro-English and not upon the lines of the great American principle of the right of Nations to their own individual free life. That principle is and always was fundamental to American doctrine and practice."[38] Rooney's viewpoint was also Kilmer's, a viewpoint he set down most forcefully in the poem "Apology," another of his works about the Rising. He elevated writers of verse to a spiritual, even celestial status. In one stanza near the end, the three poets who helped mount the Rising (Pearse, Plunkett, and MacDonagh, rather than the mistaken "McDonough" in the published version) receive consideration along with three well-known English poets: Lord Byron, Shelley, and Leigh Hunt.

> Lord Byron and Shelley and Plunkett,
>   McDonough and Hunt and Pearse
> See now why their hatred of tyrants
>   Was so insistently fierce.

> Is Freedom only a Will-o'-the-wisp
> To cheat a poet's eye?
> Be it phantom or fact, it's a noble cause
> In which to sing and to die![39]

"Apology," which Kilmer also collected in *Main Street and Other Poems*, makes "Freedom" and the "hatred of tyrants" fundamental human conditions—and worth the price of sacrificing one's life.

Kilmer's literary preoccupation with Irish figures and issues, topics to which he kept returning, developed from his adopted ethnic identity and his interpretation of what it had replaced. In a letter to his wife, Aline, herself an accomplished poet, he remarked that he had told a friend that he was "half-Irish." "For proof of this, you have only to refer to the volumes containing the histories of my mother's and my father's families. Of course I am American, but one cannot be pure American in blood unless one is an Indian."[40] Kilmer was adamant, imploring his wife in the same letter, "And don't let anyone publish a statement contradictory to this."[41]

One who challenged Kilmer's statement that he was "half Irish" was Robert Cortes Holliday, Kilmer's literary executor. In a lengthy memoir about his friend that introduced a posthumously published two-volume collection of Kilmer's poetry and prose, Holliday wryly observed that while Kilmer's "birth was not exactly eloquent of this fact," he was Irish "in the sense of keenly savouring those things which are fine in the Irish character, and with characteristic gusto feeling within himself an affinity with them."[42] Whatever the precise proportion of his ancestral blood, Kilmer took his Irishness so seriously that his son, Kenton, devoted the longest chapter of *Memories of My Father, Joyce Kilmer* to "Our Irish and Irish-American Friends and Relations." Kenton couldn't substantiate his father's "half Irish" claim, noting "I find no apparently Irish names among Dad's ancestors on the Kilmer side."[43]

Clearly, however, Joyce Kilmer selected the heritage and identity most personally meaningful to the way he saw himself in a nation of immigrants. Kenton recalled that his father "was enamored of Irish history, Irish legend and literature, and Irish and Irish-American poetry."[44] Kenton always remembered that his father would "frequent the company of Irish patriots, eager for Ireland to break free of British rule, but he also had some friends, still strongly Irish, who were for the modified autonomy called Home Rule."[45] Kenton's daughter, Miriam A. Kilmer, wrote after genealogical research about her grandfather: "His father was mostly German and English, his mother mostly

English. . . . His passionate love for Ireland and the Irish is obvious, so we may say he was Irish by adoption."[46]

Kilmer felt kinship with the Irish because they embodied traits he admired. Their love of literature, spirited and sometimes raucous embrace of life, and their commitment to family all played a part. Most compelling for Kilmer was their devotion to the Catholic Church. From his conversion in 1913 until the end of his life, Kilmer was considered (in Holliday's phrase) "the laureate of the Catholic Church,"[47] with religious themes and subjects a prime focus of his prose and poetry. Commenting on the work of Lionel Johnson, a nineteenth-century English poet and essayist, Kilmer noted: "He saw that the greatest glory of Ireland is her fidelity to the Catholic Faith, a fidelity which countless cruel persecutions have only strengthened."[48] Like Kilmer, Johnson was a convert, and both of them viewed Ireland through the lens of religion. The linkage between Catholicism and Irish identity would become even more pronounced for Kilmer during his own war service.

As a staff-level contributor to the *New York Times*, Kilmer returned to the Rising with a poignant article entitled "Irish Girl Rebel Tells of Dublin Fighting," which the *Times Magazine* published on August 20, 1916. This story—reprinted in full as an appendix at the end of this book—focused on Moira Regan, who served in Cumann na mBan, the women's auxiliary of the Irish Volunteers, relating her experiences in the GPO and as a messenger for the rebels. No doubt informed of her arrival in New York by a republican friend, Kilmer developed the narrative by means of vivid details and direct quotations that contribute both immediacy and specificity, beginning with the subject herself:

> Moira Regan is a slight, gray-eyed girl. There is a charming flavor of County Wexford in her manner and in her voice. But back of her gray eyes and charming manner there is a depth of tragic experience. For Moira Regan has worked night and day in a beleaguered fort, has breathed air redolent with gunpowder, and heard the groans of men torn by shot and shell. She has seen her friends led away to death, their bodies to be thrown into a pit of quicklime.[49]

Kilmer lets Moira Regan tell exactly what happened from her perspective during the entire two-week period:

> There are a few things that I'd like every one in America to know about this rising, and about the way in which the British officers and soldiers acted. When the rebels surrendered they were at first treated with great

courtesy. The British officers complimented them on the bold stand they had made, and said they wished they had men like them in the British Army. But after they had surrendered they were treated in the worst possible way. They were cursed and insulted, marched to the Rotunda Gardens, and made to spend the night there in the wet grass. They were not given a morsel of food.[50]

Regan went on to describe the harsh treatment the rebels received in jail, the reliance on dog biscuits for sustenance, and the cruel nature of the executions. Yet, despite or perhaps because of that treatment, there had been a "complete and amazing revival of Irish nationality. . . . [N]ow we have been awakened to the knowledge that there is a great difference between Ireland and England, that we are really a separate nation. Even the people who were not in sympathy with the rebels feel this now."[51]

Nearly four months after the insurrection ended, it continued to reverberate across the Atlantic, and not just in the pages of John Devoy's *Gaelic American*. Indeed, just a week earlier in the *New York Times Magazine* (August 13), the essay "Roger Casement, Martyr" by John Quinn, the prominent New York attorney and friend of Yeats, compared Casement to Wolfe Tone and John Brown. Though critical of Casement's "faith in Germany," as he put it, Quinn argued that Casement had "paid England's price. Now it is England's turn to pay. And England pays, and will continue to pay, in the pain of her admirers, in the silence of her defenders, in the loss of American sympathy."[52]

The attention the Rising and its aftermath generated in the American press did not escape the scrutiny of the British, who worried that it might create problems in Ireland, were it known there what was being reported. On June 1, General Sir John Maxwell, commander-in-chief of military forces in Ireland, established a Press Censor's office in Dublin, and on June 5 the censor, Lieutenant-Colonel Lord Decies, issued a directive, with "CONFIDENTIAL" in capital letters and underlined at the top, that was distributed to every newspaper in Ireland. The document, included in the "Press Censorship Records 1916–1919" in the National Archives of Ireland, warned about the republication of certain journalistic reports:

> You are requested to give careful consideration to the following before publication:
>
> 1. Resolutions and speeches of Corporations, County and Urban Councils and Boards of Guardians.

2. Letters from soldiers, connected with the late rising in Dublin.

3. Extracts from American newspapers, or private letters sent you from individuals received from America.

4. Criticisms in the form of letters from individuals on the late rising in Dublin, of a violent nature.

5. Letters sent you from men arrested in Dublin in connection with the late rising now in detention.

6. Indiscretions made by other papers either in Foreign or Home Press should not be published.

No objection will be taken to any publication of above provided the language is moderate; doubtful matter should be submitted before printing.[53]

Despite this edict—which expresses explicit concern about journalistic or personal messages originating in the United States—borders between Ireland and America proved porous. *The Gaelic American* acquired a copy of this official directive and published it in a special box on July 8, 1916, with a Devoy-sounding editorial comment as a headline: "How the Irish Press Is Gagged."[54] The *Midland Reporter*, based in Mullingar, somehow obtained Kilmer's article about Moira Regan, reprinting it in toto on September 14, roughly a month after it appeared in the *New York Times*. Two days later, Kilmer's article also appeared in the *Roscommon Herald*. Both the *Midland Reporter* and the *Roscommon Herald* were owned by Jasper Joseph Tully, and either he or someone working for him tried to defuse the explosive nature of the interview by burying it inside each weekly with a one-column headline, "Tales of the Rebellion," and by printing this brief introduction, "The New York Times, a strong pro-Ally paper, prints the following. . . ."

The press censor, however, took immediate notice, firing off an inquiry to the attorney general for Ireland, James Campbell, on September 14: "There are certain statements made which I believe are quite untrue, and the result of such an article being published cannot do any good in the country. Would you advise that the Press should be informed that all outside accounts of the Rebellion—or articles connected with it—should be submitted to the Censor before publication?"[55] The next day, Campbell responded that he thought publication of this article "a very grave offence and one which the Military Authority should at once deal with by the seizure of the printing type and plant of this paper."[56] On September 16, the censor took the matter up with the military governor in Ireland, General Maxwell, soliciting his opinion of the article. Like the attorney general, Maxwell adopted a hard line and urged enforcement of martial law: "The publication of the alleged interview in America reprinted from the New York Times is clearly a contravention of Reg. 27 of D. of R. [Defence of the Realm Act]. I would suggest dealing with this case . . . similar to the 'Liberator' of Co. Kerry, i.e., Seize the Plant and enforce a bond for restitution of the Plant and authority to republish the paper."[57]

Maxwell ultimately decided to back down from seizure of the newspapers and suggested that a strong warning from the censor would be sufficient in dealing with the republication of Kilmer's article. The censor wrote Tully on September 20, 1916:

> I am directed to inform you that the publication of your article "Tales of the Rebellion" purporting to be taken from the "New York Times" and appearing in your issue of 16th September is in contravention of the Defence of the Realm regulations, and I am further instructed to warn you that the publication of Press matter of this description renders your paper liable to suppression under the Defence of the Realm Act. You are advised in future to submit articles of this nature to the Press Censor before publication.[58]

Tully's next-day response to the warning seemed simultaneously a sincere statement of journalistic concern and a verbal smokescreen of obsequious rhetoric designed to protect his newspapers from government intervention. Given the circumstances of martial law, censorship, and the changing of public opinion after the Rising, the executions, and the arrests, either interpretation could be plausible. Tully wrote: "The article was copied from the 'New York Times,' a friendly paper, and it appeared to us to contradict rumours in circulation. If we had any suspicion that there would have been any question raised, we would have sent you the proofs before publishing it. We have no desire to cross the boundary line in these matters."[59] Tully, who had lived in America before returning to Ireland to become involved in journalism and politics, was known for his nationalist views, but he split with Parnell and was expelled from the United Irish League in 1903, ending his support for the Irish Party.

Concern over press coverage and the views of Irish America became a preoccupation for British authorities. The *New York Times* on August 22 relied on a Dublin dispatch from the *Manchester Guardian*, with the headline "Military Tightens Grip on Ireland," to report: "Newspapers have been warned that criticism of the Government and of the Administration likely to cause disaffection will not be tolerated." The same article noted that cracking down on the press co-existed with worry about public opinion and how it was being formed across the Atlantic:

> Messages to hand from the United States undoubtedly indicate an unhealthy sentiment among the Irish-American masses. For the moment it would seem as if all the good work of British and Irish statesmen for the last thirty-five years, in removing the root of poisonous bitterness from Anglo-Irish-American relations, had been undone by the recent executions and the collapse of the home rule agreement.[60]

Throughout the Rising and for months afterward, the *New York Times* played a central role in providing thorough coverage of Ireland, with Kilmer's feature stories a distinctive element. On its editorial page, however, the newspaper was unwavering in criticizing the rebels and their cause. Even the death sentence pronounced on Casement brought no sympathy on June 30. Instead, under the heading "Vanities of Martyrdom," there's an ad hominem onslaught—"How flat and unexciting the universe would be to Sir Roger Casement unless it contained, first, the fact of Sir Roger's existence, and, second, the fame of his martyrdom!"—as well as a larger judgment: "They will make a ballad of him in Ireland."[61] But other sections of the paper kept a fuller treatment of conditions and circumstances in Ireland at the forefront of reader concerns. The paper's Sunday *Magazine* was particularly noteworthy. From the Sunday immediately after the Rising began (with an article headlined "Ireland's Sudden Revolt") through the remainder of 1916—"Bernard Shaw's Solution of Ireland's Troubles" came out on November 26—ten major articles appeared. To its credit, the *Times Magazine* published competing viewpoints. For instance, "Arnold Bennett on the Irish Revolt" (May 28) blamed Irish Americans for incubating, if not instigating, the insurrection and defended Britain ("an assaulted Government has rarely shown greater magnanimity in a more dangerous crisis"), while the already-cited "Roger Casement, Martyr" (August 13) explained its subject without sarcasm or amateur psychoanalysis and with a depth of sympathy that gave human dimension to a complex figure.

How the *New York Times* covered the Rising proves instructive a century later because of its comprehensiveness. The news and feature pages, notably Kilmer's interviews, invariably cast a wide net, collecting information of every kind, while the newspaper's editorial policy remained consistent in reproving the rebels and their cause. In its ambition to be recognized as the nation's newspaper of record, the *Times* offered far-ranging coverage of domestic affairs *and* international concerns, especially matters related to the European war. Events in Ireland, with the early involvement of Germany and the armed hostilities with Britain, were initially viewed as offering a new dimension to a widening conflict. However, with the executions and activities of Irish Americans, a different story line emerged that received full, varied, and serious attention. The Rising and its consequences occurred at a critical moment in the newspaper's evolution, presenting something of a case study in itself.[62] With extensive reliance on dispatches and documents that arrived via cable—one writer has estimated that the *Times* spent $15,000 per week just on cable charges—the newspaper provided its readers with a full picture of events abroad, with a thorough airing of the intricate international angles and their American implications. As a result of such efforts, the *Times* won the first Pulitzer Prize for Public Service for (in the words of the award committee) "publishing in full so many official reports, documents, and speeches by European statesmen relating to the progress and conduct of the war."[63] The Pulitzer Prize, announced in 1918, recognized the newspaper's body of journalistic work related to the war.

By providing full and varied coverage, the *Times* was trying not only to build its reputation in America but also to differentiate its approach from the European press. On April 29, the day of the surrender in Dublin, the "Topics of the Times" column offered a comment on Casement, titled "A Familiar Form of Insanity," as well as an explanatory defense of the way U.S. newspapers go about their work. The statement endorsed what was available to the U.S. public in forming its opinion while also implying that a complete picture was missing in publications abroad:

> American papers, since the war began, have profited from the fact that whatever one Government wanted to suppress or distort another has been eager to give out accurately or to distort the other way. As a result, it has been possible here, sooner or later, to get about all of the news, and, by a little intelligent balancing of it as it comes from the various sources, to present the European situation from day to day far more accurately and fully than has been the case anywhere abroad.[64]

Kilmer's articles for the *Times Magazine* helped provide context for readers of the *Times*, from establishing the role Irish intellectuals played to summarizing what occurred during the Rising and executions, as well as the broader significance. He, of course, was not alone. Indeed, what seems most striking in retrospect is the sheer volume of coverage and the speed with which it influenced public opinion. How *The Nation*, a serious weekly with a liberal perspective founded in 1865, presented the situation in Ireland is representative of the rapid and mutable response in some American journals at the time. In its May 4 edition, the magazine pulled no punches in its criticism of "The Irish Outbreak": "That the recent outbreak was so inept as to be almost idiotic must be evident to the minds of all but the Irishmen who took part in it." At the conclusion of this unsigned editorial commentary, there was a warning similar to the one conveyed by some newspapers at the same time: "If the English are wise, they will not execute the captured rebels, but treat them as amiable and pathetic lunatics mostly in need of restraint and care."[65] In its next edition, May 11, the magazine's editors call the events "the crazy Irish rising," but now the English were subject to censure for having the rebel leaders face the firing squads in Dublin, noting that "not all things that are lawful are expedient; and we think that time will show the Irish executions to have been a blunder in public policy."[66]

A week later, the May 18 issue of *The Nation* published a letter to the editor from William Dean Howells, one of the nation's most respected literary figures, about the executions. Then seventy-nine years old, Howells wrote with a sense of tempered but pointed outrage:

> This was the golden hour for the sort of justice which we misname mercy, this was the moment, not, indeed, wholly to forget the violent madness of the Irish rising, but, above everything, not to overmatch it with the madness of English resentment. The shooting of the Irish insurrectionists is too much like the shooting of prisoners of war, too much like taking a leaf from the German classic of Schrecklichkeit; and in giving way to her vengeance England has roused the moral sense of mankind against her. What a pity, what an infinite pity. She has left us who loved her cause in the war against despotism without another word to say for her until we have first spoken our abhorrence of her inexorable legality in dealing with her Irish prisoners.[67]

For Howells and other American observers, one wrong was trumped by another, more egregious one. As a result, supporting England's cause in the war became much more difficult. For Woodrow Wilson and his administration, what had happened in Ireland presented a new, potentially volatile issue with a combination of domestic and foreign policy implications.

The *Atlantic Monthly*, which Howells edited from 1871 until 1881, and an influential national monthly from its founding in 1857, devoted three major articles to the Rising in 1916, including a moving memoir, "Easter," by James Connolly's daughter, Nora, in the November issue. However, the most telling, detailed essay, "Sir Roger Casement and Sinn Fein," was written by British journalist Henry W. Nevinson and appeared in August, the month Casement was executed. A well-known foreign correspondent, Nevinson drew on previous reportorial assignments, during which he spent time with Casement, Francis Sheehy-Skeffington ("the most violent pacifist I have known"), and John McBride ("We execute a worthless rebel, and for Ireland a heroic saint emerges from the felon's grave"), among others.[68] Similar to Howells, Nevinson focuses directly on the executions, and given the lead time for a monthly magazine to prepare an issue, he must have composed his assessment almost concurrently with the shootings in Dublin. Their meaning, though, is beyond dispute to this British journalist, explaining the Irish situation to an American audience:

> As suppressions of rebellion go, they were not many,—only fifteen,—
> but . . . they were carried out by driblets; they continued long after the
> violent danger was over, and for every man shot the ancient rage was
> rekindled in thousands of hearts. All their errors, all their offenses were
> forgotten, but the memory of those who "died for Ireland" will be cher-
> ished at every fireside. In every cottage, the pictures of "The Fifteen" will
> be framed upon the walls; and if our Law Courts add Roger Casement as
> a sixteenth, he will stand in the centre.

"Instead of being regarded as a well-intentioned but crack-brained set of people," Nevinson concluded, "they will be enshrined under that Necromancy or Magic of the Dead which is both the treasure and the plague of their country."[69]

For Americans, for all of its complexity, the Irish Question stood out as an international concern, one that brought with it serious doubts about Great Britain and the kind of relationship the United States should have with the

British government. Newspapers, magazines, and by the end of the year books kept the Rising in the American consciousness for the public's attention. What had happened three thousand or so miles away was more than a provincial preoccupation within the Irish-American community. The state of Ireland and the struggle for independence the rebels represented forced themselves on America's agenda, partly because U.S. citizens had access to information from a variety of different sources, both domestic and international, that people in Ireland and Britain never saw.

In his memoir about Kilmer, Robert Holliday says of his friend: "It is not at all improbable that had he been an Irishman born and resident in Ireland he would have been among the martyrs of Easter Week."[70] Kilmer kept returning to the Rising and the divisions it deepened in his work as a journalist, poet, and editor. In an unpublished article, "Irish-American Opinion on the Home Rule Deadlock," which is among his papers at Georgetown, Kilmer used Woodrow Wilson's speech of April 2, 1917, that asked for a declaration of war against Germany as both his lead and springboard for a consideration of Ireland's fate nearly one year after the Rising. "In the Message which made the United States a factor in the War against Germany, the Message which will send young men from Maine, California, and all the states of the Union to the trenches in France, President Wilson declared that the Nation was to fight 'for the rights of nations, great and small, and the privilege of men everywhere to choose their way of life and of obedience.'" Kilmer argued that Americans believe Ireland deserve the same rights. "This seems to us to be a thing so obvious that we can regard the recurrent obstructions to its fulfillment only with angry amazement. There are, so far as I know, only two opinions on the subject held by Americans—one, that Ireland should be a free and independent nation, and the other, that Ireland should enjoy the advantages of such Home Rule as is now possessed by Canada and Australia."[71]

Kilmer developed his argument over sixteen typed and quotation-laden pages. In the final paragraph, he looked beyond the war to its aftermath: "When the peace terms are being decided, there is no doubt that America's voice will speak resolutely and clearly on the side of Ireland. But the matter, America believes, should be settled before then, should be settled at once, so that Germany may be opposed by a union of nations of which every one honestly practices democracy."[72]

The article seems to have been written at the request of the editor of *Studies: An Irish Quarterly Review*, published by the Ireland province of Jesuit

priests, where Kilmer had contributed a poem, "Father Gerard Hopkins, S.J.," in March of 1916. Given Kilmer's full-throated support of Ireland's rights as a small nation, it is quite possible *Studies* was reluctant to provide him with a platform on Irish soil at a critical moment during the Great War. Though *Studies* might have deliberately tried to avoid controversy or possible censorship by printing Kilmer's essay—a search of the journal's archives revealed no correspondence about the article—he remained active in the U.S. publishing world as U.S. entry into the war approached. In 1917, aside from bringing out his collection *Main Street and Other Poems*, which included "Easter Week" and "Apology," he published *Dreams and Images: An Anthology of Catholic Poets*. Among the eighty-six contributors are Gerard Manley Hopkins, Hillaire Belloc, John Henry Newman, Katherine Tynan—as well as MacDonagh, Pearse, and Plunkett. In Kilmer's editorial judgment, poets didn't just march "in the Van of Irish Revolt"; they left behind verse worthy of consideration by future generations. Subsequent editions of the collection— retitled *Joyce Kilmer's Anthology of Catholic Poets* and doubling the number of contributors—retained the selections by the three leaders of the Rising. The volume remains in print today.

Kilmer, however, wasn't content to stand or sit on the sidelines, wrestling only with words. Immediately after the United States declared war on Germany on April 6, 1917, and with four children at home, he enlisted in the military. "He hated many things, but I believe that of all things he hated most a pacifist—a pacifist in anything," Holliday wrote of Kilmer. "He believed in the nobility of war and the warrior's calling, so long as the cause was holy, or believed to be holy. As he saw it, there was no question as to his duty."[73] This sense of duty co-existed with his reverence for freedom and his abhorrence of tyranny, which he had addressed in "Apology."

Initially part of the National Guard of New York, Kilmer requested a transfer to the 165th Infantry Regiment, which earlier was widely known as the "Fighting Sixty-Ninth" and was predominantly composed of Irish Americans from New York. Before shipping off to the front lines in France at the end of October 1917, he wrote a priest-friend (of which he had many): "The people I like best here are the wild Irish—boys of eighteen or twenty, who left Ireland a few years ago, some of them to escape threatened conscription, and travelled about the country in gangs, generally working on the railroads. They have delightful songs that have never been written down, but sung in vagabonds' camps and country jails."[74] Kilmer's choice of companions—the newest generation of "exiled children"—says much about him and his appreciation of Irish culture at whatever level of station or status. Whatever his own ancestral heritage, he felt right at home within the circle of his regiment.

First assigned to be a statistician and later as an intelligence observer, Kilmer got promoted from private to sergeant, but refused to be considered for a higher rank—"I'd rather be a Sergeant in the 69th than a Lieutenant in any other regiment in the world."[75] Despite the rigors of his duties in France, Kilmer continued to write when he had a free or idle moment. The most memorable work of prose that he composed at the front is a sketch about his experience and the camaraderie he shared with others in his regiment. He called it simply "Holy Ireland." One of the five poems he wrote during his service is titled "When the Sixty-Ninth Comes Back," and it features these lines:

> God rest our valiant leaders dead, whom we cannot
>   forget;
> They'll see the Fighting Irish are the Fighting
>   Irish yet.[76]

The Sixty-Ninth (or 165th Infantry) did come back—but without Kilmer. A bullet to the head from a German sniper took his life on July 30, 1918, near the French village of Seringe-et-Nesles, and he was buried in the Oise-Aisne American Cemetery close by. Kilmer's death was major news back home, especially in the literary world. The *New York Sun* referred to him as "the first of our well-known poets to fall since America entered the war."[77] England had already experienced the emotion of losing a noted poet in the Great War, a passing Kilmer lamented in his poem "In Memory of Rupert Brooke." Now the United States had to deal with a similar literary loss. The *Brooklyn Eagle* noted, "The Gael's warm blood ran in his veins, the Gael's vivid imagination thrilled him, yet in what he wrote and what he did there was the evidence of Saxon restraint, sanity, almost coldness of purpose."[78]

The Literary Digest, Poetry, and many newspaper book sections devoted pages to remembrances and original poems to mark Kilmer's death. The French awarded him the Croix de Guerre, and the British Ministry of Information released a lengthy tribute, which the *New York Times* published in full on October 27. Calling him "one of America's best-loved poets, a devout Christian gentleman, a loyal patriot, and a sincere craftsman," the governmental encomium offered three reasons why Kilmer didn't need to go off to war: "He was above the draft age, he had the responsibility of a wife and children, and his vocation as a newspaper man was generally held to be an essential occupation." The statement complimented "the Christian knight" and celebrated certain poems, including "The White Ships and the Red" about the sinking of the *Lusitania* as "one of the most righteous outpourings of wrath against the barbarism of the German methods." Predictably, perhaps, at no place in the tribute is there mention of Kilmer's putative Irishness, his writings about the Easter Rising, or his devotion to "the Fighting Irish" who were his comrades in arms.[79]

British interest in Kilmer didn't end with his death. In 1941, Duckworth, a respected British publisher for much of the twentieth century, brought out *Trees and Other Poems*. The unsigned "Publisher's Note" argued that Kilmer's work transcended his time and contemporary circumstances. Noting that the book was appearing with "the continent of Europe once more darkened by war," it noted Kilmer's enthusiasm for the English literary tradition, arguing that "there was no more sincere admirer than he of the glorious cavalcade of English poets, from Milton down to Hilaire Belloc and Rupert Brooke (for whom he wrote an epitaph, included in this book)."[80] Like the Ministry of Information statement, this collection of thirty-three poems avoids any mention of the Easter Rising or Kilmer's association with the Irish or Irish America. The British seemed willing to adopt him as one of their own as long as it was on their terms. While it noted that Kilmer had displayed a "passionate belief in the sanctity of personal freedom," one specific allegiance is avoided.

Americans, on the other hand, never forgot how much the Irish cause of independence and the larger significance of Ireland meant to one of his country's most famous casualties of the Great War. Holliday's two-volume, 561-page set of Kilmer's poetry and prose appeared in late 1918, sold out its first printing in three days, was quickly reissued, and came out four other times during the next half-century. Kilmer's poems about the Rising are included in the first volume, and "Holy Ireland," considered by critics the most accomplished prose composition of Kilmer's career, leads off Volume Two. When the 165th Infantry Regiment finally returned to America in the spring of 1919, they marched up New York's Fifth Avenue with the band playing "When the Sixty-Ninth Comes Back." Victor Herbert, the well-known Irish-born composer and first president of the Friends of Irish Freedom, had turned Kilmer's words into the lyrics of this new song. The cover of the musical score notes that "Lieut. Victor Herbert has waived his royalties on this song in behalf of

Mrs. Joyce Kilmer."[81] In death, as in life, Kilmer continued to be remembered by Irish Americans and others working to achieve independence for Ireland.

At the end of 1919, the regiment's Catholic chaplain published *Father Duffy's Story: A Tale of Humor and Heroism, Of Life and Death with the Fighting Sixty-Ninth*. In the preface, Francis P. Duffy notes, "Joyce Kilmer was to have written this book."[82] As it turned out, the twenty or so pages that Kilmer found time to draft appear as a "Historical Appendix." Trying to explain "the psychology of the 69th New York," the poet-historian quotes G. K. Chesterton's "Ballad of the White Horse":

> For the great Gaels of Ireland
> > Are the men that God made mad
> For all their wars are merry
> > And all their songs are sad.[83]

Alas, all the wars of self-adopted Gaels weren't merry. In Kilmer's case, he never saw the consequences of the Rising that so absorbed him in 1916. In *Father Duffy's Story*, the chaplain records in his diary for May 15, 1918, what might serve as a coda about the figure called in the headline of one obituary the "Hero Soldier-Poet": "Kilmer or I, or both of us, may see an end to life in this war, but neither of us will be able to say that life has not been good to us."[84] Duffy, who died in 1932, and Kilmer were reunited cinematically in the 1940 movie *The Fighting 69th*, which dramatized for a mass audience Irish-American valor and patriotism during the Great War, just as the United States faced possible involvement in the new European conflict that had begun a year earlier. In New York City, both the chaplain and the writer are remembered more permanently with monuments: an eight-foot-high statue of Francis Duffy stands imposingly in front of a much larger Celtic cross in Duffy Square, the northernmost portion of Times Square, while Kilmer is the namesake for a park in the Bronx and a triangle in Brooklyn. In addition, a plaque in Central Park reads:

> In Memoriam
> Sergeant Joyce Kilmer
> Poet of the Trees
> Killed in Action—Bois Colas
> July 30, 1918

The "Poet of the Trees" was no less the poet for Ireland's exiled children. Kilmer's adopted ethnic identity infused and animated his life and work, and the Easter Rising provided a vicarious prelude to the actual battles he would later fight, side by side, with his fellow "exiled children." His belief in freedom, devotion to the religion of his conversion, and a commitment to writing, both serious and popular, defined a career that ended long before Kilmer and his admirers might have hoped. Yet how he responded to events in Ireland during 1916 continues to guide Americans (as well as others) toward a better understanding of what happened and what it meant, without the constraints of censorship or the fog of war.

Woodrow Wilson

(Library of Congress, Prints & Photographs Division, LC-USZC2-6247)

3

Woodrow Wilson: The Denial of Exile

D ESPITE ALL THE ATTENTION DEVOTED to the Rising and the executions in America during the spring of 1916, the White House of Woodrow Wilson assiduously tried to keep its distance from what was happening in Ireland. Other affairs, international and domestic, preoccupied a president then looking ahead to what promised to be a bruising fall re-election campaign. A century later, however, this almost complete lack of engagement remains something of a mystery, if also key to the character of America's twenty-eighth president. What's clear is that Wilson's inability to answer the Irish Question haunted the end of his first term and all of his second. His political motivation to embrace Irish Catholics for their electoral support seemed at war with his personal heritage as an Ulster Protestant and Anglophile. While nationalism and unionism battled openly in Ireland, Wilson tried, in his own way, to juggle both beliefs—but ultimately failed. He personified the age-old, still unresolved tension between these two traditions that was so vital to understanding Ireland and its people who had emigrated from there.

Joyce Kilmer adopted an Irish patrimony and made it central to his identity after Easter 1916. Woodrow Wilson, though, could trace his ancestry directly back to Ireland through both of his father's parents, each from Ulster: one from County Tyrone and the other from County Down. Wilson, however, viewed his association with an ancestral homeland in an entirely different way from Kilmer's fictionalized ethnicity. For Wilson, a Scots-Irish lineage proved politically useful as he established himself within the Democratic Party. Yet, as the years passed and burdens grew heavier, how Wilson handled the American Irish and the Irish Question during 1916 subsequently became a microcosm of a presidency increasingly based on idealistic abstractions and entrenched beliefs. In the hundred years since his time in office, Wilson has come to be perceived by the Irish on both sides of the Atlantic as a figure whose grand rhetoric not only did not live up to its promise but also betrayed it.

Try as he might, and try he did, Wilson couldn't escape the pressure to do something about Ireland. In fact, the Rising delivered to the doorstep of 1600 Pennsylvania Avenue what Barbara Tuchman in *The Proud Tower* called the "Irish incubus," a problem of continuing torment that contributed to Wilson's inability to achieve the new world order he envisioned. Some have argued that had he dealt with the Irish Question more adroitly, he could have accomplished more of his international objectives and the verdict of history on his legacy would be less qualified. His papers, both published and unpublished, as well as contemporary accounts by people who had personal access to Wilson, reveal a figure with distinct public and private personae that are never reconciled. Indeed, many observers of his dealings with the Irish concluded he was duplicitous and never interested in Irish "self-determination," though it was a key Wilsonian concept. Explaining how that viewpoint evolved requires both looking back at Wilson's emergence in politics and assessing the evolving role of 1916.

Before entering politics in 1910 at the age of fifty-three as a candidate for governor of New Jersey, Wilson had been a prominent academic, with a lengthy list of scholarly and popular publications, as well as president of Princeton University for nearly a decade. Professorial in demeanor and in need of glasses from an early age, he was self-deprecating about his appearance, even writing a limerick to describe himself:

> For beauty I am not a star,
> There are others more handsome by far.
> But my face I don't mind it,
> For I am behind it,
> It's the people in front that I jar.[1]

Physical appearance aside—and his involvement in politics preceded intense concern for a figure's image; his presidential predecessor, William Howard Taft, weighed well over three hundred pounds—Wilson (who weighed 180) was widely known as what we now call a public intellectual. Articles, books, and lectures spread his views widely on domestic and foreign subjects. He was on the record as favoring home rule in Ireland—in a 1910 campaign speech he had said, "This voice that has been crying in Ireland, this voice for home rule, is a voice which is now supported by the opinion of the world. . . ."[2] During his White House years (1913–1921) Wilson never wavered from thinking that some form of self-government was necessary for Ireland.

Though shaped by academia rather than the hurly-burly of electoral politics, Wilson recognized the clout Irish Americans exerted at the ballot box, particularly in certain large cities, where Democratic Party organizations had a decidedly Celtic composition. For appearances in front of groups that emphasized Irish heritage, he tried to ingratiate himself with playful remarks about his Irishness and its effects on him. In 1909, while still president of Princeton, he told attendants at the 125th anniversary dinner of the Society of the Friendly Sons of St. Patrick in New York City about the shaping influence of his "Scotch-Irish" background. "I myself am happy to believe that there runs in my veins a very considerable strain of Irish blood," he said. "I can't prove it from documents, but I have internal evidence." That "internal evidence," he went on to say, was a "most enjoyable irresponsibility" that asserted control from time to time over his "Scotch conscience."[3] Wilson then made fun of Scotch-Irish "belligerency" before turning to more serious concerns, including the role of the president in U.S. public life—a subject he addressed in his 1908 book, *Constitutional Government in the United States*. Later, as governor and with an eye to running for president, he opened another speech to the Friendly Sons of St. Patrick (this time in Elizabeth, New Jersey) by saying: "All the Irish that is in me arises to greet you. My father's parents were born in Ireland; born farther north, perhaps, than most of you would approve of. But there was no one with more Irish in him than my father."[4]

Wilson created both rapport with and distance from his audience. In asserting his Irish background, he also noted that his Ulster ancestors were different from most "Friendly Sons," with their roots in the more nationalistic-minded and Catholic southern counties. With its strong allegiance to Britain, Ulster is, of course, distinctly different—as was Wilson's devout Presbyterianism. Wilson was saying that he was—and was not—truly Irish. That seeming contradiction on a personal level would complicate how he judged matters related to Ireland over the next decade.

To win the presidency, Wilson continued to be cagey about using his Irish "blood." Less than a month before Election Day 1912, he told a campaign rally gathered at the armory of "the Fighting Irish Seventh Regiment" in Chicago, "I have in me a very interesting and troublesome mixture of bloods. I get all my stubbornness from the Scotch [on his mother's side], and then there is something else that gives me a great deal of trouble, which I attribute to the Irish. At any rate, it makes me love a scrap; and so I knew that if I was to be privileged to speak in this armory, I would be forgiven for speaking in a somewhat militant manner."[5]

His combative bona fides established, Wilson applauded "the great liberty-loving men and women from every civilized country on the globe," including "the great Irish people" who have immigrated to the United States. Besides citing the Irish, he mentioned the Polish, Italians, Slavs, and Sicilians by name before engaging in a rousing display of call and response:

> what did they come to be free from? What was there that they wanted to get rid of in the countries which they left and hoped to find in the country in which they took refuge and made a new home for themselves? What was it that these militant people came to fight for? Why, they came to fight for a release from arbitrary power of every kind and of every degree. They came to fight against the arbitrary power of governments, the arbitrary control of aristocracy, the arbitrary privilege of classes that did not allow their privileges to be interfered with by the general interests of the people.[6]

Later, Wilson contrasted the promise of American freedom for immigrants with what he saw as the reality of life in 1912 America—after sixteen straight years of Republicans in the White House. "While these people [the new citizens] have escaped the open and avowed tyranny of special classes and of arbitrary governments, they have not escaped in America the private power of privilege and of narrow and exclusive power."[7]

During his campaign, Wilson made strong appeals to Irish Americans for their political support, using language that would lead them to believe Ireland was a place where "arbitrary power of every kind and of every degree" was being exercised and freedom was worth fighting to achieve. However, after he entered the White House—winning 41.8 percent of the vote to Progressive candidate Theodore Roosevelt's 27.4 percent, Republican incumbent William Howard Taft's 23.2 percent, and Socialist Party candidate Eugene V. Debs's 6 percent—Wilson's view changed. His "militant manner" often involved fighting with the American Irish, though he tried to avoid the perception of open warfare with such a significant constituency for the Democratic Party.

As president Wilson was principally kept informed about Irish America by his private secretary, Joseph Patrick Tumulty, who served in the capacity that is known today as chief of staff—during both four-year terms. A Roman

Catholic with savvy political instincts, Tumulty was responsible for keeping up with the constant flow of messages, the scheduling of meetings, and everything else that occupies a president's time. Tumulty's own background proved influential. Never, in his judgment, "a professional Irishman," Tumulty nonetheless kept Irish American opinion—the spectrum ranged from those who cared little about internal affairs in Ireland to those who were extreme nationalists and republicans—in perspective, helping Wilson to pursue larger goals without jeopardizing support from this vocal and vote-rich community. Having Tumulty in his position and in close proximity to the president was reassuring for Irish Americans. They knew they had access to the White House with Tumulty in such a key post.

One of Wilson's domestic objectives involved increasing patriotism and nationalistic pride by subordinating the ethnic heritage that so many first- or second-generation immigrants still embraced and celebrated. A little over a year after entering the White House, Wilson delivered a robust plea on behalf of "Americanism" at the unveiling of a statue in Washington to honor Commodore John Barry, a hero of the American Revolution. Saying he had let others talk explicitly about Barry and his accomplishments, Wilson offered what he called "a few inferences from the significance of this occasion," dilating on patriotism and its importance. In a key passage that combined a tribute to Barry and the broader theme, the president asserted that while John Barry was an Irishman, "his heart crossed the Atlantic with him." He continued:

> This man was not an Irish-American; he was an Irishman who became an American. I venture to say if he voted he voted with regard to the questions as they looked on this side of the water and not on the other side, and that is my infallible test of a genuine American—that when he votes or when he acts or when he fights, his heart and his thought are nowhere but in the center of the emotions and the purposes and the policies of the United States.[8]

According to Wilson, though "ancient affections" deserved to be preserved, they could not prevent the process of becoming "a genuine American." Divided loyalties within immigrant groups—in this case among the Irish—weakened the spirit of national unity. Interestingly, Wilson's high-minded argument brought up voting twice, a sign that electoral politics played an explicit role in the patriotic conduct of Americans. Concern for the "hyphenated"—Irish

Americans or Italian Americans—and how citizens viewed themselves in relationship to their heritage kept returning as an issue, particularly given that the war had broken out in Europe only a few months after the president spoke at the statue dedication.

Wilson wanted Americans to establish appropriate distance from their immigrant roots, and as fighting grew bloodier and more savage across the Atlantic, he also tried to maintain U.S. neutrality, which he formally proclaimed on August 4, 1914. The war, however, was worryingly immediate for millions of Americans. Ancestral allegiances competed with New World aspirations, and recent immigrants in particular closely followed what was happening on the battlefields and in the trenches, as well as how their adopted country was responding to the spreading conflict.

Despite repeated assertions that the United States would remain neutral, Wilson was often accused of favoring the Allied Powers over the Central Powers. Whether warranted or not, this perception of presidential bias placed Wilson on the side of Great Britain and at odds with Germany. At the time, according to the 1910 population statistics, 8,282,618 people (out of a total of 91,972,266) named Germany as their country of origin, with over 2.5 million born there. In addition, those from Austria-Hungary, another Central Power, numbered 2.7 million. When the more than 4.5 million people of direct Irish background, many with antipathy to Britain, were added, the total was nearly 15.5 million who, to one degree or another, might have some reservations about showing partiality for the Allies. The same census figures showed just over 3.2 million of the U.S. population who named the United Kingdom (without counting Ireland) as their country of origin.[9]

As far as some observers were concerned, Wilson's familial background, with its Ulster and Scottish heritage, placed him in the British corner and his life before politics reinforced that impression. Wilson scholar Arthur S. Link named Edmund Burke, Walter Bagehot, and Herbert Spencer as important influences on Wilson's political philosophy.[10] In *Thomas Woodrow Wilson: A Psychological Study*, Sigmund Freud and William C. Bullitt, who worked with Wilson at the 1919 Paris Peace Conference before resigning over policy differences, were more explicit: "All his heroes were British: Burke, Bright, Bagehot, Gladstone."[11] Later they wrote: "Four times after 'breakdowns' he attempted to overcome his habitual symptoms by visits to the British Isles. His experience in Ireland was confined to a few days of contempt; but Scotland he loved, the English universities moved him to ecstasy and the English Lake District became the home of his heart."[12] Moreover, Wilson's admiration for Britain's parliamentary system was a matter of public record. Some of his academic writing, particularly his early work *Congressional Government: A Study in American Politics* (1885), praised the close association between the legislative and executive functions in the House of Commons, with its emphasis on persuasive rhetoric in debating policy.

Notwithstanding his Anglophile attachments (either ancestral or intellectual), Wilson tried to navigate his administration on a neutral course, even as some German Americans and Irish Americans detected a tack toward the British side as the war intensified. The German navy's U-boat campaign targeting British ships tested Wilson's approach, particularly when U.S. citizens or goods were in jeopardy. The sternest challenge to his strategy of noninvolvement came with the sinking of the *Lusitania*, the largest ship in the Cunard fleet, on a return voyage to Britain from New York. Because over a hundred Americans perished, Wilson began to feel both domestic and British pressure to respond aggressively. Former president Theodore Roosevelt left no doubt where he stood after the attack: "It seems inconceivable that we can refrain from taking action in this matter, for we owe it not only to humanity but to our own national self-respect."[13] Despite the outrage that the American press amplified with massive coverage—Joyce Kilmer's "The White Ships and the Red" took up a whole page of the *New York Times Magazine* on May 16—Wilson held his fire and refused immediate comment. In his first public remarks after the ship's sinking (four days earlier), he made no mention of the *Lusitania* or the firestorm its sinking had provoked. Instead, as he did so often, he took the higher road, the one leading to principles and ideals: "The example of America must be the example not merely of peace because it will not fight, but of peace because peace is the healing and elevating influence of the world and strife is not. There is such a thing as a man being too proud to fight."[14]

Ultimately, Wilson sought an apology from Germany and assurance that such attacks wouldn't occur in the future. The policy of neutrality remained in place while messages shot back and forth between the two governments. The man in the White House listened to his inner voice rather than to the bellicose calls from those outside, the nation's top politician acting more like the academic of his earlier life. Count Johann Heinrich von Bernstorff, the German ambassador to the United States, sized up the president in his memoir, *My Three Years in America*: "President Wilson, who by inclination and habit is a recluse and a lonely worker, does not like company."[15]

Choosing to keep his own counsel marked not only Wilson's commitment to neutrality throughout his first term but also his approach to Ireland during his eight years in the White House. The German ambassador's comment is descriptive without being judgmental. A. Scott Berg quotes, in his biography of Wilson, Oklahoma Senator Thomas Pryor Gore, an early ally of the president who later opposed U.S. involvement in World War I and the proposed League of Nations: "Wilson had no friends, only slaves and enemies."[16]

While the submarine warfare by Germany alienated many Americans, the British actions, including a naval blockade of Germany that restricted the flow of American merchandise, also raised concerns for the Wilson administration. In effect, the president was forced to deal with problems coming from both sides of the war. In each case, the impact on U.S. citizens and interests proved considerable. In a letter dated May 16, 1916, and written just after the last executions of the rebel leaders in Dublin, which he said had caused a "great shock" to American public opinion, Wilson told his adviser and, in the words of the salutation, "My dearest Friend," Colonel Edward Mandell House, that relations with the British government had reached a "turning point" and "we should get down to hard pan." He then wrote:

> The United States must either make a decided move for peace (upon some basis that promises to be permanent) or, if she postpones that, must insist to the limit upon her rights of trade and upon such freedom of the seas as international law already justifies her in insisting on as against Great Britain, with the same plain speaking and firmness that she has used against Germany. And the choice must be made immediately. Which does Great Britain prefer? She cannot escape both. To do nothing is now, for us, impossible.[17]

Wilson's phrase about "the great shock" revealed his awareness of the Rising and its aftermath, but he did not elaborate. His principal subject is the role the United States might play in bringing the war to an end. As before with the *Lusitania*, achieving peace was uppermost in his mind, the abiding pursuit. Later, in May, he delivered a speech to the League to Enforce Peace that asserted, without being specific, "every people has a right to choose the sovereignty under which they shall live" and (as he noted in campaigning during 1912) "small states of the world have a right to enjoy the same respect for their sovereignty and for their territorial integrity that great and powerful nations expect and insist upon."[18] He went on to propose that his country would be willing to occupy a place on the world stage by noting "that the United States is willing to become a partner in any feasible association of nations formed in order to realize these objects and make them secure against violation."[19] Criticized by Europeans for not addressing the war's causes and its objects, Wilson positioned himself and his country on the side of peace while advocating an "association of nations" devoted to maintaining global security. This speech contained the seeds of policy proposals that took root and became consequential later in his presidency. With Dublin still reeling after the recent insurrection, the Irish and their kinfolk in America heard encouraging phrases on behalf of individual sovereignty and "small states of the world." Colonel House brought up the Rising in a letter to Wilson of June 7, 1916, echoing the president's letter of May 16 that the "execution of the Irish rebels had accentuated opinion against Great Britain." House also offered his advice that the British government should refrain from releasing a rationale for what they did in Dublin. In a conclusion that in retrospect seems stunning in the magnitude of its misjudgment, he wrote: "Things are soon forgotten these tragic days and the quicker that is forgotten the better."[20]

Both Wilson and House used the word *opinion* in referring to the impact felt in the United States from the punishment the British inflicted on the Rising's leaders. The extensive press coverage must have had some reverberations in the White House at the same time as the president was making his best effort to be perceived as peacemaker in the European conflict. Renominated in mid-June for a second term at the Democratic Party's convention in St. Louis, Wilson's approach going into his campaign combined passive neutrality with a commitment to active peacemaking. As time grew closer to the November election, the compelling slogan someone suggested that the incumbent use—"He kept us out of war"—would reinforce the relationship between Wilson and his policy. However, before Americans cast their ballots, the White House had to take into account the sea change in thinking on the part of a key Democratic voting bloc: the American Irish.

Given the amount of media attention devoted to the Rising, the response of Irish America received a full airing, revealing the depth of the outrage and sympathy for those either directly involved (the dead, wounded, or arrested) or through the loss of property. The anti-British sentiment that grew in the

United States after the Rising strengthened Wilson's hand to maintain neutrality. In addition, the president had serious policy differences with London during 1916 that showed his ability to keep personal preferences about English life distinct from governmental activities. Angered by the publication of a "blacklist" that named eighty-seven American companies involved in trade with the Central Powers, and thus no longer able to transact business with the British, Wilson wrote Colonel House on July 23, 1916, that he was "about at the end of my patience with Great Britain and the Allies." He went on to say that he was "seriously considering asking Congress to authorize me to prohibit loans and restrict exportations to the Allies." He told House that he and the State Department were "compounding a very sharp note. I may feel obliged to make it as sharp and final as the one to Germany on the submarines."[21]

Besides the blacklisting, Anglo-American relations were already on rocky footing as a result of a maritime blockade and the searching of letters and parcels carried by neutral ships crossing the Atlantic. Wilson was genuinely at odds with the British at a time before what later became referred to as "the special relationship" between the United Kingdom and the United States didn't yet exist. That relationship developed during World War II, over two decades later, and largely because Winston Churchill sought closer cooperation among English-speaking peoples. In 1916 and for a variety of reasons, Wilson sought transatlantic distance.

Given all of the governmental controversies and the stormy reaction to the Rising, the British kept a close eye on activities in America. Perhaps the country's most valuable source of information and interpretation came from the letters and assessments written by Cecil Spring Rice, who served as Britain's ambassador in Washington from September 1912 until January 1918. What made these diplomatic dispatches noteworthy was their acuity in analyzing American public opinion and political machinations. Government ministers and others at Whitehall received Spring Rice's detailed assessments, which read like the work of a veteran reporter, with clockwork regularity. By contrast the U.S. State Department had to request field reports about the Rising from its consuls based in Ireland. The report from Dublin didn't arrive in Washington until early December 1916, by which point it was of little to no use.[22]

Possibly because of his own Anglo-Irish heritage—in one of his poems he wrote, "I am an Irishman, you see, / That is what expresses me"—Spring Rice took a keen interest in what was happening in Ireland and among the

American Irish. Well connected on both sides of the Atlantic (he served as Theodore Roosevelt's best man at his marriage in London in 1886), Spring Rice devoted much of his ambassadorial time to composing his reports for the Foreign Office from Washington, D.C. His reluctance to seek public attention was itself newsworthy. The *New York Herald* began a Sunday magazine profile on June 25, 1916: "Erin's sons are renowned for their eloquence rather than for their reticence. Yet the Irishman to whom the British Empire has confided the care of its diplomatic interests in the United States in this the greatest crisis of its existence has earned for himself renown among Americans as the most silent Ambassador ever sent to Washington by any foreign Power." Though the feature appeared two months after the Rising and at a time when the British were being widely rebuked for the executions, the writer, F. Cunliffe-Owen—perhaps in honor of his subject's silence—entirely avoids the subject.[23] However, in his own dispatches, Spring Rice kept returning to the U.S. reaction to the events in Ireland, and particularly their impact on Irish Americans. His observations, gleaned from press accounts, personal conversations, and staff reports, provided contemporaneous evidence of American opinion as it evolved over several weeks. On April 28, shortly after the news broke, Spring Rice was both measured and matter-of-fact in describing the U.S. reaction. On the whole, he found public opinion "satisfactory," continuing: "The press seems to be agreed that the movement is suicidal and in the interests of Germany alone. The attitude of the majority of the Irish is uncertain, but if the movement spreads the effect here will be very serious indeed. All are agreed that it will be dangerous to make Casement a martyr."[24]

Just a month later, on May 30, Spring Rice adopted a decidedly different tone and approach, raising warning flags and signaling a no-win situation for the English in dealing with Casement. It was bad enough that the executions had been spread out, as the American public might have excused them had they been done in "hot blood." As for Casement, who most agree had acted "almost like a madman," it would be "far better" to make him "ridiculous than a martyr," in Spring Rice's judgment. "There is no doubt whatever that the Germans here look forward with great interest to his execution, of which they will take full advantage."[25]

Then, two weeks later, and just as Wilson was being nominated for a second term at the Democratic Convention, the ambassador wrote in his dispatch that enmity directed at Britain continued to grow among the American Irish. His sense of alarm was tempered with suggestions to improve the situation, principally by distributing funds to the "sufferers by the revolt" and settling the issue of home rule. But as for the Irish in America, there was nothing to be done. "They have blood in their eyes when they look our way." While Spring Rice noted that even England's bitterest enemies did "not wish to take sides with the destroyer of Belgium," the English cause among the Irish in America was "a lost one."[26]

All the passages quoted here come from the second volume of *The Letters and Friendships of Sir Cecil Spring Rice*. Many of his unpublished dispatches are in the holdings of the National Archives at Kew, and the ones during this period reinforced or amplified his judgments about the shifting U.S. opinion caused by the Rising and, more significantly, by the executions. He also addressed the possibility that the rebels in Ireland didn't act alone, noting on May 1: "A question that will be debated exhaustively is how far the movement [in Ireland] originated in this country or received support from American citizens. . . . No one here doubts the complete cooperation of German and Irish societies in this country in a policy of hostility to Great Britain."[27]

In a coded telegram dated August 1, Spring Rice reported that he had made an "informal verbal agreement" with Michael Francis Doyle, Casement's American lawyer, that neither would say anything about Casement's scheduled hanging two days later. His last sentence refers to Doyle and provokes puzzlement: "He tells me privately that Clan Nagael [*sic*] want Casement executed."[28] When so many American politicians, journalists, and groups were working to save Casement from the gallows, why Clan na Gael, the most extreme organization devoted to independence for Ireland, welcomed the death sentence seems a mystery. By this time, John Devoy and others could have decided that Casement was too mercurial and too much of a risk to the larger cause. In his biography of Casement, Angus Mitchell speculates that Devoy blamed Casement for betraying secrets about the Rising, though it later seemed possible that it was Devoy's cables that had been intercepted, tipping off the British command.[29] In any case, the Clan had financially supported Casement in Germany and also during his London trial.

Throughout the dispatches Spring Rice prepared, he repeatedly discussed American press coverage of the events in Ireland and the ways the American Irish responded to what was happening there. How sensitive were policymakers in the Foreign Office to the news treatment, with its criticism of British statements and actions? One "American Press Résumé," assembled on May 25 and printed for the cabinet to consider, covered ten full pages of closely spaced type. "CONFIDENTIAL" appears underlined and in boldface at the top of what is basically a collection of articles from easily available public sources.[30] Among Prime Minister Herbert Henry Asquith's papers at Oxford during this period are U.S. newspapers with articles and editorials about Casement's fate. All the concern over the journalistic coverage showed the extent to which London thought American public opinion was taking a turn against the British at a key time for the war being fought in Europe. Neutrality was one thing; hostility could prove more consequential and difficult to overcome in the future.

To survey U.S. thinking and the nation's mood, Spring Rice looked beyond newspapers and kept an eye trained on the conduct of domestic politics and Wilson's fortunes. Early in 1916 (January 13), several months before the Rising, he informed Edward Grey, the foreign minister: "The best politicians in the country [the United States] are the Irish, and the professional Irish politician is against us."[31] After the firestorm of criticism following the executions, he advocated a strategy of deliberately staying out of the spotlight, writing on July 31 that, with the presidential election on the horizon and Congress in session, and with "the Irish in a particularly pugnacious mood and both sides hungering for the German vote," it would be a good idea "to lie as quiet as possible and to occupy as little attention as we can."[32]

While the British sought to steer clear of any action that might prompt negative publicity, Wilson and his administration followed a somewhat similar course during the summer and fall of 1916, yet for a different reason. Wilson biographer Ray Stannard Baker quotes Wilson's remarks delivered early in the campaign: "From this time until the seventh of November it is going to be practically impossible for the present Administration to handle any critical matter concerning our foreign relations, because all foreign statesmen are waiting to see which way the election goes, and in the meantime they know that settlements will be inconclusive." Baker, a journalist and friend of the president, then directly commented on Wilson's effort to keep international affairs at bay by observing: "In consonance with this conviction he avoided every possible controversy upon foreign affairs."[33] The candidate, who tried to make voters aware that he had done whatever possible to avoid getting involved in the war abroad, wanted his electioneering to stay confined to matters within the U.S. borders.

In his speech after being renominated as the Democratic Party candidate, he noted: "I am the candidate of a party, but I am above all things else an

American citizen. I neither seek the favour nor fear the displeasure of that small alien element amongst us which puts loyalty to any foreign power before loyalty to the United States."[34] Without raising the concept of hyphenated Americans, Wilson made his point, and he drove it home later in the month. Jeremiah A. O'Leary, president of the American Truth Society and proponent of both Irish independence and the German side in the war, accused the president of "truckling to the British Empire" and jeopardizing Democratic votes in November. Wilson immediately shot back: "Your telegram received. I would feel deeply mortified to have you or anybody like you vote for me. Since you have access to many disloyal Americans and I have not I will ask you to convey this message to them."[35] He was asked about O'Leary's message and "the hyphenate issue" at a press conference, and his six-sentence reply contained two references to "damn fools." "A telegram like that is the most silly indiscretion that a man could possibly commit."[36] In the postscript to a letter Colonel House sent to Wilson the next day, he commented, "Your telegram to O'Leary is the best thing so far in the campaign and will do more good than you can realize."[37]

Wilson's presidential pique, which received extensive news coverage, stands in marked contrast to his usual public response to a potentially controversial matter. Though O'Leary never mentioned Ireland or Germany in what he wrote the president, the American Truth Society was well known for being pro-German, and O'Leary was a prominent figure in Irish-American circles. Indeed, among Joseph McGarrity's papers in the National Library of Ireland is a memorandum McGarrity drafted about 1916. He recalls he was "bound to secrecy" about the Rising "until the newspapers finally got the story." McGarrity then related how what was happening in Ireland became known in the United States: "Jeremiah A. O'Leary of New York had called some of the New York Newspapers and asked the Editor why he was suppressing the news of a Rebellion now going on in Ireland, and after persistent calling the Editors began to seek for the story. . . ." McGarrity went on to say that the fighting was "two or three days on before the newspapers in America were in a position to give it to the world, the rest is history."[38]

In the months before and after Wilson's assertive reply to O'Leary, the president had engaged in political bobbing and dodging when Irish-related issues landed on his desk. Actually, a pattern developed that continued throughout the remainder of his first White House term and well into his second—a consistent approach of rhetorical sympathy without policy substance. For public occasions and statements that might be quoted in the press or elsewhere, Wilson maintained an attitude of sincerity and conscientious concern. The American Irish were led to believe the president understood their viewpoint in seeking remedies to their problems and to the larger resolution of Ireland's future. In private, however, Wilson operated differently. What he said or did showed a deliberate resolve to keep at arm's length almost every matter explicitly related to Irish-American interests. Indeed, away from the scrutiny of the press and citizenry, he displayed flashes of anger and antipathy that reveal ethnic-group animus of considerable proportion. The man who wanted the world to regard him as a peacemaker wasn't above maneuvering behind the scenes to allow certain conflicts to fester. As time passed, it became increasingly difficult for him to maintain one stance in public and another in private.

The key person trying to project Wilson's image of concern vis-à-vis Ireland was Joseph Tumulty, whose fingerprints can be detected on many of the documents that went out from the White House in Wilson's name. An examination of the Woodrow Wilson Papers in the Library of Congress reveals that the Easter Rising and Roger Casement's case generated numerous telegrams and letters seeking presidential involvement and help. The day before Pearse's surrender, Michael Francis Doyle, a Philadelphia attorney with Democratic connections who later represented Casement in London, wired Wilson, requesting a meeting to talk about Casement and "if possible to enlist your interest on his behalf on the grounds of humanity." On May 2, Wilson wrote to Tumulty rather than to Doyle: "We have no choice in a matter of this sort. It is absolutely necessary to say that I could take no action of any kind regarding it."[39] That direct statement would seem to close every door; however, Tumulty handed off the matter to the State Department and, subsequently, drafted a form response that anyone who contacted the White House about Casement would receive. Its wording made Wilson appear quite different from what the president had written to his secretary. With concern for Casement's fate growing in Congress and among the public, Tumulty instructed the White House secretarial staff on July 3 to send "the following form reply under his signature":

> The President wishes me to acknowledge receipt your telegram in the case of Sir Roger Casement and requests me to say that he will seek the earliest opportunity to discuss this matter with the Secretary of State. Of course he will give the suggestion you make the consideration which its great importance merits.[40]

Though noncommittal and not specific about "the suggestion" offered, the cordial message reflected an open-minded willingness to deal with Casement's situation at the highest levels of the administration. It was really all a façade.

When Tumulty gave Wilson a letter Doyle had sent from London about Casement's trial with the information that "a personal request from the President *will save his life*," the president in his reaction of July 20 was even more emphatic than he had been on May 2. The handwritten response reads: "It would be inexcusable for me to touch this. It w'd [would] involve serious international embarrassment."[41] Wilson's hands-off approach to intervening on behalf of Casement foreshadows his refusal to introduce Ireland as a subject at the 1919 Paris Peace Conference. Though he played his Irish card to win political acceptance, he stopped at jocular lip service when faced with a life-or-death decision or a major policy initiative. During his inaugural address as president of Princeton in 1902, Wilson asserted in an often-quoted statement: "We are not put into this world to sit still and know; we are put into it to act."[42] On Ireland and Irish issues, however, he knew but sat still.

From evidence in Wilson's papers in the Library of Congress, it becomes clear Tumulty wasn't alone in attempting to make Wilson look more favorable in Irish eyes. The Knights of St. Patrick in San Francisco sent the president a lengthy telegram on May 17, 1916, proposing that the U.S. government intervene with the British to end secret trials and executions of Irish prisoners. The text of the appeal was published by the *San Francisco Chronicle* on May 20, and near the beginning, it says that the "request is made on behalf of numberless American citizens whose ancestry, like your own, is Irish." The concluding paragraph raised a point often made in the United States during the spring of 1916: "The only offense of the Irish revolutionists was the same aspiration for liberty which inspired Washington in the American Revolution."[43] For over a month, the Knights of St. Patrick waited to receive acknowledgment of their telegram, and Senator James D. Phelan of California took up the matter directly with Tumulty. On June 28, after a conversation about the lack of a reply, the senator (who served just one term, from 1915 to 1921) sent the secretary a letter with background about the situation *and* a proposed response from the president to be forwarded to the Knights of St. Patrick.

What Phelan wrote on behalf of Wilson—"Pursuant to your suggestion this morning, I offer the enclosed"—made the intended signatory, Wilson, appear not only conscientious in his duties but also sympathetic to the Irish rebels. The letter, submitted on plain white paper and typed identically as the cover note to Tumulty accompanying it, said that concerning Irish prisoners, "it is needless for me to say that I have done everything, so far as representations go, to provide for their humane and just treatment." The next sentence brought the subject closer to home, though there is no specific mention of any particular case: "Where the fate of an American citizen was involved, I have secured favorable action. . . ." Then, the text assumed a grand Wilsonian tone:

> My natural sympathies are with men struggling for freedom, and concerning whose sincerity as patriots, seeking solely the welfare of their country, can not be questioned. In view of the conditions in other lands, Americans should be doubly thankful for the form of Government which has been transmitted to them by their ancestors, won by valor and sacrifice, under which they enjoy self-government.[44]

Any president, of course, receives so many messages and pleas that answering each one is impossible. In this instance, however, what was said in Wilson's name was strikingly at variance from what we know the president was thinking and writing at the time. The statement, undoubtedly drafted by Phelan or someone on his staff with just a couple minor, handwritten changes by Tumulty, accomplished its immediate goal of replying to an Irish-American organization at a critical time.

On July 11, Robert P. Troy, president of the Knights, responded directly to Wilson (referring twice to "your esteemed letter") and acknowledged the president's "friendly suggestion . . . to the British Government in behalf of clemency for the prisoners who were concerned in the recent Irish uprising." Troy went on to write: "I have taken the liberty of assuring our members at all times that we could depend upon you to take such action as would be consistent with discretion and established diplomatic precedents."[45] The ghosted letter had served its purpose. The Knights of St. Patrick thought they had a dependable ally of Irish ancestry in the White House and said as much. The reply arrived on July 17, and a handwritten notation, presumably by Tumulty, says "copy sent to Sen. Phelan" the next day. Troy's and the Knights' trust in Wilson prompted them to contact the White House again a few days later in July. According to a report in the *San Francisco Chronicle* (July 22, 1916), the Knights of St. Patrick, "pioneer Irish organization of the Pacific Coast," had appealed to Wilson, asking that he use a "friendly suggestion" to the British to seek clemency for Casement.[46] By that time, of course, Wilson had decided to make no "friendly suggestion" of any kind to help Casement.

Over the years, some historians have taken Wilson at what they thought were his words. After citing the inspiring passage about Wilson's "natural sympathies are with men struggling for freedom," Francis Carroll remarked, "It cannot be known how specifically Wilson was referring to Irishmen struggling for freedom or men in general, nor can it be known the extent to which this statement, with its strong pro-Irish implications, was motivated by purely political reasons; certainly it manifests as much warmth for the Irish cause as his statements in his early career."[47] To know now that a senator and presidential aide orchestrated the letter between themselves—one wonders if Wilson ever saw it or was even told about it—puts even greater emphasis on its political urgency. More broadly and beyond its immediate usage, the statement suggested that the man in the White House considered the Irish cause, with people "struggling for freedom," as harmonious with his worldview and worthy of his support.

Like Spring Rice and others in Washington, Tumulty was sensitive to the profound change in Irish-American opinion after the Rising, and he understood as well as anyone else how careful the White House had to act in dealing with it. In communicating with the State Department on June 9 about a possible response to Phelan for the Knights of St. Patrick, Tumulty told Frank L. Polk, counselor at the State Department, "I would like to discuss this matter with you before a reply is made to the Senator. There is so much dynamite in it that we ought to proceed with care."[48] The "dynamite" had the potential to detonate domestically and make the "exiled children" think twice about supporting the incumbent Democratic president a few months before the 1916 election. However, as it turned out, there was no explosion. Wilson carried California by fewer than four thousand votes, and in the general election he narrowly defeated Charles Evans Hughes (49.2 percent to 46.1 percent, or 277 Electoral College votes to 254).

From his renomination in June, the president wanted to be perceived as the tireless worker for peace, with strict neutrality his guiding star. Taking sides on Casement would have endangered the White House strategy of maintaining deliberate distance from controversial foreign matters. Although the administration received criticism for delaying the transmission of a Senate resolution requesting clemency for Casement, the White House vigorously denied the charges and worked to make the campaign concentrate on affairs at home. Despite all the attention to European hostilities, America's highest elected official was content to attend to business in the forty-eight states. Nonetheless, the Rising produced political and policy aftershocks that reverberated during the president's second term and demanded his attention. Try as he might to command the world stage as a war leader with ethereal plans for the future, Wilson could never seem to disentangle himself from the Irish Question. Yet, given everything happening across the Atlantic, it was only a matter of time before Wilson and his administration were forced to deal more openly with international affairs.

Despite the spirit and practical application of his campaign slogan, Wilson's hand was forced by events, and he could no longer keep the United States on the sidelines of the war. Germany announced a new and unrestricted submarine offensive on January 31; a month later, a telegram from Arthur Zimmermann, the German foreign minister, was revealed, proposing an alliance between his country and Mexico against the United States. Military skirmishes with Mexico had taken place during Wilson's presidency in 1914, and the prospect of increased conflict, with German provocation, angered Americans. Moreover, with U.S. ships now the targets of U-boat torpedoes, neutrality no longer seemed an option. On April 2, 1917, Wilson asked Congress for a declaration of war, telling the House of Representatives and the Senate, "The world must be made safe for democracy." Four days later, Congress approved the president's request by wide margins in both chambers, and the United States was engaged in the European war.

On April 10, as the White House prepared for combat abroad, Wilson wrote on his own typewriter a letter to Secretary of State Robert Lansing suggesting that a "confidential message" be sent to the U.S. ambassador to Great Britain, Walter Hines Page. What Wilson wrote showed a realistic and political concern for Ireland in both its relationship to Britain and its influence within Irish America's "exiled children." The president urged Lansing that the message to Page should instruct him to tell Prime Minister Lloyd George that the only thing standing between "an absolutely cordial" relation between the United States and Great Britain was "a satisfactory method of self-government for Ireland." He went on:

> This appeared very strikingly in the recent debates in Congress upon the war resolution and appeared in the speeches of opponents of that resolution who were not themselves Irishmen or representatives of

constituencies in which Irish voters were influential, notably several members from the South. If the people of the United States could feel that there was an early prospect of the establishment for Ireland of substantial self-government a very great element of satisfaction and enthusiasm would be added to the cooperation now about to be organized between this country and Great Britain. Convey this information unofficially of course but as having no little significance. Successful action now would absolutely divorce our citizens of Irish birth and sympathy from the German sympathizers here with whom many of them have been inclined to make common cause.

Page now knows the Prime Minister well enough to know how to say these things to him frankly, and if a way could be found now to grant Ireland what she has so often been promised, it would be felt that the real programme of government by the consent of the governed had been adopted everywhere in the anti-Prussian world.[49]

By remarkable coincidence, just three days after Wilson sent his private letter to Lansing, Ambassador Spring Rice wrote the Foreign Office in London, stressing the centrality of Ireland's fate to Wilson and the United States. The Irish Question remained a thorn in the side of the administration because it served "as a proof that it is not wholly true that the fight is one for the sanctity of engagements or the independence of small nations." Politics lay at the base of it. "The President is by descent an Orangeman and by education a Presbyterian. But he is the leader of the Democratic Party in which the Irish play a prominent part, and he is bound in every way to give consideration to their demands."[50]

That the messages of Wilson and Spring Rice came at virtually the same time provides evidence of the place the Irish Question held in both Anglo-American relations *and* American domestic politics. Given the joint awareness as U.S. involvement in the war began, the expectation for some kind of resolution is clearly on the mind of public officials with memories of what happened in Dublin less than a year before. Though he often preferred back-channel secrecy for such overtures, Wilson consistently supported and pushed for home rule in Ireland. At this critical moment, it would have helped to divide two strong groups of hyphenated citizens in the United States—Irish Americans and German Americans—and given the war effort a boost. In the broader context, it also might have led to a greater sense of self-determination among the Irish. On April 18, Page sent a telegram to the president about the proposal: "I took up this subject in a confidential conversation with the Prime Minister at my house last night. He instantly understood and showed that he already knew the facts that I presented and was glad that the President had instructed me to bring the subject up. He had had the American situation in mind during the whole discussion of home rule and he was doing his best."[51]

Home rule for Ireland kept returning as a subject of debate in the British government, but words never led to implementation. Wilson's nudge didn't do the trick in 1917, even when Britain might have been inclined to be receptive. As the war effort was mobilized and fighting in Europe intensified, the American Irish subordinated ancestral considerations to the cause of victory. Solidarity of singular purpose prevailed while the Yanks in the Fighting Sixty-Ninth (like Kilmer) and other divisions served abroad. But the work of the commander-in-chief demanded more than the creation of a united home front. Nonetheless, the issue of home rule for Ireland became a recurring subplot in Anglo-American relations.

On May 12, 1917, the *New York World* reported, "Persons who are in a position to speak with authority say that the President has gone as far as the proprieties permit in bringing to the realization of the British Foreign Secretary the importance of the Home Rule proposition in this country."[52] In June, British Prime Minister Lloyd George announced what was called the "Irish Convention" to address self-government in Ireland. Meeting in Dublin from July 25, 1917, until April 5, 1918, the convention—involving some hundred delegates of widely varying viewpoints (from nationalists to Ulster unionists, though not Sinn Féin)—ended in failure; however, it bought time for Wilson and others. As long as delegates talked and presented proposals, the administration could point to formal proceedings abroad that were trying to address the Irish Question. The president had protection during a critical period in the war when he wanted to project a resolute unity of purpose at home.

Wilson, however, couldn't entirely dodge consideration of Ireland's future, what historian George Dangerfield referred to as "the damnable question." At a White House ceremony on January 10, 1918, that involved Senator Phelan, Wilson was given a statue of Robert Emmet, the Dublin-born Irish nationalist who led an ill-fated rebellion against the British in 1803. Like the Rising leaders of 1916, he, too, had been executed. In making the presentation, Phelan used the occasion to revisit Ireland's contemporary situation. While praising the president, Phelan also put Wilson on the spot:

> Robert Emmet was a poor potter, and he died for his country. And the men of Irish blood of America, American citizens here represented, think it is most opportune in the history of the world that attention should be called to his sacrifice, and more particularly to the cause in which he made the sacrifice. There should be a good feeling among all nations, especially among those allied in the war—and they have all made professions. In fact, Mr. President, you have been their spokesman in favor of recognizing the national right of a country of homogeneous people to independence and autonomy—certainly autonomy. And we feel that, at this time, while presenting to you the image of an Irish rebel, from our point of view, we are presenting to you the representative of a nation in rebellion against the oppression which has been put upon them for centuries. And I don't think it is inappropriate here to say, from my knowledge of history, that no greater indignity, no more atrocious acts, have ever been committed against a people as have been committed against the people of Ireland. That is all back in the past. The world up to the beginning of the war had become enlightened, and we are willing to forget the past if we can be the beneficiaries of that enlightenment which you, sir, are endeavoring to preserve and treasure.[53]

Wilson responded to Phelan by retreating behind the cover of the Irish Convention and with platitudes about Emmet, arguing that what he did "in his time would not be necessary to do in our time." Nonetheless, "without any partisanship of any kind," we could all appreciate "the spirit which leads a man to go the full length of sacrifice for the purpose that he holds most dear."[54] At a cabinet meeting the following day, however, Wilson unloaded. According to a diary entry by Josephus Daniels, secretary of the navy during both terms, "WW indignant at speech by Phelan, in presenting small bust of Emmett [*sic*], wishing the President to help Ireland secure its rights. At this time, with England fighting with us, such talk almost treasonable. President said he so mad he could hardly restrain himself."[55]

The same day as the cabinet meeting, the president had what was termed an "interview" with Hanna Sheehy-Skeffington, an Irish nationalist, pacifist, and suffragette. She was the widow of Francis Sheehy-Skeffington, a prominent journalist who had been gunned down by a British officer during the Rising, even though, as a pacifist, he was not involved in the fighting and had been trying to stop the looting of Dublin businesses. Like other nationalists and republicans (such as Nora Connelly, Liam Mellows, and Diarmuid Lynch), Hanna Sheehy-Skeffington traveled to America after the Rising to rally support for Ireland in an environment sympathetic to the cause for independence. During a year and a half in the United States, she spoke "at over two hundred and fifty public meetings" in (by her count) twenty states, returning to Dublin in June 1918 to write a short but engrossing memoir, *Impressions of Sinn Féin in America*.

Given her background and allegiances, it seems puzzling that Wilson was willing to see her, though she credited Bainbridge Colby, a prominent lawyer and political figure who later served as Wilson's last secretary of state, and Joseph Tumulty as intermediaries on her behalf. Her principal objective in meeting Wilson was to deliver a petition from Cumann na mBan, the Irish women's republican paramilitary organization, and signed by Constance Markievicz, Margaret Pearse (P. H. Pearse's mother), and others. The document, which somehow reached Sheehy-Skeffington without being stopped by British censors in Ireland, "put forth the claim of Ireland for self-determination, and appealed to President Wilson to include Ireland among the Small Nations for whose freedom America was fighting."[56]

In her account of the interview, Sheehy-Skeffington took pride in being "the first Irish exile and the first Sinn Féiner to enter the White House, and the first to wear there the badge of the Irish Republic, which I took care to pin in my coat before I went."[57] She reported Wilson's hope that "the Lloyd George Convention then sitting in Ireland" would solve the Irish Question, but she says that two weeks after her interview "it collapsed like a badly-built house of cards." What was most striking, however, was her profound faith that Wilson would pursue a solution at the post-armistice Peace Conference. Sheehy-Skeffington had several months to reflect on her time with the president and what he might do at the end of hostilities in Europe: "President Wilson is not the type that will lead, pioneer-like, a forlorn hope, or stake all on a desperate enterprise; but, on the other hand, he is one who by tradition (he has Irish blood in his veins) and by temperament, will see the need of self-determination for Ireland as well as for other nations." Sheehy-Skeffington was confident that Wilson would not be allowed to "turn a deaf ear."[58]

Sheehy-Skeffington's faith in Wilson was also reflected in a letter she sent to John Devoy shortly after the meeting. "The president was personally very courteous and acknowledged smilingly his Irish blood," she wrote. "I asked him to consider our claims as a small nation governed without consent. He took the petition and seemed interested." Later in the letter Sheehy-Skeffington advised Devoy (his hatred of Wilson notwithstanding) to use editorials in *The Gaelic American* "to plead for Ireland" and to put pressure on Congress on behalf of the Irish cause.[59] Generally, her feeling was that Irish Americans were, as she put it in her memoir, "Hot Air Harps" who talked about the situation in Ireland without moving beyond words. To her, Wilson and his rhetoric were more promising. As it turned out, if not a "Hot Air Harp," Wilson proved something of a "Celtic Chameleon."

During the same week (on January 8, 1918), Wilson delivered a speech to a joint session of Congress that spelled out the fourteen points he wanted addressed at the end of the war. Ireland was not mentioned, but his fifth point (before specifying proposals for Russia, Belgium, France, Italy, Austria-Hungary, etc.) asserted his view of "[a] free, open-minded, and absolutely impartial adjustment of all colonial claims, based upon a strict observance of the principle that in determining all such questions of sovereignty the interests of the populations concerned must have equal weight with the equitable claims of the government whose title is to be determined."[60] Like his remarks about "every people" and "small states" to the League to Enforce Peace in late May 1916, Wilson's references to "all colonial claims" and "interests of the populations concerned" could logically apply to the Irish.

A little over a month later, on February 11, 1918, Wilson returned to the Capitol for another speech to a joint session of the House and Senate that both reacted to the German and Austrian responses to Wilson's points and amplified his thinking about the postwar world. In one section, he focused directly on a concern that independence-minded Irish and Irish Americans considered critical to their cause: "National aspirations must be respected; peoples may now be dominated and governed only by their own consent. 'Self-determination' is not a mere phrase. It is an imperative principle of action, which statesmen will henceforth ignore at their peril."[61]

In the wake of the Rising, growing numbers of Irish people on both sides of the Atlantic certainly thought "self-determination" was more than "a mere phrase." Wilson, however, harbored a different view. While physical-force nationalists regarded Ireland as a vassal of Britain, a colony under the lion's paw, Wilson approached Ireland as essentially a domestic concern for the

British. For Fenians such as John Devoy, the Irish had suffered from English subjugation since the twelfth century as a result of invasion from across the Irish Sea and by papal fiat. The story of Ireland was the story of English oppression.[62] Wilson, with his doctorate in history and political science—the only U.S. president thus far who has earned a Ph.D.—could never see Ireland as a separate country unto itself or in the way the narrative had evolved during the past two centuries. To him, it was just one of the many "British isles."

Moreover, Wilson's lofty yet imprecise language had the potential of creating false impressions. Writing in his diary on December 30, 1918, more than six weeks after the armistice, Secretary of State Robert Lansing trenchantly observed that the more he thought about the president's assertion of self-determination "the more convinced I am of the danger of putting such ideas into the mind of certain races. It is bound to be the basis of impossible demands on the Peace Congress and create trouble in many lands." To Lansing the phrase was "simply loaded with dynamite. It will raise hopes which can never be realized. It will, I fear, cost thousands of lives." In the end, in Lansing's view, it had been a "calamity" that Wilson had ever uttered it.[63]

Although the Peace Conference at Versailles didn't formally convene until January 18, 1919, Wilson was already looking ahead, setting down in words definite plans for reshaping the world as he thought it should be. But more than a year before details of the eventual peace treaty were formulated, the president had made one decision that, in terms of the future, would haunt his upcoming months in Paris and the remainder of his time in the White House. In a sentence buried near the end of a multipage "Most Secret" memorandum of February 4, 1918, written by William Wiseman, the head of Britain's intelligence office in the United States and liaison between the administration and London, Wiseman reported that during a three-hour session with Wilson the president assured him "that as far as he was concerned he would not allow Ireland to be dragged into a Peace Conference."[64] In Wilson's thinking, though he refrained from saying so publicly, the Irish Question remained what it had always been: a domestic matter to be resolved internally by political leaders in the United Kingdom.

The precise extent to which the Easter Rising directly affected Wilson's approach to Ireland remains unknown. He took note of it in 1916 (though not nearly to the degree that Spring Rice did), but efforts at peacemaking and keeping a tight focus on domestic issues for his reelection campaign took precedence. Two years later, however, the Rising returned as an issue, when the British government provided the United States with a series of decoded messages, showing a direct connection between the German government and individual Americans (namely John Devoy, Daniel F. Cohalan, and Joseph McGarrity) in the planning and financing. On May 19, 1918, Secretary of State Lansing sent Wilson the thirty-two telegrams and letters that revealed the secret relationship with "Sinn Fein agents in this country" (beginning on September 25, 1914, and ending January 18, 1917). Although the documents proved German and American involvement in the Rising, Lansing argued against the U.S. government releasing them, noting: "The Irish situation is very delicate and anything which we might do to aid either side [the British or Sinn Féin] in the controversy would, I fear, involve us in all sorts of difficulties with the Irish in this country. . . . [P]ublishing these papers at this time would be construed as a direct assistance to Great Britain in the matter of conscription in Ireland."[65] The Irish Conference in Dublin had recently ended without an agreement for self-government. Enacting conscription without first establishing home rule was politically impossible in American eyes.

After the failure of the Irish Conference, Wilson no longer had an excuse to hide behind when the subject of Ireland arose. One of the first overtures to the president came from his ally yet single-issue irritant Senator Phelan, who proposed (on June 29, 1918) "a frank statement of Ireland's right to autonomous government (without necessarily defining the kind) and the prompt granting of it" as part of a Fourth of July address.[66] In responding, Wilson fell back on reassuring rhetoric that avoided taking a definite stand. "I realize, of course, the critical importance of the whole Irish question, but I do not think that it would be wise for me in any public utterance to attempt to outline a policy for the British Government with regard to Ireland. It is a matter, of course, of the utmost delicacy, and I must frankly say that I would not know how to handle it without risking very uncomfortable confusions of counsel."[67]

Privately, Wilson was of course less guarded and Colonel House didn't refrain from recording conversations between himself and the president.[68] Though the two ultimately had a falling out in 1919—like Devoy, maintaining friendships or even working relationships proved difficult for Wilson—House enjoyed maximum access to the president in 1918.[69] In his diary for August 16, 1918, he wrote:

> In speaking of the Irish he surprised me by saying that he did not intend
> to appoint another Irishman to anything; that they were untrustworthy
> and uncertain. He thought Tumulty was the only one he had come in

contact with who was. It is curious that he should pick him as an exception to the rule. Dudley Malone [a Wilson appointee who turned on the president for his lukewarm support of women's suffrage in his first term] and some others have brought him to this frame of mind and he does the Irish an injustice.[70]

Wilson's frustration may have derived from the efforts of Phelan and others pushing for assistance on behalf of Ireland. Whatever the motivation, it is telling a president would express a generalization of this kind about an entire "race," one to which he had politically appealed on ancestral grounds in the past. House was also convinced that Wilson might run for a third term.

> I am opposed to a third term in ordinary circumstances but after looking over the different possibilities, I have come to believe that it may be necessary for the President to undertake another four years. The end of the war is drawing too near the end of his term to make it possible for him to properly solve the many problems arising at the Peace Conference, and the after war problems which are certain to need wise solution. There is no one but the President who has the proper background and outlook.[71]

Over the years, House had worked with several politicians, helping four to become governor of his native Texas. He knew the breed and the temptations of ambition. With unbounded self-regard in matters pertaining to peacemaking and committed to a new world order made possible with a functioning League of Nations, Wilson hadn't closed any doors in his mind or with others. Like Franklin D. Roosevelt pondering the possibility of an unprecedented third term in 1940, the incumbent president had unfinished business he thought he alone could accomplish.

Wilson had indeed entertained the thought of a potential candidacy for the better part of two years, even up to the Democratic National Convention in the summer of 1920, when Ohio Governor James M. Cox was nominated on the forty-fourth ballot. The press kept the prospect in front of the public during this period, and Wilson himself wrote Tumulty from Paris on June 2, 1919, requesting his secretary's opinion of an editorial in the *Springfield Republican* about a possible third term. Though Tumulty opposed another campaign, he advised against making a formal statement—and as a result the matter remained open. Indeed, when Wilson decided to make his cross-country speaking tour in September of 1919 to generate support for the Treaty of Versailles and the League of Nations, some commentators saw it in political terms—namely the mission of a candidate rallying voters for 1920. Wilson dealt with Ireland and appeals from the American Irish as though he planned to run another race. Yet by this point his avoidance of the Ireland Question had turned a sizable percentage of Irish Americans against the president, his objectives, and his party.

The American Irish were by no means alone. Wilson's second term was much less successful than his first, when (among other accomplishments) he and Congress reduced tariffs, enacted banking reform, created the Federal Reserve, bolstered anti-trust regulation, and established the Federal Trade Commission. Wilson called the progressive agenda of his first term the "New Freedom," and it was overwhelmingly oriented to domestic initiatives. After his reelection in 1916, international concerns and crises consumed more of the president's attention, and the world became a stage he thought he could command. Given the circumstances, his ambition, too, didn't stop growing.

In retrospect, though, it is remarkable that he seriously contemplated another term after the disastrous results of the 1918 mid-term elections. With the war in Europe in its final days and victory within reach, Wilson composed an open letter, released on October 25, in which he inserted himself directly in the middle of the campaign. Saying it is "no time either for divided counsel or for divided leadership," he phrased the possibility of the rival party winning in stark personal terms: "The return of a Republican majority to either House of the Congress would, moreover, certainly be interpreted on the other side of the water as a repudiation of my leadership."[72] Republicans and many independents accused Wilson of questioning their patriotism, and when the votes were counted, his opponents had won majorities in both the House and the Senate. The president's attempt to build support for himself and his agenda backfired, making his postwar plans much more difficult to accomplish.

The mid-term elections of 1918 took place on November 5, and the armistice was signed in France just six days later. With the sense of national unity no longer an imperative among immigrants and their offspring, Wilson started to feel pressure from ethnic groups, notably the Irish, for settlement of issues the war had delayed. For instance, the Government of Ireland Act of 1914, which was to become statute on September 18, was suspended because Britain had declared war on Germany a month earlier. The end of hostilities could finally lead to home rule, and the American president could help to make it happen—or so many of his fellow citizens thought. On December 2,

1918, Senator Thomas J. Walsh of Montana, a strong White House supporter who managed the critically important Western portion of the president's 1916 campaign, wrote a lengthy appeal to Wilson, arguing for "a speedy solution of the question of self-government for Ireland." Walsh's letter set the tone for the multitude of messages delivered on paper and in person to the president about the Irish Question. The war had been fought, Wilson had led everyone to believe, to make the world safe for democracy and to gain self-determination for small nations. Now Ireland deserved that kind of Wilsonian attention and emphasis. Walsh even issued a warning for failing to act: "If the Peace Congress dissolves without a reasonably satisfactory settlement there will not be a controversy between this country and Great Britain, however trivial, that will not be fanned into what may some day be a consuming flame."[73]

In his response, Wilson (who departed from Washington on December 4 on the first trip to Europe ever taken by a sitting president) made no mention of his earlier decision to keep Ireland out of the Peace Conference.

> I appreciate the importance of a proper solution of the Irish question and thank you for the suggestions of your letter of yesterday. Until I get on the other side and find my footing in delicate matters of this sort I cannot forecast with any degree of confidence what influence I can exercise, but you may be sure that I shall keep this important interest in mind and shall use my influence at every opportunity to bring about a just and satisfactory solution.[74]

Wilson wasn't showing his hand. Adding to the complexity of the situation in Ireland, what the British refer to as the Anglo-Irish War and the Irish call the War of Independence began on January 21, 1919, just three days after the Peace Conference formally opened.

While Wilson was in France, Tumulty stayed in Washington, keeping the president informed on activity in Congress and the domestic press coverage. The Irish Question remained a front-and-center concern, with a House of Representatives resolution urging the United States at the Peace Conference to present the case for "the right to freedom, independence, and self-determination of Ireland."[75] However, no matter whether at the White House or abroad, Wilson was not inclined to act, telling Tumulty on January 30, 1919: "I frankly dread the effect on British public opinion with which I am daily dealing here of a Home Rule resolution by the House of

Representatives and I am afraid that it would be impossible to explain such a resolution here. . . . It is not a question of sympathy but of international tactics at a very critical period."[76]

Wilson always seemed to find a way of not dealing formally with Ireland, though in the past he had been a strong and consistent proponent of home rule. As the Peace Conference progressed, Ireland bedeviled Wilson with such regularity that a weaker figure might have relented and pushed for some kind of resolution to reduce the pressure so he could concentrate on other issues, such as establishing the League of Nations. Wilson, however, didn't budge. In his mind and despite the ramifications of the Rising, Ireland simply wasn't a subject for the Peace Conference, and he did whatever he could to ensure that it didn't receive formal consideration.

Wilson took a three-week break from conference proceedings in late February and early March 1919 to return to the States. Criticism among Republican senators to treaty proposals was already mounting, and the future of Ireland was being debated more openly in Congress and among the general public. Upon his arrival in Boston on February 24, he spoke about "the cause of liberty" in language intended to inspire not only an American audience but also people in other countries with postwar aspirations of self-determination. Near the end of his remarks, Wilson said: "We set this nation up to make men free, and we did not confine our conception and purpose to America, and now we will make men free." Doing otherwise would diminish the country. "I have fighting blood in me, and it is sometimes a delight to let it have scope, but if it is challenged on this occasion it will be an indulgence. Think of the picture, think of the utter blackness that would fall on the world. America has failed. America made a little essay at generosity and then withdrew." It was the country's moral obligation to "set up light to lead men along the paths of liberty."[77] After painting a bleak future for a world without U.S. leadership, the president mentioned by name the Polish, Czecho-Slovaks, Jugo-Slavs, and Armenians. He never brought up Ireland. His Boston audience may have thought it was implicit. Didn't some of his "fighting blood" come from ancestors who had emigrated from Ireland, as he had proudly announced years before when he entered politics?

On March 1, Wilson received strongly worded letters from two close associates about the need to take up Ireland as an issue on his return to Paris, and Tumulty urged the president to meet with a delegation of Irish Americans, noting "Your attitude in this matter is fraught with a great deal of danger both to the Democratic party and to the cause you represent." The secretary, who made a point of saying that he was "not a professional Irishman," remained sensitive to domestic politics and to the Wilsonian worldview, concluding that "your refusal to see this delegation will simply strengthen the Sinn Fein movement in this country."[78] Though involving relatively few Americans three years before, the Easter Rising was responsible for setting in motion what had become a "movement" in the United States to support independence for Ireland, and Wilson's closest link to the Irish-American community understood the need to maintain friendly relations with a critical voting and opinion-forming constituency.

Moreover, George Creel, who headed the U.S. Committee on Public Information (the wartime propaganda department of the government), wrote Wilson the same day from his post in Paris, and his letter, like Tumulty's, offered a warning. To Creel, Ireland posed "one of the most important questions with which you will have to deal." The Irish in America were going to unite and would be joined by every German American "eager to take advantage of the opportunity to embarrass our relations with Great Britain." Creel made clear to Wilson that Sinn Féin controlled Ireland "absolutely, with the exception of four counties in Ulster, and in two of these counties it has forty percent of the voting strength." The old home-rule leaders were gone, and the cry was now for an Irish republic.[79]

Tumulty and Creel weren't alone in trying to get Wilson to concentrate on the Irish Question, and several other appeals to provide help can be found in the president's papers. He ultimately consented to meet with the delegation of Irish Americans, as Tumulty wanted, doing so in New York on March 4, the day before his return to France. The *New York Times* told its readers that Wilson was asked to propose at the Peace Conference that Ireland should determine its future form of government. Wilson balked at expressing any opinion or potential action, according to the account, but the delegates left the twenty-five-minute session thinking the president was "favorable to the Irish cause."[80] Interestingly, what newspapers reported about the meeting came from a statement provided by the Irish-American group. Included in the summary are direct quotations attributed to the president. At one point, he tells the committee, "I agree with your argument. Yes. I agree with what you say." Later, in talking about whether the Irish Question should be addressed in Paris, he was less forthcoming: "when this case comes up I will have to use my best judgment as to how to act."[81]

In public, Wilson continued to convey concern, creating the perception that he was working on the matter. However, away from agenda-driven delegations or argument-making correspondents, the president presented a much different face. The diary of his physician, Dr. Cary T. Grayson, contains a lengthy entry for March 4, offering a more revealing and comprehensive account of the New York meeting than any newspaper coverage. Grayson wrote that Wilson was adamant that Daniel F. Cohalan, a justice on the New York State Supreme Court, brother-in-law of Jeremiah O'Leary, and an opponent of Wilson's presidential nomination in 1912, be excluded from the delegation. "I will not attend the meeting if Cohalan is there because he is a traitor," the president is quoted as telling policemen protecting him. Concluding what he wrote about the session, Grayson observed: "The President heard the committee courteously but made no promises. The President said it was a domestic affair for Great Britain and Ireland to settle themselves, and not a matter for outside interference."[82] What is not clear from this diary entry is whether Wilson delivered his opinion about not wanting to interfere in "a domestic affair" during the meeting. Given the generally positive and optimistic statement of the delegation, it seems more probable the president said it to Grayson afterward.

As the president and his party set sail on the *George Washington*, Grayson added a postscript about the previous night. The doctor and Wilson were talking about the meeting, and the discussion turned from the Peace Conference to a wider perspective:

> In referring to the Irish meeting last night, at which an effort was made to get the President to promise that he would bring their cause before the Peace Conference, he said that the Irish as a race are very hard to deal with owing to their inconsiderateness, their unreasonable demands and their jealousies. He predicted that owing to the dissatisfaction among the Irish-Americans and the German-Americans with the Democratic administration, unless a decided change was brought about, it might defeat the Democratic party in 1920.[83]

In the back of his mind, Wilson might have entertained secret hopes about a third term, but he was realistic in contemplating the political repercussions of failing to solve the Irish Question. Moreover, away from the public stage and Irish Americans he wanted to impress, the president wasn't inclined to raise his own heritage.

An even more informative account of Wilson's reaction to the New York meeting can be found in *My Diary at the Conference of Paris* by David Hunter Miller, who served as a legal adviser to the U.S. Commission at the Peace Conference. Miller recounts talking with Wilson in Paris about the treaty then being drafted. What Miller recorded shows the president without his mask of feigned sincerity and seems similar to his private reaction several months earlier when he received the statue of Emmet: "He then spoke of the Irish question and said that he had been made very angry by a delegation of the Irish who had visited him while in the United States and had asked him to promise to ask the Peace Conference to make Ireland independent." According to Miller, Wilson said he would explain matters to Prime Minister Lloyd George, and if the prime minister wanted nothing done about Ireland, then "he would do nothing." Miller wrote that Wilson was aware that if he did not raise the issue of Irish self-determination, the Irish would start

> a campaign against the League on this ground, and that this would raise a racial and religious question which would have far-reaching conse-quences. Of course, he said, it would be overwhelmingly defeated by the Irish and would insure the success of the League, and that his first impulse had been, from his fighting blood getting up, that he had wanted to tell them (the Irish) to go to hell, but he realized that while that might give some personal satisfaction it would not be the act of wisdom or the act of a statesman.[84]

Wilson found it impossible to elude pleadings on behalf of the Irish at the Peace Conference. He even attempted humor as a way to handle the situ-ation, quipping to Lloyd George, "I gave you the solution of that question if you had only followed it out, namely, give them Home Rule and reserve the moving-picture rights."[85] The president's attempt to be droll by refer-ring to the potential for slapstick from the Irish having local governmen-tal control didn't amuse Lloyd George. Writing in his *Memoirs of the Peace Conference*, Lloyd George commented: "Wilson had no humour and his wit was synthetic."[86]

While the former prime minister tried to be fair in assessing his American counterpart at the Peace Conference, the portrait he drew was mostly unflat-tering. Early in his rendering of Wilson, Lloyd George complained, "Whilst we were dealing every day with ghastly realities on land and sea, some of them visible to our own eyes and audible to our ears, he was soaring in clouds of serene rhetoric."[87] Later descriptions were equally as revealing—"He was the most extraordinary compound I have ever encountered of the noble visionary, the implacable and unscrupulous partisan, the exalted idealist and the man of rather petty personal rancours."[88] Lloyd George went so far as to call Wilson's participation at the Peace Conference "a mistake," mainly because "he was not of a trustful disposition. That was his most disabling weakness—his pervasive suspiciousness. He believed in mankind but distrusted all men."[89] Impolitic in the extreme, the allies could also be rivals.

Endless rounds of meetings with international delegations filled Wilson's time in Paris. However, the Irish Question continued to come up in negotiations with the British, and beginning in mid-April of 1919, representatives of the American Irish arrived in France to push the president and those around him for formal consideration at the Peace Conference. Called the American Commission on Irish Independence and appointed during the Third Irish Race Convention in February 1919, the three prominent, politically connected figures had as their objective U.S. approval for leaders of Dáil Éireann, including its president and survivor of the Rising, Éamon de Valera, to make the case for self-government. The Dáil was established in January 1919 as, in effect, the revolutionary parliament in Ireland after Sinn Féin won 73 of the 101 seats in the 1918 election. Refusing to participate in the House of Commons at Westminster, these nationalists formed their own assembly in Dublin, despite British opposition, and had sent Sean T. O'Kelly to Paris in hopes of making an appeal to the president, which never occurred. The commission, led by Francis Patrick Walsh, met with Wilson shortly after arriving—and that session was about the only time the trio didn't prompt critical reactions from the president or others participating in the conference.

The commissioners, including Edward F. Dunne, the former Democratic governor of Illinois, had hurt their cause with the American delegation during a side trip to Ireland, where (in Colonel House's opinion) they "made incendiary speeches" advocating an Irish republic. Press coverage of what they said circulated in Ireland and Britain, putting both the British and Americans on the defensive at the Peace Conference. Although they kept hounding the president and his inner circle to schedule time for a consideration of Ireland, the requests went unheeded. In his diary (for May 21), Ray Stannard Baker noted: "The Irish-Americans . . . are back here from revolutionary Ireland & like every group of restless agitators came first to our office.

They get everybody they come into contact with into hot water. They have written a letter to the Colonel [House] in which they try to involve both him & the President in the squabble."[90]

The commission pursued recognition for Ireland with relentless energy. For Wilson, absorbed in nuances of the treaty and his dream of a League of Nations, distraction from his larger purpose was irritating, if not exasperating. On May 29, Baker visited the president at his residence in Paris, and they talked about postwar boundaries in Austria and support of the League among "oppressed minorities in the world." In his diary for that day, Baker notes: "All the minorities except the Irish," said the president. "Yes," I said, "the Irish seem very unhappy. Walsh & Dunne are in my office every day with a new letter or manifesto." The president responded, almost savagely, "I don't know how long I shall be able to resist telling them what I think of their miserable mischief-making. . . . They can see nothing except their own small interest."[91]

Throughout its time abroad, the Irish-American contingent got deeper and deeper under Wilson's skin. Just two days after his outburst about the League, Baker, again in his diary, recorded that the president talked about the "mischief makers" and how he might try to neutralize their impact back in the United States. "I have one weapon I can use against them—one terrible weapon, which I shall not use unless I am driven to it," he said, "unless it appears that the Irish movement has forgotten to be American in its interest in a foreign controversy." He paused, and then said, "I have only to warn our people of the attempt of the Roman Catholic hierarchy to dominate our public opinion, & there is no doubt about what America will do."[92] Even raising religion as a potential "weapon" revealed the near desperation of Wilson's thinking. All the nationalist lobbying and agitation backed the frustrated president into a corner, compounding a domestic problem at the very moment that he was preoccupied with what shape the world might take after the conference.

Back at the White House, Tumulty took a more dispassionate view, worrying that not addressing Ireland could weaken U.S. support for the League of Nations. Yet even that threat did not push Wilson to search anew for some way to act. On June 8, the president responded at length to his secretary: "The American Committee of Irishmen have made it exceedingly difficult, if not impossible, to render the assistance we were diligently trying to render in the matter of bringing the Irish aspirations to the attention of the Peace Congress." Wilson was convinced that by going to Ireland and in the process inflaming English opinion, the committee had undermined its cause. He said, "I made an effort yesterday in this matter which shows, I am afraid, the utter futility of future efforts. I am distressed that the American committee should have acted with such extreme indiscretion and lack of sense, and can at the moment see nothing further to do."[93]

Two days after criticizing the "American Committee," Wilson did schedule a meeting with Walsh and Dunne. In his diary, Dr. Grayson provides a detailed account, noting that Walsh informed American journalists in Paris that he might seek the impeachment of Wilson if the president didn't allow representatives from the rebel government of Ireland to speak at the Peace Conference. After listening to Walsh state his case, Wilson, as might be expected, absolved himself of blame, arguing that their trip to Ireland and own "speeches in advocacy of the Irish Republic aroused the ire of the British government and made extremely difficult, if not impossible, the matter of securing any concessions your way."[94]

Walsh responded that the commission sought for Ireland "a republican form of government" similar to the one in the United States, which fought for its independence from England, and he then "read extracts from the President's speeches, in which the latter had pled for self-government and freedom for oppressed peoples." Wilson reacted to hearing his own words quoted back to him by trying to correct and change the perception he seemed to have conveyed:

> "You do not mean to have me think, Mr. Walsh, that you as an American construed this speech as referring directly to Ireland," inquired the President. "I certainly did think so," declared Walsh; "in fact, Sir, when I read your speech at the outset of the war I made an address in Kansas City in which I declared that what you said actually fitted in with what was happening in Ireland." "Yet," continued the President, "you must have known as everyone else knew that what I said at that time referred distinctly and decidedly to the problems affecting the nations that were involved in the war, and especially the smaller nations that had been the victims of the Central Powers."

According to Grayson's report of the meeting, "Walsh insisted that he had believed, and still believed, that the president had voiced an appeal for justice to all nations, Ireland included."[95]

Near the end of the meeting, Wilson retreated to the strategy of having these potential opponents feel sorry for him because the burdens of his office made all that he would like to accomplish impossible. "I wish that I could make plain to you all that I feel. You cannot realize how difficult has been the task that has been set for me to do and how it has hurt me inside to realize that I have not been able to carry through to completion the entire program which I outlined."[96] Grayson continued to describe the scene and Wilson's self-defense, building to the observation that the president's "wonderful command of the English language was never so emphasized as it was in this conference with two men, who were plainly hostile to him upon their arrival, and yet whose animosity had been disarmed by the frank, free and open manner in which the President explained the terrible difficulties of the great task that had confronted him over here."[97]

This account showed Wilson directly dealing with a problem that threatened the outcome of the treaty and America's involvement in the League of Nations. The Easter Rising unleashed forces in Ireland that, in his mind, weren't relevant at the Peace Conference. Internal strife of this kind didn't qualify for consideration. Others had interpreted his rhetoric differently. The former academic's abstract language created misunderstanding not only among Irish Americans but also among the Irish themselves. In fact, in late 1918 and before the December election that Sinn Féin dominated, the Irish Parliamentary Party circulated a leaflet, "Ireland's Appeal to President Wilson," that relied on statements from Wilson's speeches as the bases for "Free Self-Determination." Published by the United Irish League in Dublin, the pamphlet (available at the National Library of Ireland) emphasized, in Wilson's phrase, "the right of small nations," and ends in language that is both strong and definite: "We appeal to you, sir, because in every hour of our history our race has stood by the flag of your nation, and your nation has never refused us its aid, its sympathy, and its accord with our national aspirations."[98] The moderate, constitutional party of John Redmond and John Dillon drew hope from Wilson's speeches—just as the Sinn Féin–oriented American Irish did. In a very real way, Wilson's own words came back to haunt him. Yet what sounded so hopeful to others meant something quite different to the speaker himself.

As one scholar has put it, Wilson "was at home in phrases, abstractions, ideas, not in raw reality."[99] To a certain extent, this judgment of the mature Wilson, who was immersed in international affairs, echoes what

Arthur S. Link wrote concerning the years before 1902, when Wilson assumed the presidency of Princeton. Link states:

> Wilson's political thought during this period was of course chiefly derived from historical study and theoretical speculation. The student will look in vain among his speeches or writings for any indication that Wilson understood even faintly the workings of the political machine, the activities of the ward heeler, or the multifarious ramifications of everyday political practice.[100]

Visionary and idealist, Wilson saw the world, near and far, through the eyes of an academic—with an academic's bookish and restricted myopia. For all his intelligence and international concern, Wilson could be blind to the nuance of "raw reality"—notably the tangled issues the Irish Question posed for the Irish, the British, and Irish Americans.

Back at the White House, Tumulty gauged the growing hostility in the United States as a result of the avoidance of the Ireland Question at the Peace Conference. Republicans and even some Democrats were voicing opposition to the treaty, but Wilson refused to tamp down the resistance by taking a stand. On June 18, Tumulty sent a one-line telegram to the president: "Just a word for Ireland would help a great deal."[101] Nine days later at a press conference in Paris, Wilson was asked about Ireland, and his response encompassed seventeen words without much meaning: "The Irish question takes new shape every day. I am a good deal at sea about it."[102] The same day, June 27, he sent Tumulty a telegram that referred to "the Irish question," how it might be resolved, along with the domestic politics related to it:

> I firmly believe that when the League of Nations is once organized it will afford a forum not now available for bringing the opinion of the world and of the United States in particular to bear on just such problems [as Ireland]. The Republicans will commit another great blunder if they make use of the Irish agitation and will endanger the lining up of the whole country along religious lines. That would be a calamity which would not be compensated for by the defeat of the Republicans.[103]

History proved him wrong on every count.

Shortly after Wilson's second term ended, Tumulty published a memoir in which he devoted an entire chapter to Ireland, beginning it with an assessment that contrasted how the president was perceived by those following what he did from the outside versus the view of others in close proximity to the Oval Office. "To one standing on the side-lines in the capital of the nation and witnessing the play of the ardent passions of the people of the Irish race," it seemed as if Wilson was "woefully unmindful" of their dreams to be free of British domination. "But to those, like myself, who were on the inside of affairs, it was evident that in every proper and legitimate way the American President was cautiously searching for efficient means to advance the cause of self-government in Ireland and to bring about a definite and satisfactory solution of this complicated problem."[104]

Tumulty's staunch defense of Wilson included an anecdote about the president's reaction to Edward Carson, when the Ulster Unionist leader in Westminster threatened to refuse recognition of home rule. Quoting Carson's statement that "I do not care two pence whether this is treason or not," Tumulty reported Wilson as stating, "He ought to be hanged for treason." If Prime Minister Asquith didn't call Carson's bluff, "the contagion of unrest and rebellion in Ireland will spread until only a major operation will save the Empire." Then there is the invocation of another president of Northern Irish heritage. "A little of the firmness and courage of Andrew Jackson would force a settlement of the Irish question right now," Tumulty quoted Wilson as saying.[105]

Wilson never went beyond the viewpoint that home rule was the answer to Britain's problem with Ireland. The faithful secretary parroted his boss's pronouncements about "a delicate diplomatic situation" that made it impossible "to espouse the cause of Ireland" and forced the president "to move quietly and by informal conferences." To be sure, Wilson comprehended the complexities involved, but there's no evidence that he pushed for a genuine resolution. Near the end of his memoir-cum-brief, Tumulty even argued that "Ireland has never had a truer friend than Woodrow Wilson."[106] However, the evidence seems to indicate that Wilson was largely indifferent to Irish self-determination.[107]

The Treaty of Versailles was signed on June 28, and Wilson arrived back in America on July 8 to a hero's welcome: a ticker-tape parade in New York City and a cheering throng, estimated at 100,000, at Washington, D.C.'s Union Station. Two days later, the president addressed Congress. His campaign to ratify the treaty and gain support for the League of Nations had begun in earnest. The effort, of course, would lead to Wilson's decision to make a physically demanding cross-country speaking tour in September. Three weeks into it, he became ill in Colorado, and Dr. Grayson urged an immediate return to Washington. Then, on October 2, the president suffered a massive cerebral hemorrhage that, in effect, rendered it impossible for him to appear in public or conduct the day-to-day duties of the president. The Senate rejected the treaty, which Wilson would not allow to be changed, on November 19, 1919, and then for a second time four months later, on March 19, 1920. The United States, therefore, never joined the League of Nations. The president, who championed "peace without victory" before his nation entered the European hostilities, had achieved peace but without the treaty victory he so fervently desired.

The Senate Republican crucial to shattering Wilson's postwar dreams was Henry Cabot Lodge from Massachusetts, the chairman of the Foreign Relations Committee after the 1918 elections flipped congressional control to the GOP. Killing the Treaty of Versailles and preventing participation in the League of Nations pitted Lodge against Wilson. At one point on the Senate floor, Lodge said, "I have loved but one flag and I cannot share that devotion and give affection to the mongrel banner invented for a league."[108] No longer to be taken for granted by Democrats, the American Irish played a critical role in the campaign against the treaty. The Friends of Irish Freedom circulated over a million pamphlets and sponsored newspaper advertising in opposition to Wilson in places where he spoke on behalf of the League.[109]

So much had changed in a relatively brief time. English writer H. G. Wells described how the world viewed Wilson during his participation at Versailles: "He ceased to be a common statesman; he became a Messiah. Millions believed him as the bringer of untold blessings; thousands would gladly have died for him." A few sentences later, however, Wells offered a more considered (and less considerate) judgment from more extended scrutiny: "The essential Wilson, the world was soon to learn, was vain and theatrical, with no depth of thought and no wide generosity. So far from standing for all mankind, he stood indeed only for the Democratic Party in the United States—and for himself."[110] The president, who previously emphasized the value of working with Congress (even meeting members in the President's Room of the Capitol), decided to go directly to the people when his party lost the majority in both chambers. Though creative and flexible in trying to generate support, Wilson was unwilling to modify the treaty's substance. By not bending to alternative approaches, the president could show little except extensive press coverage after six intense months of performing on the world stage.

Wilson's decline, both physically and politically, is a story that has been told often since his death on February 3, 1924, in Washington, D.C.[111] Doubts about Democrats occupying the nation's highest office lingered, and Republican presidential candidates were elected three straight times—in 1920, 1924, and 1928. Incredibly, even in his weakened and frail state, Wilson entertained ideas of running for the White House in both 1920 *and* 1924.[112] What is less well known, however, is Wilson's own interpretation of who was responsible in dashing his dreams for a world that he had worked so hard to shape. Included in one volume of the president's published papers is a letter from William Edward Dodd about a meeting the University of Chicago historian and future ambassador to Germany had with Wilson in early 1921, just before leaving the White House and shortly after the formal announcement in late 1920 that Wilson was the recipient of the 1919 Nobel Peace Prize. Dodd, a friend and Wilson biographer (and fellow Virginian), remarked at the beginning "the President is sure a broken man." As Dodd went on, it becomes clear that the president's physical frailty was one aspect of a larger human collapse, intellectually and emotionally. Long-cherished goals were now reduced to the psychic rubble of noble but failed intentions. A brooding bitterness made this clearly fragile figure seek consolation in assigning fault to others, both individuals and groups. Wilson identified Lloyd George as "the real cause of the defeat," and the president's thinking is preoccupied by one abiding concern: "Wilson can not talk ten minutes without reverting to Paris. That word means the summation of a life struggle to him. There he had the world for his parish; there he says the world abandoned him."[113]

In continuing to describe the session, Dodd reported the president's "insistence the Irish had wrecked his whole programme for adoption of the work at Paris." Gone was any attempt to cushion personal opinion with diplomatic language: "'Oh, the foolish Irish,'" he would say. "'Would to God they might all have gone back home.'"[114] Wilson's consolation, according to Dodd, was a sense of fellowship with a former British prime minister, who had his own problems with Ireland: "Wilson reverted to Gladstone, whom he has always considered a sort of political saint to himself. Gladstone he said was right in most he tried to do. You know how perfectly the Irish trouble defeated Gladstone in his life-work. . . . Wilson is another Gladstone and he feels it."[115]

Especially during the postwar phase of his second term, Wilson had refused to concentrate on the Irish Question, even though it seemed to dog him—from America to Europe and back again twice. Despite the leadership he tried to exert on the world stage and the radical changes within Ireland after the Easter Rising and the executions, Wilson kept dodging in public while fuming and fulminating in private. Finally, over time, public opinion in the United States and elsewhere crystallized: Wilson was not inclined to do anything of lasting consequence for Ireland. Though he blamed the American Irish for the failure to ratify the treaty and involve the United States in the League of Nations, they, in turn, blamed him for abandoning Ireland at a critical juncture. From either perspective, the centrality of the Irish issue was undeniable, leading to another not insignificant question: How could a president, seriously contemplating a third term, be so obstinately close-minded in addressing an important political constituency's dominant concern?

As the American Commission for Irish Independence tried, without success, to place Ireland on the agenda of the Peace Conference, Colonel House jotted in his diary a comment that might help explain both the pre-presidential Wilson and the figure who occupied the White House for eight years. "One of the great defects of the President's character is his prejudice and self-will," House observed.[116] The consummate idealist, global peacemaker, and champion of democracy was unable to overcome his own unwillingness to bring the fate of Ireland to the world's attention at a turning point in history, when the effort could have proved decisive for what he also wanted to achieve at home. Assessing Wilson, especially as a war leader, Winston Churchill wrote, "He did not truly divine the instinct of the American people."[117] When it came to Ireland, Wilson was equally unable to recognize a cause with the potential of advancing his ambitious international agenda.

As a politician, Wilson no doubt wanted to have it both ways—maintaining an image of concern without doing anything concrete. In this case, the sensible politics of taking steps to satisfy the longing of millions of Irish Americans could have translated into support for the broader governmental and global program he longed to accomplish. As years passed, he seemed to deny his divided sense of exile. Though he had worked as a candidate and later to project the perception that his own Irishness could bridge nationalist and unionist thinking, the reality of his own inaction came to define him. This inaction could have derived from his Ulster ancestry or his deeply held conviction that hyphenated Americanism had no place in U.S. public affairs. Whatever the case, the Irish Question was an issue that demanded a definite policy stand, but the president decided to do nothing.

On June 11, 1919, the day when Wilson met Walsh and Dunne in Paris, Éamon de Valera arrived in New York for an eighteen-month stay to build support and to raise money for an Irish republic. A Rising leader now engaged in politics, de Valera embarked on a speaking tour that, in contrast to Wilson's, rallied Irish America, engendering hope for an independent Ireland. Denied a hearing in Paris, de Valera brought the revolutionary spirit of 1916 to the republic of his birth, a place he considered vital to the new nation he was struggling to help establish across the Atlantic.

Éamon de Valera

John Devoy (right) and Roger Casement (left) in 1914, when Casement was visiting the United States to raise funds and build support for the Irish nationalist cause. This picture aroused suspicion among the British and others that "Sir Roger," as he was widely known, might be involved in the clandestine revolutionary activities of Devoy and Clan na Gael.

(Courtesy of the John Devoy Memorial Committee)

POBLACHT NA H EIREANN.
THE PROVISIONAL GOVERNMENT
OF THE
IRISH REPUBLIC
TO THE PEOPLE OF IRELAND.

IRISHMEN AND IRISHWOMEN: In the name of God and of the dead generations from which she receives her old tradition of nationhood, Ireland, through us, summons her children to her flag and strikes for her freedom.

Having organised and trained her manhood through her secret revolutionary organisation, the Irish Republican Brotherhood, and through her open military organisations, the Irish Volunteers and the Irish Citizen Army, having patiently perfected her discipline, having resolutely waited for the right moment to reveal itself, she now seizes that moment, and, supported by her exiled children in America and by gallant allies in Europe, but relying in the first on her own strength, she strikes in full confidence of victory.

We declare the right of the people of Ireland to the ownership of Ireland, and to the unfettered control of Irish destinies, to be sovereign and indefeasible. The long usurpation of that right by a foreign people and government has not extinguished the right, nor can it ever be extinguished except by the destruction of the Irish people. In every generation the Irish people have asserted their right to national freedom and sovereignty; six times during the past three hundred years they have asserted it in arms. Standing on that fundamental right and again asserting it in arms in the face of the world, we hereby proclaim the Irish Republic as a Sovereign Independent State, and we pledge our lives and the lives of our comrades-in-arms to the cause of its freedom, of its welfare, and of its exaltation among the nations.

The Irish Republic is entitled to, and hereby claims, the allegiance of every Irishman and Irishwoman. The Republic guarantees religious and civil liberty, equal rights and equal opportunities to all its citizens, and declares its resolve to pursue the happiness and prosperity of the whole nation and of all its parts, cherishing all the children of the nation equally, and oblivious of the differences carefully fostered by an alien government, which have divided a minority from the majority in the past.

Until our arms have brought the opportune moment for the establishment of a permanent National Government, representative of the whole people of Ireland and elected by the suffrages of all her men and women, the Provisional Government, hereby constituted, will administer the civil and military affairs of the Republic in trust for the people.

We place the cause of the Irish Republic under the protection of the Most High God, Whose blessing we invoke upon our arms, and we pray that no one who serves that cause will dishonour it by cowardice, inhumanity, or rapine. In this supreme hour the Irish nation must, by its valour and discipline and by the readiness of its children to sacrifice themselves for the common good, prove itself worthy of the august destiny to which it is called.

Signed on Behalf of the Provisional Government,

THOMAS J. CLARKE.

SEAN Mac DIARMADA,   THOMAS MacDONAGH,
P. H. PEARSE,   EAMONN CEANNT,
JAMES CONNOLLY.   JOSEPH PLUNKETT.

The Proclamation that was read by P. H. Pearse, president of the Provisional Government and commander-in-chief, on Easter Monday, April 24, 1916, the first day of the Rising. The phrase "supported by her exiled children in America" appears in the second paragraph.

Almost always photographed in profile, P. H. Pearse, president of the Provisional Government, formally surrendered on Saturday, April 29, and was the first Rising leader to be executed by the British (on May 3, 1916).

(Library of Congress, Prints & Photographs Division, LC-USZ62-67823)

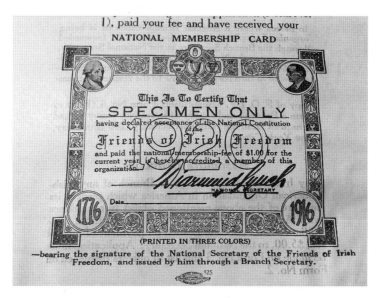

In U.S. news accounts and in speeches supporting the republican cause in America, Pearse was compared to George Washington—and 1916 was likened to 1776. For years, the membership card of the Friends of Irish Freedom made these parallels visually explicit. Diarmuid Lynch, national secretary of the FOIF, was believed to be the last person to escape the bombed and burning GPO.

(Courtesy of the American Irish Historical Society)

IRISH REBELLION, MAY 1916.

THOMAS J. CLARKE,
Executed May 3rd, 1916.
One of the signatories of the "Irish Republic Proclamation."

A naturalized American citizen, Thomas J. Clarke worked with John Devoy in New York City to rally the "exiled children" before returning to Ireland to become involved in planning and conducting the Rising. He stands alone (because of his seniority) as first signatory of the Proclamation and was the second rebel leader (after P. H. Pearse) to be executed on May 3, 1916.

(BMH CD256/3/1 to the Bureau of Military History 1913-1921, Military Archives)

Two views of the destruction in Dublin following the Rising and the British military's response. The General Post Office, occupied by the rebels as their headquarters, suffered extensive damage, as did the Dublin Bread Company, near the GPO.

(Courtesy of the National Library of Ireland)

Though James Connolly could be highly critical of the United States, this lecture poster, intended to attract audiences in Ireland, features him as "The Irish-American Orator." He was the last rebel leader to be executed in Dublin on May 12, 1916.

(Courtesy of the National Library of Ireland)

WESTERN UNION
No. 148

ANGLO-AMERICAN DIRECT UNITED STATES
CABLEGRAM

No.	Service Instructions.	Time Received. 3.36AM	Receiving Office. See back of Form for Telephone Number.
	Via Western Union.	A.D.	
	Handed in at	No. of Words.	
B 571/14 PHILADELPHIA 37			

No inquiry respecting this Message can be attended to without the production of this paper.

To CLT JOHN REDMOND PARLIAMENT HOUSE LDN

IRISH EXECUTION HAVE ALIENATED EVERY AMERICAN FRIEND AND

CAUSED RESURGANCE OF ANCIENT ENMITIES YOUR LIFE WORK

DESTROYED BY ENGLISH BRUTALITY OPINION WIDESPREAD THAT

PROMISE OR HOME RULE WAS MOCKERY

MICHAEL RYAN

CABLE LETTER.

Please hand your Reply direct to this Office.

John Redmond, the leader of the Irish Parliamentary Party in the House of Commons for almost two decades, received this cable from Michael J. Ryan, the former president of the United Irish League of America, which had supported Redmond and his commitment to home rule for many years. Redmond and Ryan had a falling out over Redmond's robust backing of Britain in the Great War; however, Ryan's wording left little doubt about Irish America's reaction to the executions.

One of the numerous souvenir postcards that appeared across Ireland in the wake of the Rising to honor the leaders and what they did. No reason is given for the commutation of the death sentence for "ED. de VALERA," and the subject continues to raise conflicting explanations.

(Courtesy of the National Library of Ireland)

This cartoon, titled "Surrendered" and drawn by John Scott Clubb, appeared in the *Rochester Herald* on May 2, 1916 (the day before the first executions in Dublin). It shows the Rising as a military defeat and also points out the possibility of German involvement. At the time, Éamon de Valera's mother, Catherine (Coll) Wheelwright, lived in Rochester, New York.

(Library of Congress, Prints & Photographs Division, LC-USZ62-84113)

Sir Cecil Spring Rice, the British ambassador to the United States, informed the Foreign Office in London about a conversation he had with American attorney Michael Francis Doyle, who had assisted in the defense of Roger Casement during his trial for treason. The last line—"that Clan Nagael [sic] want Casement executed"—is intriguing, given the efforts of many U.S. citizens to save Casement from the death penalty.

(Courtesy of the National Archives, Kew)

GLOBE EXTRA!
CASEMENT
IS EXECUTED

Irish Revolutionary Pays Penalty on Gallows

British Government Unmoved By Appeals For Reprieve

ROGER CASEMENT.

Doomed Man Cheerful During Last Hours---Had Become a Catholic

Roger Casement's arrest (on April 21, 1916), near Tralee in County Kerry, received front-page coverage in the United States, as did his hanging in London's Pentonville Prison on August 3, 1916. The *Boston Globe* published an extra edition, carrying details of his execution, shortly after it occurred. Knighted in 1911, Casement had retired from Britain's consular service two years later and devoted himself to working on behalf of Irish nationalism.

(Courtesy of the *Boston Globe*)

To Editors,

All newspapers.

You are requested to give careful consideration to the following before publication :-

1. Resolutions and speeches of Corporations, County and Urban Councils and Boards of Guardians.

2. Letters from soldiers, connected with the late rising in Dublin.

3. Extracts from American newspapers, or private letters sent you from individuals received from America

4. Criticisms in the form of letters from individuals on the late rising in Dublin, of a violent nature.

5. Letters sent you from men arrested in Dublin in connection with the late rising now in detention.

6. Indiscretions made by other papers either in Foreign or Home Press should not be published.

No objection will be taken to any publication of above provided the language is moderate; doubtful matter should be submitted before printing.

(Sd.) DECIES.

Headquarters,
 Irish Command,
  Dublin.
June 5th, 1916.

Lieut-Col.,

PRESS CENSOR.

Joyce Kilmer wrote journalism and poetry about the Easter Rising. One of Kilmer's articles for the *New York Times Magazine* was reprinted in Ireland, in contravention of the press censor's "confidential" directive to the editors of Irish newspapers. The censor's statement reflects worry among British authorities about American reaction to the Rising, and the newspapers that published Kilmer's article received threatening warnings for violating the directive.

(Courtesy of the National Archives of Ireland and its Director. National Archives of Ireland, Chief Secretary's Office, Press Censorship, No. 128, June 5, 1916)

President Woodrow Wilson tried to keep his distance from affairs he considered internal matters within the "United Kingdom of Great Britain and Ireland." However, his long-time private secretary, Joseph Tumulty, behind Wilson here, was both Irish American and Catholic. Tumulty tried, without much success, to temper Wilson's attitude toward the Irish and Ireland.

(Library of Congress, Prints & Photographs Division, LC-USZ62-53914)

California Senator James D. Phelan, whose mother and father emigrated from Ireland, pushed President Wilson to become actively involved in the Irish Question, much to Wilson's disdain. Phelan, a Democrat, served just one term and was defeated for re-election in 1920.

(Library of Congress, Prints & Photographs Division, LC-F81-2198)

RECOLLECTIONS OF
AN IRISH REBEL

⚜

THE FENIAN MOVEMENT
ITS ORIGIN AND PROGRESS. METHODS OF
WORK IN IRELAND AND IN THE BRITISH
ARMY. WHY IT FAILED TO
ACHIEVE ITS MAIN OBJECT.
BUT EXERCISED GREAT
INFLUENCE ON IRE-
LAND'S FUTURE

PERSONALITIES OF THE ORGANIZATION

The Clan-na-Gael and the
Rising of Easter Week, 1916

⚜

A PERSONAL NARRATIVE
by
John Devoy

After the Easter Rising, John Devoy began writing his memoir, *Recollections of an Irish Rebel*, which appeared posthumously in 1929. Note the omission of "Germany" in relation to "Easter Week, 1916" on the published title page.

(Courtesy of the National Library of Ireland)

SERGEANT JOYCE KILMER
165TH INFANTRY (69TH NEW YORK),
A. E. F., FRANCE, MAY, 1918

JOYCE KILMER

EDITED WITH A MEMOIR
BY ROBERT CORTES HOLLIDAY

VOLUME TWO
PROSE WORKS

NEW YORK
GEORGE H. DORAN COMPANY

Joyce Kilmer enlisted in the military right after declaration of war by Congress in 1917. He was a member of the 69th Infantry Regiment (nicknamed the "Fighting 69th" and called "the Fighting Irish" by Kilmer in his poem "When the Sixty-Ninth Comes Back"). The first essay in the posthumous two-volume collection, *Joyce Kilmer*, is titled "Holy Ireland" and was composed during a break in combat near the front in France.

(Courtesy of the Hesburgh Library of the University of Notre Dame)

This poster, printed in 1919 and intended to promote the Irish Victory Drive, as well as influence the proceedings of the Paris Peace Conference, mentions the Ourcq River in France (top right). Kilmer was killed during a reconnaissance mission near the Ourcq on July 30, 1918.

(Courtesy of the National Library of Ireland)

Éamon de Valera (middle) flanked by John Devoy (right) and Judge Daniel Cohalan, early in de Valera's eighteen-month campaign in America, mid-1919–late 1920, to support independence for Ireland. Before long, differences of opinion and policy divided Devoy from de Valera, and they became enemies.

(Library of Congress, Prints & Photographs Division, LC-B2-4954-9)

Éamon de Valera arrived as a stowaway in New York on June 11, 1919. Proclaimed "the President of Ireland" by American supporters, he toured widely and received gifts and honors, including Native American recognition, at events where he spoke.

(Reproduced by kind permission of UCD-OFM Partnership)

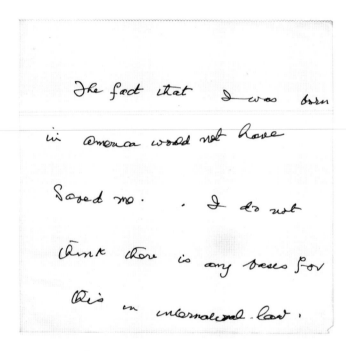

The fact that I was born in America would not have saved me. . I do not think there is any basis for this in international law.

In the summer of 1969, Éamon de Valera, then serving his second term as the elected president of Ireland, drafted a statement about his escape from execution after the Rising. Having written that "I have not the slightest doubt that my reprieve in 1916 was due to the fact that my court-martial and sentence came late," he goes on to say, "The fact that I was born in America would not have saved me."

4

Éamon de Valera: The Myth of Exile

THE FOURTEEN REBELS WHO HAD fought in the Easter Rising and faced British firing squads during the ten-day period between May 3 and May 12, 1916, were shot in what is called the "Stonebreakers' Yard" of Kilmainham Jail in Dublin. Ceasing to be used as a prison in 1924, Kilmainham now serves as both a monument and a museum to Irish nationalism and independence. Among the featured displays for the 1916 exhibit is a poster-size photograph of Éamon de Valera with this caption: "Eamon de Valera (1882–1975) under arrest at Richmond Barracks soon after surrender. Sentenced to die like the other leaders, de Valera would have been the fifteenth man executed at Kilmainham had he not been saved by his American citizenship."

A few miles from Kilmainham, the National Gallery of Ireland includes in its collection a bust of de Valera, completed while he was visiting the United States in 1920. The identifying plaque refers to him as "the most prominent Irish politician and statesman of the twentieth century." The brief description of de Valera—who was either head of government or head of state for more than three decades—goes on to say: "For his part in the Easter Rising of 1916 he was sentenced to death but escaped the death penalty because he was an American citizen." And the biographical introduction to the vast collection of de Valera's papers at the Archives of University College Dublin notes in its first paragraph: "He joined the Irish Volunteers in 1913 and during the rebellion of 1916 commanded the 3rd Battalion at Boland's Mill. Sentenced to death, de Valera was reprieved partly because of his American birth."[1]

By contrast, however, within the papers themselves and in de Valera's own script is a statement he wrote in 1969 at the age of eighty-six: that his reprieve was due to the timing of the executions and British Prime Minister Asquith's decision to halt them after a certain point, aside from the ringleaders, "which they interpreted as those who had signed the Proclamation." De Valera was firm on one point: "The fact that I was born in America would not have saved me."[2]

At the heart of the ambiguity of de Valera's reprieve—an act, or non-act, that helped thrust him into the forefront of the fight for Irish independence—is his connection to the United States. Indeed, although de Valera did elude execution, he has never been able to escape the perception that his American background was a basis for his reprieve, contributing to the complexity of a figure who casts the longest shadow on Ireland during the twentieth century.

Discovering even the most mundane facts about de Valera demands exegesis. Born on October 14, 1882, in New York City, de Valera's original birth certificate gave his name as "George de Valero." A corrected birth certificate, listing the name of "Edward de Valera" and dated May 23, 1916, is included among de Valera's papers at University College Dublin.[3] This document was issued twelve days *after* de Valera's death sentence was commuted to "penal servitude for life" and eleven days after the final two executions at Kilmainham. Another "Corrected Certificate" for "Edward de Valera" that was "Approved by Commissioner of Health June 30, 1910" was issued by the State of New York, which probably means the 1916 document in his papers was actually a duplicate sent to Ireland for verification to British authorities after de Valera's arrest. In addition to the different birth certificates, two baptismal records exist—one for "Edward De Valeros" and an amended one for "Eamon de Valera." One of de Valera's biographers, Tim Pat Coogan, noted that he was told the changes may be in the handwriting of de Valera's eldest son, Vivion de Valera.[4]

Sloppy recordkeeping, of course, was not uncommon, but it is nonetheless curious that *both* the first and the last names required correction. His father, Juan Vivion de Valera, was born in Spain and might not have been scrupulous in his English spelling; however, his mother, Catherine Coll, had immigrated to America from Ireland in 1879. Why she didn't catch the mistakes on such significant documents seems somewhat puzzling. At any rate, the Church of St. Agnes on 43rd Street in New York features a plaque with a Celtic cross and this inscription: "At This Baptismal Font The Irish Patriot Eamon de Valera Was Baptized on December 3, 1882."

Whatever the case, the boy lived in the United States for just over two years before his mother's brother, Edward Coll, took him to Bruree in County Limerick to be raised by his grandmother and other members of the family. When he went to school, he was registered under the name of "Edward Coll" rather than "Edward de Valera." "Edward" eventually turned into the Irish version "Éamonn" as a result of his participation in the Gaelic League and other aspects of the Gaelic Revival. For several years, Eamonn included two "n's"—but that was subsequently reduced to one, as de Valera became more involved in public life. Interestingly, the 1922 edition of David T. Dwane's biography spelled his subject's first name with the double "n," while the 1927 version used one.[5] Throughout his long political career, de Valera consciously shaped his identity, including the choice of the American characteristics he wanted to emphasize at a particular time. Making a name for himself, literally, helped to begin that process, and it took years until he arrived at whom he wanted to be.

His non-execution was the defining moment. In his authoritative study *Easter 1916: The Irish Rebellion*, Charles Townshend notes that de Valera escaped death for reasons "that are still not clear."[6] Nonetheless, we can say that certain actions took place at just the right time that happened to benefit de Valera, who surrendered with his battalion from his position at Boland's Mill on Grand Canal Street in Dublin a full day after Pearse. Initially held under arrest in Ballsbridge several miles from the Rising leaders, de Valera's court-martial was delayed and did not take place until May 8. By then many of the most prominent rebels had already been executed, and revulsion directed at British authorities was reaching a boiling point. Moreover, at the request of de Valera's family, the U.S. consulate in Dublin was contacted to see if his American heritage might have any bearing in the consideration of de Valera's case, a fact he pointed out in his 1969 statement.[7] The lateness of the court-martial and the mounting pressure to bring the death sentences to an end became the salient factors in de Valera's reprieve.

In his book on W. E. Wylie, who, as a second lieutenant in the Territorial Army and a barrister, witnessed many of the court-martial proceedings after the Rising, León Ó Broin draws on Wylie's unpublished memoir. On May 8, according to Wylie, the commander of the British forces, General Sir John Maxwell, showed him a telegram from Asquith, saying the prime minister wanted the executions to end. According to Ó Broin, "Maxwell asked Wylie who was next on his list for court martial, no doubt wondering whether there was anyone on it likely to be executed."

> "Somebody called de Valera, sir."
> "Who is he?" said Maxwell. "I haven't heard of him before."
> "He was in command of Boland's bakery in the Ringsend area."

"I wonder would he be likely to make trouble in the future?" Maxwell went on.

"I wouldn't think so, sir, I don't think he is important enough. From all I can hear he is not one of the leaders."

"All right then," said the Commander-in-Chief. "Stop now except for the public trials, and come up and dine tonight. I have another job for you."[8]

Wylie went on to acknowledge that he "was far off the mark" in judging whether de Valera might cause future trouble, and he speculated about the nature of de Valera's charisma.

> He had the 1916 halo. He had an unusual name. He had a cold reserved personality. He was a bit of a mystic, and an idol to the ordinary peasant and man in the street, and he was above all an absolute fanatical idealist about some things. His mind could not compromise on what he deemed to be principles. He was prepared to sacrifice himself and any one, indeed everybody else, rather than give away an inch. He looked into his own heart to find what Ireland wanted, and his heart told him about an independent people, the Irish language, the past wrongs of Ireland, Gaelic culture, and lot of other things we should all forget and forgive. I find him a difficult man to place.[9]

Wylie maintained that he was not responsible for prosecuting de Valera at his court-martial. Forty-eight years later, in 1964, however, de Valera happened to see Wylie at a lunch and said to him, "You prosecuted in 1916, and a man is enquiring from me at present what I said and how I defended myself at that time. I cannot recollect anything about it, or who was there or what was said." In his mid-eighties at the time (de Valera was then eighty-one), Wylie reported that he had replied: "You were not prosecuted at that time, and there is nothing to remember."[10] Despite Wylie's denial a prosecution took place—during which de Valera's death sentence was commuted to a life sentence—but what seems curious is de Valera's admission that he "cannot recollect anything" about the proceedings. As noted, in 1969, five years later, he had composed a detailed memorandum on the subject. Why was de Valera so definite about what happened in 1969 but inquisitive, and seemingly without any recall about it, in 1964? What prompted the change in approach, and what, if anything, happened during the intervening five years to clarify his memory? Perhaps de Valera seemed to think it was finally necessary to pro-vide his own personal account after reading and hearing all the conflicting stories that surrounded his reprieve since 1916.

By then, various explanations about how he had escaped death had appeared for decades in journalistic reports, biographical studies, and historical accounts from the time of the Rising onward. Perplexingly, in the archive containing de Valera's 1969 statement denying an American role in the commutation of his sentence are three articles from American newspapers about his cap-ture and court-martial, which tell an entirely different story. Though lacking in attribution as to the sources of their information, the articles emphasized the crucial importance of de Valera's heritage to the change in his punish-ment. "Citizenship in U.S. Saved Valera's Life" read the headline in the *Boston American* on July 9, 1916. In the body of all three stories (the first is dated July 3, 1916, the second July 7, 1916, and the third July 9, 1916), what is reported is virtually identical: "On Sunday evening, April 30, [*sic*] De Valera was called for trial before a court martial and sentenced to be shot at dawn. As soon, however, as General Maxwell learned that De Valera was an American citizen he post-poned the execution and later commuted it to penal servitude for life. . . . [T]he prestige of American citizenship was not lost upon Maxwell."[11]

The same day that the *Boston American* published its story about de Valera, the *Boston Globe* offered a more detailed account. Appearing on page 4 under the headline "American Led Irish Rebels," it was framed as a domestic dis-patch with local relevance about an international issue. "It is only now, two months after the uprising, that some of the stirring events which marked the passing of the short-lived Irish Republic are coming before the people of this country."[12] Except for two paragraphs, which credit the information as com-ing from an "eyewitness, Dr. Myles Keogh," the article used third-person reporting to focus on "Edward de Valera," calling him "a great student of the Irish language," "ardent lover of the land which gave his mother birth," and an individual with "all the qualities of mind and soul that distinguish a leader of men." The part chronicling his activities as a commandant during the Rising includes this observation: "An English solder who was a prisoner in the [Boland] mill describes de Valera as tall, dark and of remarkable courage." Discussing the court-martial, the story, which carries no byline, reported: "As soon, however, as Gen. Maxwell learned that de Valera was an American citi-zen, he postponed the execution, and later commuted it to penal servitude for life."[13] The phrasing in the *Boston Globe* about the reprieve was almost exactly the same as the other two, which means that the different newspapers were most probably relying on a widely distributed wire-service dispatch. Nonetheless, it concluded with a stronger American angle:

> Some of de Valera's friends have heard that he has been denied the privilege of communicating with his friends and relatives. De Valera's mother is at present ill at her home in America. Upon medical advice news of his condition has been kept from her.
>
> An effort is now going to be made to have some action taken through Washington officials to have de Valera's sentence shortened and the punishment mitigated, as has been done in other cases.[14]

This story and the other ones that circulated in July of 1916 were the origin of the explanation for his reprieve. They were written with a specific purpose in mind, which was to influence American public opinion. That in itself is a dimension of the larger story.

While de Valera was serving prison time in England, his family on the other side of the Atlantic was working assiduously to find a way to secure his freedom. The central figure in the effort was de Valera's half-brother, Reverend Thomas J. Wheelwright, a Redemptorist priest living in Rochester, New York, where de Valera's mother also resided. (She had married Charles Wheelwright, an immigrant from England, in 1888, three years after de Valera was sent to Ireland.) One portion of de Valera's papers contains numerous letters from Father Wheelwright, requesting the intervention of senators and other governmental figures in a reduction of the life sentence given to his half-brother. Joseph Tumulty, President Wilson's secretary, received one of the appeals, and other members of the priest's order wrote members of Congress. Though the responses (also in the papers) expressed concern, they repeated the point that the issue required State Department consideration. One letter, dated July 18, 1916, from Senator James Wadsworth of New York included the formal judgment from State:

> The fact that Mr. De Valera may be an American citizen constitutes no reason for clemency in his case, or for a request by this Government for clemency on the part of the British Government. There appears to be nothing to indicate that his trial was not fair or that he was in any way discriminated against, and there would, therefore, appear to be no reason for action by this Department on behalf of Mr. De Valera.[15]

At no time during the letter-writing campaign did de Valera's family receive formal encouragement. The extensive documentation of what was being done on his behalf in the United States stands in contrast to what is known about the overtures for help to American representatives in Ireland. In his hand-written statement of 1969, de Valera noted: "It is of course true that my wife was encouraged by friends and did make representations to the American consul here."[16]

Besides the account in his own hand, de Valera's papers include a formal-looking document on the stationery of the president of Ireland, "Reprieve of Eamon de Valera," which incorporated phrases and sentences to what de Valera himself had drafted and amplified them. For example, the sentence "The fact that I was born in America would not have saved me" became "The fact that I was born in America would not, I am convinced, have saved me" in the official rendering that is signed and dated July 3, 1969. His handwritten statement about his wife's "representations" to the consul was expanded by the observation in the formal copy: "He was sympathetic, I understand."[17]

More extensive revision is evident in the next section of his "Reprieve." In his own script, he noted: "The American administration refused to intervene when later the question of freeing me from prison was raised."[18] In the note for the historical record: "Similarly, my mother and American friends, including Joe McGarrity no doubt, made representations to Washington. I do not know if they got any reply, but I feel certain that the Administration took no official action."[19] Although Father Wheelwright was the central figure in contacting Washington officials, he is not mentioned—an odd omission. Had de Valera, then eighty-six years old, simply forgotten? Were members of the president's staff who might have polished the prose and presentation unaware of the half-brother's involvement? In 1916, it is highly doubtful that de Valera had even met McGarrity. Of perhaps even greater significance, however, is the last paragraph in the official statement. Not a word of it is part of de Valera's handwritten notes:

> By the way, Thomas Ashe was court martialed the same day that I was. He, too, would have been executed, I have no doubt, had he been tried earlier because of the part he took at the Battle of Ashbourne, Co. Dublin, where he was in charge, and where a number of Royal Irish Constabulary were killed. He was not an American citizen, and it could not be suggested, therefore, that it was on that account he was reprieved.[20]

The year after this 1969 statement was prepared, the authorized biography *Eamon de Valera* by the Earl of Longford and Thomas P. O'Neill was published. In describing the Rising and its aftermath, the authors build on de Valera's final sentence just quoted to dramatize his reputation as a surviving commander:

> Two commandants escaped the firing squad because of the delay in bringing them to trial. They were Thomas Ashe and Eamon de Valera. It has been suggested that the latter was reprieved because of his American birth. There is no evidence of this, and the fact that he and Ashe were both tried and reprieved on the same day supports the view that it was the effect of the executions on public opinion and the delay which saved them.[21]

The repeated references to his American birth or citizenship must have bothered de Valera. Although he acknowledged his wife made "representations" to the "sympathetic" U.S. consul, he did not investigate the consequences, if any, of the action. Edward L. Adams, then the consul in Dublin, wrote to the State Department that "by intervention . . . a sentence of death was commuted to imprisonment for life. Mrs. De Valera afterwards called at the Consulate to express her gratitude."[22] Adams was perhaps taking more credit than he deserved in this case, and it's not clear that he would even know the extent to which his "intervention" played a role for the change in de Valera's sentence. Either way, it seems clear this report and references to it were factors in convincing the public that U.S. involvement helped save de Valera. In *American Opinion and the Irish Question 1910–23*, for example, Francis M. Carroll credits Adams for being "instrumental in reversing the death sentence of the court martial," a sign that it was widely known.[23]

In his biography of de Valera, Owen Dudley Edwards argued that his subject never acknowledged that the consul could have been a factor in the reprieve. De Valera linked his commutation to Ashe's, though, according to Edwards, "Ashe had been responsible for far less slaughter in the affray at Ashbourne than de Valera's campaign in the city." In his analysis of what saved de Valera, Edwards focused on Maxwell, the British commander, who was "more alive to the delicacies of placating American opinion, in the hope of American entry into the war, than any other British general, perhaps than any person in the British government." Edwards added that Maxwell's daughter Philae had fallen in love with and would eventually marry a young American named

C. N. Carver, who had attended Cambridge and after the war broke out worked at the U.S. embassy in London, and then became an aide to Colonel House. "As a soldier, Maxwell knew how vital respect for the representations of American officialdom would be to ensure that so indispensable a potential ally was not needlessly alienated." In Edwards's view, "De Valera was probably right in see-ing a connection between Ashe's pardon and his own, but it was the converse which applied." Ashe's life had been saved by de Valera once he "had been made an exception to the principle of execution for the leaders."[24]

In looking back as president of the Republic of Ireland, de Valera offered a blanket denial that his American background was influential to any degree in deciding his fate. Actually, an examination of H. H. Asquith's papers at Oxford University supports de Valera's basic premise that the lateness of his court-martial proved decisive to his commutation. Asquith's files about what is referred to in one document as "this most recent German campaign" pro-vide the distinct impression that another front in the war had opened up in Ireland, and there are several tally reports about the number of people killed, wounded, taken prisoner—and executed. These battle counts stick out in the correspondence Asquith received about what was also called the "Rebellion in Ireland." On May 9, 1916, John Dillon, an Irish Parliamentary Party member of the House of Commons, wrote the prime minister, "I am quite convinced that hundreds of perfectly loyal men have been arrested. . . . All this will of course be dragged out and discussed, with infinitely mischievous results." Dillon went on to report that he was receiving "American cables" and that "the effect on the Irish in America will be horrible." Dillon underlined the word *horrible* twice.[25] The same day Dillon wrote Asquith, General Maxwell sent a telegram from his headquarters in Dublin:

> Please inform Prime Minister that the Courts under the Defence of the Realm Act in regard to rebellion in the City of Dublin are practically finished. . . . I have confirmed no death sentence unless I have been con-vinced by the evidence that the convict was either a leader of the move-ment or a commander of rebels, who were engaged in shooting dowm [sic] His Majesty's Troops or subjects. Today there still remain to be tried Conolly [sic] and MacEgmont [sic]. If convicted they must suffer extreme penalty. This will be the last to suffer extreme penalty as far as I can now state. Any cases of proved murder of soldiers and police in the execution of their duty which have or may occur, are of course expected by me.[26]

De Valera's name does not appear in the documents sent to Asquith at this time, even though de Valera's death sentence was commuted the day the telegram was composed. The day after Maxwell reported that the court-martials were "practically finished," he reiterated—and defended—his position for the executions of Connolly and Mac Diarmada in another telegram:

> In view of the gravity of the rebellion and its connection with German intrigue and propaganda, and in view of the great loss of life and destruction of property resulting therefrom, the General Officer Commanding-in-Chief Irish Command has found it imperative to inflict the most severe sentences on the known organisers of this detestable rising and of those Commanders who took an active part in the actual fighting which occurred. It is hoped that these examples will be sufficient to act as a deterrent to intrigues and to bring home to them that the murder of His Majesty's subjects or other acts calculated to imperil the safety of the realm will not be tolerated.[27]

For the second time in two days, Maxwell does not acknowledge de Valera's role as a commandant during the Rising. Connolly and Mac Diarmada were the last two leaders executed—one day after Asquith had arrived in Dublin for a personal assessment of what had occurred.

At the same time, from his cell at Kilmainham, de Valera wrote farewell letters to friends: "Tomorrow I am to be shot."[28] In the Neil Jordan film *Michael Collins*, which opens with evocative Easter Week battle scenes, de Valera (played by Alan Rickman) is portrayed writing in his cell, as a voiceover provides the statement he is supposed to be composing: "The fact that I was born in America might save my hide. Either way I am ready for what comes. The Irish Republic is a dream no longer. It is daily sealed by the lifeblood of those who proclaimed it. And every one of us they shoot brings more people to our side."[29] After his reprieve, with or without the factor of his birth as a consideration, de Valera was moved to Mountjoy Prison in Dublin before being transferred to Dartmoor Prison in England. In all, he served time in six different jails or prisons after his surrender and arrest at the conclusion of the Rising.

Father Wheelwright began his letter-writing initiative on behalf of de Valera in June of 1916. On July 1, the U.S. Embassy in London contacted Britain's Home Office about "the present status of the case of Mr. Edward de Valera" and whether his "claims to be an American citizen" were accurate. Edward Bell in the embassy inquired twice (July 1 and August 8) for the information, and on August 12 he received a statement back from the Home Office with a report quoting "the Governor of the Prison" about de Valera: "The prisoner gives New York as his place of birth. He states that he has asked his mother to find out whether his father—who was a Spaniard—became an American citizen. If so, he (prisoner) claims to be such. If not, he is a Spaniard. He further states that he did not become a British citizen, but he would have become an Irish citizen if that had been possible."[30]

The letters from the embassy and de Valera's prison records are available at the National Archives in Kew. Despite all the efforts of his family in the United States, the documents reveal that de Valera never pushed his American heritage for any personal advantage. Indeed, by associating himself with the father he never knew, he complicated how others might perceive him. In effect, and most significantly, he challenged the British authorities to figure him out in terms of his citizenship and his overall identity. Moreover, given his incarceration and the censorship of the mail that existed during the war, it is questionable that de Valera even knew the extent of the endeavor to gain leniency for him that was taking place across the Atlantic. While his family played the American card wherever and however they could, de Valera was engaged in an entirely different game.

Though he was released from prison on June 15, 1917, in a general amnesty for those incarcerated after the Easter Rising, he was arrested again nearly a year later (on May 17, 1918) in what was called the "German Plot." British authorities accused certain Irish republicans of conspiring with Germans against the United Kingdom. Jailed in England's Lincoln Prison, de Valera made a daring escape, involving a key for a locked prison door delivered in a cake, on February 3, 1919. His post-Rising exploits were contributing to a biography that seemed closer to an adventure novel.

Interestingly, his reluctance to make his U.S. roots a principal element in his life extended to his first trip back to America since his childhood. In June 1919, after being elected Príomh Aire of Dáil Éireann—which translates as prime or chief minister of the assembly of Ireland—de Valera stowed away on a New York–bound ship. His plan was to travel throughout the States, promoting the cause of an Irish Republic. During his first press conference at the Waldorf Astoria Hotel on June 23, the man presented as "President of the Republic of Ireland" was asked: "Are you an American citizen?" De Valera responded, "I am an Irish citizen." The next question probed more deeply: "Did you foreswear allegiance to the United States?" This time, he took an even more definite stand: "I ceased to be an American when I became a soldier of the Irish republic."[31]

Of course, in 1919 it was legally impossible to be an Irish citizen (until 1922 a person from Ireland was considered a British subject), and "the Irish republic" was a nationalistic dream rather than a recognized governmental entity. The Dáil of which de Valera was a part was a rebel assembly at the time—in its way (as mentioned previously) similar to the Continental Congress for the thirteen colonies that began meeting in 1774 before the American Revolutionary War—and de Valera wasn't really who he was billed as being.

Patrick McCartan argued that Joseph McGarrity was responsible for the title—President of the Republic of Ireland—that de Valera used during his eighteen months in the United States. McCartan, a member of the Dáil and Sinn Féin's representative to the United States until 1921, was close to McGarrity and personally involved in many aspects of the visit. According to McCartan, before being introduced at the first press conference, de Valera worried about misrepresentation: "De Valera pointed out that he was not President of the Republic of Ireland, but only Chairman of the Dáil. McGarrity contended that it was the same thing, and that we had already made him President of the Republic in the minds of the American people."[32] McCartan developed what the strategic decision of conferring presidential status actually meant. From their own history since George Washington took office in 1789, Americans understood the role of president in a republic—so that is what de Valera became:

> We had styled de Valera President of the Republic of Ireland. He had assumed that title. The Press conceded it to him. He had been received as our President by the chief executives of many American cities and States. He had been acclaimed as such by hundreds of thousands of American citizens. As such he had issued and sold bonds of the Republic of Ireland and had pleaded for its recognition.[33]

As was the case with the stories about his American background being the reason for his reprieve, de Valera became "President of the Republic of Ireland" on the basis of repeated references to this fabricated designation. Some newspapers, notably the *New York Times*, couldn't resist placing the phrase "self-styled" before "President of the Irish Republic"; however, as de Valera crisscrossed the country, the "exiled children" and others by and large treated him as a head of state.[34]

For de Valera, politics and power had become animating concerns since the Rising and his escape from execution. As with Woodrow Wilson, the security of an academic life—de Valera, of course, had been a teacher before the Rising—gave way to the vagaries and vicissitudes of political involvement and intrigue. Others helped to "create" him, but his own ambition kept driving him to contest elections and to seek positions of leadership. His rise prompted attention from historians, biographers, and journalists to explain where he came from and how he had emerged as such a political force in such a short time. His connections to America couldn't be avoided, yet what was reported often proved either partially correct or completely inaccurate. One of the chapters in Edwards's *Éamon de Valera* is titled "The Man from God Knows Where," and the phrase was not only apt but also cautionary. The search for answers produces more questions.

In de Valera's case, biographical statements often hedged rather than affirmed, leaving a reader unsure and wondering why. George Dangerfield in *The Damnable Question*, published not long after de Valera's death, presented de Valera's enigma by noting the competing explanations and then offering the author's judgment: "Eamon de Valera had his death sentence commuted to penal servitude for life on 11 May, either because he had been born in America or (as he himself believed) because of the unfortunate effect the executions were already having on public opinion. The fact that Thomas Ashe also escaped the firing squad on that day—and he was both a commander and an organizer— supports the latter view."[35] Dangerfield's careful phrasing comes after de Valera had offered his account for escaping execution late in his presidency; however, by 1969 other stories had firmly taken root and had gone unchallenged for decades. De Valera became a personality and subject of attention in the wake of the Rising, and he was rarely out of the limelight for nearly sixty years, certainly among biographers. In David T. Dwane's *Early Life of Eamonn De Valera*, the reader is forced to untangle facts from stories that bear a striking similarity to the ones Mason Locke Weems wrote about George Washington in his biography published in 1800, involving Washington's congenital inability to tell a lie about chopping down a cherry tree. Early in Dwane's book, published in 1922, one anecdote he told strains credulity but suggests heroic consistency:

> It is related that one day he toddled across the street to where a wealthy Englishman dwelt. We are not aware whether this Englishman was a professional gentleman or a large store-keeper, but at any rate he approached

young de Valera and proffered him the choice of two flags. One was the
Union Jack and the other had emblazoned upon it the Stars and Stripes.
After a short pause de Valera accepted the American flag. "Come, now,"
said the Englishman in merry mood, "give me back that flag and take
this one." "No, no," muttered de Valera, tightening his grasp of the one
he had. "Well, then, you will take both," replied the Englishman, at the
same time giving effect to the statement by sticking the Union Jack in
the pocket of his tunic. He had no sooner done so, than young de Valera
plucked it out, and throwing it on the ground, folded his arms, and faced
his would-be benefactor with an air of stubborn independence.[36]

As though this were not enough to make his point, Dwane connected the
boy to the past (an "old Fenian" in exile) and to a future of "freedom and
advancement":

> it [tossing the flag to the ground] had the effect of arousing the innate
> patriotic feelings of an exiled Irishman—an "old Fenian"—who had
> been watching the incident from near by. Uttering such words as "maith
> anpáiste," "maith an buachaill," "maith an fear," he rushed up and tak-
> ing the little lad in his arms in a wild embrace hugged and kissed him as
> if he were a long lost child.[37]

Such childhood tales naturally foreshadowed adult narratives that help define
a public figure. However, when the author (Dwane) got to the Rising, he
became, like Dangerfield, more cautious in recounting what happened. There
are, he said, "doubts as to whether this was due to his American citizenship,
or to the fact that he was the last commandant to surrender."[38]

After his return from America, de Valera became embroiled in a succes-
sion of political battles, notably the debate over the treaty with Great Britain
that followed the truce in the War of Independence. The truce was declared
July 11, 1921, and the next month de Valera pushed for a change in the 1919
Constitution of the Dáil to establish the office of president of the Republic.
Rather than being chairman of the Irish cabinet or, in effect, prime minister,
the president would be head of state. Two years after Americans had invented
the title, de Valera assumed it. However, de Valera's opposition to the Anglo-
Irish Treaty (signed in London on December 6, 1921, and ratified ten days
later by Britain's Parliament) put him at odds with many in the Dáil. (Among
the treaty's provisions was the opportunity for the six northeastern counties

of Northern Ireland to remain in the United Kingdom, continuing the partition of the island that had begun with the Government of Ireland Act of 1920.) After the treaty's ratification in Dublin by a 64 to 57 vote on January 7, 1922, de Valera resigned as president on January 9. The pro- and anti-treaty divisions ultimately provoked the Irish Civil War, which began in June of 1922 and lasted nearly a year.

For the first several years of the Irish Free State established by the treaty, de Valera was at odds with those in government—to the delight and satisfaction of John Devoy and his followers in the United States. Devoy never stopped looking to the homeland he left almost a half-century earlier, and de Valera always kept the country of his birth in his sights while working to develop Ireland. After their falling out and the unequivocal enmity between these two outsized figures, the "exiled children" faced a difficult choice in allegiance, with many deciding to follow the younger American-born leader rather than the aging Fenian. One historian points out that membership in the Devoy-backed Friends of Irish Freedom plunged from over 100,000 in 1920 to 20,000 the next year after de Valera established his rival organization, the American Association for the Recognition of the Irish Republic, during his controversial eighteen-month stay in the United States that ended in late 1920.[39]

Although without a dominant governmental position after the treaty split, de Valera continued his involvement in politics throughout the 1920s. In 1926, he was instrumental in founding a new party, Fianna Fáil, which evolved into a considerable force in the general election of 1932, bringing de Valera to office as president of the Executive Council that year. In this role, essentially the prime minister of the parliament—the title was changed to "Taoiseach" in late 1937—de Valera was the head of the Irish government from March 9, 1932, until February 18, 1948. Later, in the 1950s, he served two more times as Taoiseach—before being elected head of state as president of Ireland in 1959, an office he occupied for two seven-year terms, retiring in 1973 at the age of ninety. Historians and political observers, with sound reason, refer to the period from 1932 to 1973 as the "Age of de Valera."

From the Rising onward, de Valera was constantly in the public eye, and his life story was told and retold with each electoral victory or defeat, and also on other occasions. A recurring fact, particularly in U.S. outlets, was of course his connection to America by virtue of his birth. For example, shortly after de Valera assumed the presidency of the Executive Council in 1932, the *Washington Post* (on March 13) devoted a lengthy article to what the headline referred to as the "Thrilling Drama" of a "Man Condemned by England for 1916 Revolution Now Holds World Spotlight." Exploring the American angle, the writer, David Rankin Barbee, noted that the United States had "quite a stake in this man, for he is a native of the sidewalks of New York, same as Al Smith." He went on to report: "When he was proclaimed 'president' of the 'republic of Ireland' during the World War, or just after it, the British government investigated this matter and published the fact that the 'mythical' republic of Ireland had a 'president' who was not even an Irishman. But neither was St. Patrick, and many a Frenchman and many a Spaniard bearing Irish names are but exiles from Erin, having migrated after the battle of the Boyne."[40] The article went on to establish how the Rising had shaped de Valera's preparation for future battles, and that his death sentence had galvanized public opinion. Senators and representatives

> in Congress officially protested against the execution of a man born in America. England sometimes blunders, but this was not one of those times. She looked through the hole in the grindstone and saw a nation whose friendship she needed in an angry mood. She had no idea of inflaming that anger. So she sent De Valera and his comrades to prison for life.[41]

Actually, of course, the letter-writing campaign didn't begin until well after the court-martial and commutation. It was the summer of 1916, with de Valera imprisoned in England, before American newspapers devoted coverage to him. At the beginning of his article, Barbee mentions that he had seen de Valera speak at the National Press Club in Washington during a visit to the United States in 1931—this trip raised money to launch the newspaper *The Irish Press*. One wonders whether he had heard the story at that time or had come across it elsewhere. In any case, five months later, the *Washington Post* carried another profile of de Valera, calling him "The Irish Enigma" in large type and pointing out in the subhead: "Foundation for Power of Ireland's President Was Laid in America." This article, published on August 14, described the condemned man "as he lay in his cell in a Dublin prison, stoically waiting to be led out to his death," when word reached him that the sentence had been commuted to imprisonment for life. "The fact that his American birth made him technically still a citizen of the United States had saved him from the firing squad."[42] Fifteen years later, the "fact" of de Valera's birth was still cited as the reason for his reprieve.

De Valera's return to power in 1932 became a comeback story that U.S. journalists simply couldn't resist. *Time* magazine devoted a cover article to his ascent (April 11, 1932) and the *New York Times Magazine* (May 1, 1932) called him "the Irish Don Quixote," who (because of his reprieve) "has lived to embody in his own person the legend of Irish republicanism" and "the dream of 1916." The most detailed profile appeared in the *Saturday Evening Post* (May 28, 1932), which probed the different facets of his links to America, including his early years in New York and his visit in 1919–1920. In the section about his tour of the United States a decade earlier, Francis Hackett explained:

> Here he was installed in the Waldorf-Astoria as president of the Irish Republic; and not only could he not be deported, being an American citizen, but on all sides he had allies and compatriots—police officials, customs officers, hotel clerks, taxi men, congressmen, millionaires, bishops, journalists, publicity experts, a whole nation in exile, a nation in whom the love of Ireland lived like the power of life in a corm.[43]

In this article, "Eamonn De Valera"—with the double "n" for the first name and the "D" of the surname capitalized throughout—Hackett dramatized his subject's role in the Rising and built to the court-martial scene, at which the military tribunal learned that de Valera has been born in America: no British military tribunal cared "to execute an American citizen in May, 1916, when England was courting America to be an ally. De Valera's death sentence was changed to life imprisonment, and in a short time he was out on amnesty."[44]

American newspapers and magazines rarely missed the opportunity to associate de Valera's escape from execution with the fortuitous happenstance of his birthplace. The second *Time* magazine cover story about him in less than a decade appeared March 25, 1940, and referred to de Valera as the "Prime Minister of Freedom." While there's some hedging about why de Valera had survived after the Rising, the basis for the clemency was still a "fact" and that fact was "that this young rebel was born in the U.S. of a Spanish father and an Irish mother and might technically even be considered a U.S. citizen, was an important argument for a Great Britain just then anxious for U.S. aid in the War."[45]

Interestingly, American sources weren't alone in either attributing or suggesting that de Valera's birthplace had been a factor in commuting his sentence. When he became president of the Executive Council, book-length

biographical and analytical works came out in the 1930s from publishers
based in Ireland and Britain. Dublin's Talbot Press, which kept Dwane's
Early Life in print a decade earlier, published Seán Ó Faoláin's *The Life Story
of Eamon de Valera* in 1933. Ó Faoláin, a prominent short story writer and
founding editor of the literary periodical *The Bell*, put his emphasis on de
Valera as an "enigmatic" character in a dramatic narrative, noting in the prologue that "somehow or other, one never seems to be able to penetrate behind
the brown mask of his lined features, and, as was also true of the last great
leader of the Irish race before him, Charles Stewart Parnell, he eludes you and
you leave him with his secret, as unsolved a riddle as the Sphinx."[46] A sense
of mystery pervades Ó Faoláin's rendering. After de Valera's surrender at the
end of the Rising, we are told: "It seemed as if no power on earth could save
De Valera, and from the moment of his arrest he had, himself, no further
hope of life." With darkness descending and the language becoming more
purple with each descriptive phrase, "the six roaring rifle-barrels of the firing
party" were ready to take aim—but then Ó Faoláin reports that "the horror
aroused in the country, the protests in the British Parliament, and, perhaps,
the gallantry of his fight, preserved him, as if by a Divine Providence, to lead
his people in the great struggle that was to follow, and to lead them as he leads
them to-day."[47] Whether by virtue of the late surrender, Divine Providence, or
his "American citizenship," de Valera survived and discovered how to use his
life in a cause greater than himself.

The same year—1933—that Ó Faoláin's work appeared, Denis Gwynn's *De
Valera* came out in London. More solidly biographical (and stylistically restrained),
De Valera followed Gwynn's earlier studies of (among other subjects) Roger
Casement and John Redmond. A journalist as well as a history professor, Gwynn
probes de Valera's life in depth, explaining at one point that while de Valera's exe-
cution "seemed inevitable" an "unexpected intervention" saved his life.

> John Redmond in London had been unable to receive any direct reports,
> apart from brief telegraphic messages sent over the Government's wire
> from the Viceregal Lodge, which alone remained in action. But he
> realised immediately that reprisals would create a fierce revulsion of
> feeling in Ireland. Appealing to the precedent of General [Louis] Botha's
> leniency towards General [J. B. M.] Hertzog and his insurrection at the
> outset of the war [the Second Boer War], he implored Asquith to prevent
> executions, and sought for any conceivable pretext to reduce the severity

of the reprisals which General Maxwell had in contemplation. It was discovered that de Valera was an American citizen; and Redmond made full use of the opening which this gave. Representations were made by the American consulate in Dublin at the same time, and de Valera's sentence was not announced until May 11. He had been formally sentenced to death, but like a number of others (including W. T. Cosgrave), his sentence was commuted to penal servitude for life.[48]

Introducing the possibility of Redmond's involvement in the proceedings adds a new facet to the de Valera reprieve story. Gwynn combines Redmond's appeal to Asquith with de Valera's American citizenship. Gwynn's point, however, was not necessarily to bring clarity. He opens the first chapter ("The Dublin Insurrection, 1916") with "Few public men have been the subject of so much controversy in regard to their nationality and antecedents as Eamon de Valera."[49]

Of all of the early, extended works that tried to come to terms with de Valera, Desmond Ryan's *Unique Dictator: A Study of Eamon de Valera* (1936) remains illuminating for its insights and its attention to the evolution of de Valera's *persona*, complete with the surrounding myths and legends. To employ "dictator" in his title—at the moment Hitler and Mussolini were providing new meaning to the term—took a certain boldness on his part, but Ryan's overall aim was to take a broader view of his subject. In his chapter "The Legend Grows," he zeroes in on de Valera's actions after the Rising, but a reader receives a rounded view of what happened following the surrender and why:

De Valera had vanished behind the stone walls with stoical dignity. In Richmond Barracks on the day of his court-martial he had taken a calm leave of his friends and given away even his fountain pen and the last buttons on his tunic and said to Batt O'Connor with a last clap of his hands to imitate rifle-fire: "You know I am expecting that!" Although he felt bound in honour to obey the call to arms, de Valera never concealed his doubts as to its wisdom on the eve of that enterprise in which he had played such an outstanding part. In Richmond Barracks, he candidly said he was glad he had only to carry out his orders and not vote for or against. Then he was snatched from death. The general belief was that Spain and the United States had spoken an unofficial word on his behalf; and by some it is claimed that John Redmond had a share in his reprieve.[50]

Legend and fact are blended in the life or lives of Éamon de Valera. Ryan qualifies his factual recitation by inserting the phrases "general belief" and "it is claimed." An "unofficial" U.S. role receives mention, and there is the unattributed assertion by Gwynn of Redmond's involvement. The complete story remains elusive, which results in either inaccuracy or speculation. By that time, it was more than a little curious why de Valera didn't have an authoritative account of his emergence as a public figure readily available for anyone wanting to write about him.

This is particularly puzzling because de Valera participated in the publication of Dorothy Macardle's comprehensive, thousand-page volume *The Irish Republic*, which was first published in 1937 and included a preface he was credited with writing. Describing the public reaction to the court-martials and sentences, Macardle notes that even those who "opposed their cause" were repelled by the execution of the rebels. That opposition was building among the Irish in America, in the British colonies, "and even among Irish soldiers in the trenches." She goes on: "The executions were 'becoming an atrocity' as the *Manchester Guardian* declared. This was probably the reason why the sentence of death, conveyed to Ashe and De Valera on May 10th, was followed immediately by the announcement that it had been commuted to penal servitude for life."[51]

Macardle does not mention de Valera's birth or citizenship as a factor, and her account in that sense is similar to what de Valera wrote in 1969 that he benefited from his case coming late. Given the author's proximity to de Valera, the book would have been a perfect vehicle to set the historical record straight and avoid further amplification of stories without factual foundation. Here again, however, there is ambiguity. One conclusion is that de Valera himself wanted to maintain an aura of mystery and that his often-asserted life-saving association with America strengthened him in his political and governmental pursuits.

From his early involvement in public life, de Valera understood the importance of Irish America to the development of Ireland, and his own transatlantic tie created a personal bond. He was the child of an exile returned home—but he never forgot from where he came. In 1937, de Valera told John Cudahy, the U.S. minister to Ireland, "Without the moral support of American opinion, the Irish Free State could never have become a reality."[52] The support, of course, was more than moral, and de Valera was a beneficiary of financial resources from Americans at several key times. He raised a reported $5.5 million in bond sales to help finance the fledgling Irish government he envisioned during his eighteen-month tour in 1919–1920, and he returned between 1927 and 1931 to solicit support for launching a newspaper favorable to his agenda—and to himself. De Valera realized how influential the delivery and control of a political message could be, saying at one point: "Any government that desires to hold power in Ireland should put publicity before all."[53] As it turned out, *The Irish Press* began publishing in September 1931, and de Valera took office as president of the Executive Council in early March 1932, after the February election. Those two developments do not seem entirely coincidental. It is also probably not a complete coincidence that de Valera's friend in America, Joseph McGarrity, published a weekly newspaper, with the title *The Irish Press*, from March 23, 1918, to May 6, 1922.[54]

Right before taking office, de Valera delivered a radio broadcast to "old friends of our cause in the United States." As Franklin D. Roosevelt learned through his "Fireside Chats," which began in 1933, radio broadcasting allowed direct, intimate communication to people in their homes. De Valera took to the American airwaves again on February 12, 1933, to celebrate Lincoln's birthday and to connect that president's life to Ireland almost a century later. "The veneration in which Abraham Lincoln is held by the American people is shared in no small measure by the people of Ireland," de Valera stated. "Having ourselves so long striven for freedom, we honour him as the liberator of a race. Having had to suffer the partition of our territory, we revere him as the preserver of the unity of a nation."[55] De Valera kept a bust of the martyred president in his office.

Once de Valera assumed power in 1932, he held it without interruption for almost sixteen years. In 1944, M. J. MacManus published *Eamon de Valera*, which treats its subject with authority and subsequently appeared in two later editions (1957 and 1962). The chapter about "Easter Week" noted that "protests were beginning to be raised in the House of Commons and in the British and American press" over the executions at Kilmainham; however, MacManus does not go any further in explaining the reprieve.[56] In its review of the book (June 17, 1944), however, the *Christian Science Monitor* was more explicit, the reviewer stating flatly: "He [de Valera] fought in the Rising and escaped execution only because of his American birth. He received a life sentence instead."[57] Why the reviewer (the byline at the end offers just the initials "R. M. F.") inserted the facts about the "American birth" suggests that the story about de Valera was such common knowledge in the United States at the time that it was taken for granted and repeated without verification—even though the biography under review made no such claim.

In the headline and in the body of the article, de Valera was called "Eire's Man of Destiny." His "destiny," however, was forever tethered to the country of his birth. Though de Valera in 1919 told reporters "I ceased to be an American when I became a soldier of the Irish republic," he directed an official at the Department of External Affairs to draft a formal statement in 1946, responding to an inquiry from *Collier's*, a popular U.S. weekly, about his citizenship. In part, the statement says:

> The Taoiseach never deliberately "renounced" it at any time. As far as I am personally aware, the Taoiseach's American citizenship was recognised to exist, by himself and other interested parties, long after he attained his majority (e.g. in 1916). . . . As an American citizen by birth, his American status is much more firmly rooted than that of a naturalized American . . . we may assume that no change has taken place in the Taoiseach's natural-born status.[58]

At age sixty-three, and after all his dealings with what he called "our best friend," de Valera wasn't simply going to abandon his transatlantic connections, and he wanted other people to know that he was even more American than a naturalized citizen, such as Tom Clarke—or even John Devoy.

De Valera led Fianna Fáil to victories in six elections—then lost in 1948 before coming back as Taoiseach from June 1951 through June 1954, and later from June 1957 through June 1959. Shortly after the 1957 election, the *New York Times* devoted its "Man in the News" feature to de Valera, who was identified in the headline with the two words "Legendary Irishman." Noting "how dominant he is" and that he occupies a "place in all Irish hearts," the profile of the seventy-four-year-old figure is laudatory, a counterpoint to much of the coverage he received in the same newspaper as he emerged in politics four decades earlier.

> To the younger generation of Irish men and women "Dev," as he is popularly known, has become an elder statesman and something of a legend. Their parents perhaps may remind them that he is the last surviving commandant of the Insurrection of 1916, one who directed the fight against the British from Boland's flour mills in Dublin and who was saved from execution only by questions over his then United States citizenship.

> Watching this serious-visaged man sitting at his place in the Dail, it
> is not easy to visualize him as the young republican chief who in 1919
> crossed the Atlantic disguised as a stoker to raise a loan of $5,000,000
> in the United States, or the man who escaped from Lincoln Prison in
> England with the aid of a key sent in to him in a birthday cake.[59]

The stories mix and merge here, proving again that most of the legends were
born in the United States.

The same year de Valera was elected to begin his last term as Taoiseach,
1957, Charles Callan Tansill, a professor of American diplomatic history at
Georgetown University, published *America and the Fight for Irish Freedom
1866–1922*. In it, Tansill is harshly critical of de Valera while praising John
Devoy and Daniel Cohalan. Nonetheless, there's a brisk matter-of-factness to
his treatment of the executions: "The seven leaders who had signed the proclamation announcing the birth of an Irish Republic were quickly shot, and eight
others who were judged to be their chief supporters were hurried before firing
squads. De Valera was reprieved only because there was a possibility that he
was an American citizen."[60] Of course, Tom Clarke was executed, and he, too,
was an American through the naturalization process. By not considering de
Valera as one of the "chief supporters," Tansill maintains his bias at the same
time he repeats, without verification or amplification, the most often reported
reason that de Valera escaped the firing squad.

During fourteen years in the largely ceremonial position as president of
Ireland—he was seventy-six years old when he moved into Áras an Uachtaráin
(the presidential residence across from the home of the U.S. ambassador in
Dublin's Phoenix Park) and ninety when he retired from public service—
de Valera continued to dominate the political landscape. Since the Rising,
in effect for well over a half-century, he played a central role in Irish affairs,
whether holding a major office or leading the opposition. Everything he said
and did received attention, and for the entirety of his life, truth and legend
co-habitated.

In the end, however, de Valera's salvation from execution in 1916 stood
out in this respect. Two years after de Valera's election as president in 1959,
Seán T. O'Kelly, who preceded him, published "Memoirs of Seán T." in serial
form in *The Irish Press*. Like de Valera, O'Kelly was involved in the Rising and
later was one of de Valera's closest political allies, helping to found Fianna

Fáil and serving as vice president of the Executive Council throughout de Valera's time, and then as Tánaiste (or deputy prime minister) until June of 1945, when he was elected president of Ireland.

In the concluding two paragraphs of his first-person account about the aftermath of the Rising (which appeared under the eight-column headline "Shadow of Death Hangs Over All"), O'Kelly focused on de Valera. "Why the British commuted the death sentence I don't know," he maintained, going through the usual litany of pressure from all quarters, including the United States, whom England was working hard to entice into joining the war. "All I say now is thank God his life was saved. He was spared to render further service to the cause of the liberation of Ireland. This service he gladly and successfully has given over many long years. . . . May he long be spared in health to be Ireland's President."[61]

O'Kelly had worked side by side with de Valera for decades, and yet even he "cannot say" what was responsible for de Valera's clemency. In addition, *The Irish Press* was the newspaper de Valera founded and that his family later controlled. Indeed, his son Vivion de Valera was the paper's managing director in 1961, a post he held from 1951 until 1982.

Finally, and as we saw with the discrepancies in his 1969 account—a sort of last will and testament, though he would write an actual will the following year—complicating anyone's understanding of what actually happened was de Valera's own memory of his reprieve. In fact, in 1963, during John F. Kennedy's only trip to Ireland as president of the United States, and not long after he became the first foreign head of state to honor the Rising's executed leaders at Arbour Hill Cemetery, the first Irish Catholic to occupy the White House wanted a precise piece of information from his host. In their book *"Johnny, We Hardly Knew Ye,"* Kennedy aides Kenneth P. O'Donnell and David F. Powers report that during his last night in Ireland, the president and his party attended an informal dinner with de Valera at which "the conversation was sparkling and the laughs plentiful." Kennedy could not resist asking de Valera the question that had been asked for decades. Why had he not been shot in 1916? "De Valera explained that he had lived in Ireland since his early childhood, but he was born in New York City, and because of his American citizenship, the British were reluctant to kill him. 'But there were many times when the key in my jail cell door was turned,' he said, 'and I thought that my turn had come.'"[62] Kennedy, according to the account, "listened, spellbound."

In the article "Obsessive Historian: Eamon de Valera and the Policing of His Reputation" for the *Proceedings of the Royal Irish Academy*, Patrick Murray described in arresting detail de Valera's "preoccupation with his own history." One of the more telling sections of the 2001 article involved a story about the noted Irish historian F. S. L. Lyons:

> In 1964, as one of a group of historians, Lyons was summoned to Áras an Uachtaráin to ask de Valera a few questions about his career. The questions had to be submitted in writing on the previous day, and the answers were predictable and in line with his public statements. What Lyons thought remarkable, however, was that, at the age of eighty-two, de Valera, "who submitted unweariedly to six or seven hours of inter-rogation, not only possessed a phenomenal memory, but also revealed an obsessive concern to set the record straight as he saw it," and that he did not seem to realise that his "transparent anxiety might be regarded by the historians as evidence of a very different kind than that which he sought to press upon them."[63]

De Valera's session with the historians took place not that long after his din-ner with Kennedy—and during the same year, 1964, he told W. E. Wylie he couldn't "recollect anything" about his court-martial. With Kennedy, how-ever, his memory had been very sharp. Clearly he had wanted to entertain Kennedy, in whom he saw at long last a U.S. president who genuinely loved Ireland, rather than seeing it merely as a pawn in a geopolitical game, as well as to establish an American bond.

In the end we are left with unanswered questions, and most of them revolve around the degree to which de Valera identified with Ireland's "exiled chil-dren." As with the others, he struggled with a dual identity, waiting until 1969—just four years before retiring from governmental service—to put his official version into words. Kennedy had brought him closest to choosing his American birth as a reason for his survival.

Five months after de Valera entertained Kennedy, he represented Ireland at the assassinated president's funeral in Washington, D.C. And five months later, de Valera returned to the United States on a state visit that included a speech to a joint session of Congress and a White House dinner given by President Lyndon Johnson. In his toast, Johnson spoke directly to de Valera: "you have come back to the country of your birth, home to the people who claim you as

one of their own." In response, de Valera broached the question of a hyphenated citizenship, in the form of an amusing anecdote:

> There is a time when the phrase hyphenated American was used—most
> of you people are too young to remember those days—but there was a
> certain sting in the phrase and it hurt our people, so, as a counter, I am
> 100 percent American. When I was pronounced on one occasion in an
> American assembly to be the 100 percent American in the room, it hap-
> pened like this. I had been accepted or made a chief of the Chippewa
> Tribe. As a matter of fact, I have been made a chief of two Indian tribes.
> But this man speaking of me pronounced that I was the 100 percent
> American in the room, that I was born in America and I was an Indian
> chief.[64]

By 1964, the dagger of hyphenation, which Wilson sharpened and wielded
to shame Irish Americans into embracing American unity, was no longer a
weapon in the opinion of this twice-proclaimed Indian chief.

Besides this formal occasion, de Valera expressed his affection for America
two years later in an interview conducted in Dublin for an oral history project
of the John F. Kennedy Library. He recalls being asked on a visit to the United
States how anyone could love two countries: "I said, 'Now look here, a man
can love his wife and love her the best in the world, but that doesn't prevent
him at all from having a very deep love for his mother. And for us, as for a lot
of our people, this was the mother country.' "[65]

In 1966, to recognize the fiftieth anniversary of the Rising, the
Washington Post published a detailed article of news analysis in its Easter
Sunday (April 10) edition. From the headline—"Easter Rising Showed All
Colonials the Way"—and into the text, the Irish received credit for beginning the movements for nationalistic independence through guerrilla
warfare that helped define the history of the twentieth century. Far-flung
empires, such as Britain's, confronted homegrown threats on a global
scale, and Ireland started the trend. "It [the Rising] had no chance of succeeding, it was greeted with derision by the Irish, and yet within five years
its chief goal was realized." Again, the account returned to de Valera's
death sentence, commuted "because he happened to have been born in
America." "He is a man of formidable abilities. But it can be said that his
status as sole survivor among the leaders assured him a prominence that
he has had ever since."[66]

According to de Valera's papers in the UCD archives, his "last will" was written in January 1970, six months after he drafted the statement about his reprieve. It was a time of looking back, summing up, and setting the record straight from *his* vantage point. Despite his formal recollection about his reprieve and its amplification in his authorized biography, when de Valera died on August 29, 1975, several journalistic outlets relied on information in their libraries (or, in news parlance, "morgues") to prepare obituaries and editorial tributes.

For example, an Associated Press dispatch with a Dublin dateline included this background for the wire service's subscribers around the world: "He was condemned to death along with 15 others for his part in the rebellion but because of his American birth his sentence was commuted to life imprisonment." And for drama, the dispatch recounted the moment of his capture in 1916: "I am De Valera. Shoot me, but spare my men."[67]

The Observer in Britain likened de Valera to French leader Charles de Gaulle and reported de Valera hadn't been executed in 1916 "probably because he could claim American citizenship."[68] In an editorial, "A Maker of Ireland," the *New York Times* also noted the similarity to de Gaulle, concluding about de Valera: "The British spared his life in 1916 in deference to American public opinion—and not only Ireland was the beneficiary."[69] The obituary in the news section of the *New York Times* on the same day takes a somewhat different tack and goes into greater detail: "The major reason for his salvation was probably public opinion: people in Britain as well as Ireland were becoming sickened by daily news of further executions. Most commentators would agree, however, that his dual citizenship helped spare his life."[70]

The *Irish Times* in its extensive, biographical report about "[t]he controversial giant of modern Ireland," came closest to telling what most probably happened; however, even in its report, there's the passing mention of an American connection, illustrating the inevitability, and even the necessity, of recognizing it in some way: "De Valera's men were the last to surrender and he was detained under arrest. His reprieve from a death sentence is attributed to that delay rather than to his American birth."[71]

In its obituary, the *Irish Times* reflected the judgment that the late nature of the court-martial proved decisive in the context of the other capital sentences. This viewpoint, which saw de Valera's American birth or citizenship as inconsequential to his reprieve, is reflected (and receives emphasis) in a number of more recent biographical and historical studies by (among others) Pauric

Travers, Tim Pat Coogan, T. Ryle Dwyer, Ronan Fanning, Thomas Bartlett, and Seán Enright. Fanning's entry in the *Dictionary of Irish Biography* says de Valera's "escape owed more to luck" than any other factor,[72] and Bartlett, in his magisterial *Ireland: A History,* states: "only de Valera among the senior military commanders had his sentence commuted, not because of his America birth, as sometimes claimed, but because by the time he was tried the politicians had finally managed to wrest the initiative back from a military command bent on swift retribution."[73] In *Easter Rising 1916: The Trials*, Enright raised the possibility of "representations to the American Consulate and that President Wilson intervened directly with Asquith" or that "Maxwell was swayed by de Valera's American citizenship," as initial press accounts reported.[74] In this case and others, it is almost as though the rumors of some kind of American involvement, which circulated for a century, demand retelling—even if for the purpose of refuting them. Enright, a Crown Court judge in Britain and a legal historian, then focuses on the facts of de Valera's case, including details from the Trial Register:

> The truth of the matter is probably far more prosaic. De Valera's men surrendered on the Sunday afternoon when Richmond Barracks and Arbour Hill were overflowing with prisoners. De Valera's men were moved to the RDS [Royal Dublin Society] at Ballsbridge, in the south of the city. De Valera remained there until the afternoon of Tuesday 2 May, when he and his men were marched to Richmond Barracks. By this time all prisoners likely to be tried had been assigned a number and there was a long queue of prisoners awaiting trial.[75]

Rather than birthplace, it had been a matter of numbers. This detailed account, including the critical fact that "de Valera's fate became tied up with political considerations at Westminster,"[76] corroborates what de Valera wrote in 1969: "I have not the slightest doubt that my reprieve in 1916 was due to the fact that my courtmartial and sentence came late."

Despite all the evidence contradicting an American role in de Valera's reprieve, the suggestion or assertion continues to appear in scholarly and popular treatments of the Rising and the people involved in it. For example, explaining the role of 1916 events in the context of the Great War, Martin Gilbert notes in *First World War* (1994), "Fifteen of the rebel leaders were executed. A sixteenth, Eamon de Valera, a mathematics professor, was saved from execution because he was an American citizen."[77] The 1998 historical novel by

Morgan Llywelyn, titled simply *1916*, contains this passage: "On the eleventh [of May], the death sentence of Eamon de Valera was commuted to life imprisonment out of deference to his American citizenship."[78] Terry Eagleton, in *The Truth About the Irish* (1999), says, "De Valera had been born in New York, a fortunate accident which was to save him from a death sentence."[79] In the introduction to *Modern Ireland* (2003), published by Oxford University Press, Senia Pašeta writes, "The highest ranking survivor of the Easter Rising, de Valera's American citizenship had saved him from execution and placed him at the front of the queue of potential successors to the nationalist throne."[80] Michael Doorley notes in *Irish-American Diaspora Nationalism* (2005): "De Valera took part in the 1916 Rising but later escaped execution because of his American birth."[81] *A Pocket History of Ireland* (2010) by Joseph McCullough includes this sentence: "An Irish-American, Eamon de Valera had been one of the leaders of the Easter Rising and only escaped execution because of his dual citizenship and the intervention of the American ambassador."[82]

In *Story of Ireland* (2011), the companion book to a BBC television series, Fergal Keene recalls in his autobiographical introduction, "We were taught through the medium of Irish, and the history we learned stressed the sufferings of the Irish and their ultimate triumph over the foreign invaders. We had also been visited at school by the President, Eamon de Valera, a veteran of 1916, who only escaped execution because he had been born in America."[83] Though Fanning attributed "luck" to de Valera's survival in the *Dictionary of Irish Biography*, he subsequently offered another, more definite reason altogether in *Fatal Path* (2013): "Fifteen executions were carried out between 3 and 12 May: all seven signatories of the proclamation and all the Volunteer commandants except one were shot. Éamon de Valera escaped death because of his American birth."[84]

Many other sources, both in print and on Internet websites, state with unequivocal authority that de Valera owed his long life after 1916 to his American birth. The persistence of the claim reflects how deeply rooted it had become during de Valera's rise to power and throughout his decades in high office. His activities in the Rising, combined with his American heritage, had become so intertwined in the public narrative about him that even he didn't want to invite questions as he established himself as a political figure in Ireland and throughout the wider world. Only at the end did he try to correct any suggestion that his American tie had provided his deliverance from a British firing squad. The story by then had outlived its political usefulness.

In *Ireland 1912–1985*, J. J. Lee observes: "It may safely be predicted that the paradoxes of de Valera will intrigue historians for generations to come. Exploration of the recesses of that cavernous mind reveals ever more complex, ever more fascinating, formations."[85] For anyone to occupy a nation's center stage for several decades takes a self-dramatization that combines political acumen and adaptability. From a relatively early age, de Valera understood the importance of America to the cause and course of an independent Ireland. He wanted to keep the "exiled children" in the United States in his corner—and his own biography helped strengthen those transatlantic ties. In the twilight of his career, he attempted to set the record straight. By then, however, people in Ireland, the States, and elsewhere thought they knew what had occurred in 1916. Today, a century later, the American genesis of the Rising's most prominent survivor remains an essential part of the story (with its mythic elements) that defines him on both sides of the Atlantic. De Valera's long shadow extends from the land of his birth to the republic he helped found and shape.

Epilogue

THOMAS J. CLARKE, WHO BECAME an American citizen in 1905, occupies the first position on the list of signatories of the 1916 Proclamation. However, a narrative of U.S. connections to the Easter Rising comes full circle with several accounts identifying Diarmuid Lynch, another naturalized American citizen, as the last person to leave Dublin's General Post Office (GPO) when it was engulfed in flames following nearly a week of fierce fighting. A member of the Irish Republican Brotherhood's supreme council and an active participant in planning and staging the Rising, Lynch (like Éamon de Valera) received a death sentence at his court-martial before it was commuted, in his circumstance, to ten years of penal servitude. Lynch's story, with its Irish and American dimensions, helps explain how the transatlantic ties preceding 1916 continued to be critical in the turbulent years following the Rising.

Called "a forgotten Irish patriot" in a 2013 biography,[1] Lynch's reprieve was front-page news on May 21, 1916, with the *New York Times* crediting the intervention of Woodrow Wilson in his case. According to this dispatch, the State Department received a cablegram from the U.S. Embassy in London that reported, "Mr. Lynch's life was saved by a margin of less than four hours."[2] Given that the last executions in Dublin had taken place on May 12, and that the sentence of de Valera had already been reduced, a last-minute decision seems highly doubtful. After his release from prison in England in June 1917 as part of the amnesty for those sentenced after the Rising, Lynch returned to Ireland, resuming his republican activities in senior posts for the IRB, Sinn Féin, and the Irish Volunteers. However, not long afterwards, he was re-arrested and deported to the United States, where he had lived for over a decade, until 1907.

Back in America—he stayed until 1933—Lynch was appointed secretary of the Friends of Irish Freedom (FOIF), which was created just before the Rising. He resumed his association with John Devoy, Daniel F. Cohalan, and other nationalistic-minded Americans and raised funds promoting the cause of Irish independence. When de Valera came to the United States in 1919 and tried to exert control over Irish-American efforts on behalf of Ireland, Lynch broke with his fellow rebel fighter and remained loyal to Devoy and those supporting the old Fenian. Though the FOIF suffered from de Valera's establishment of his rival organization, the American Association for Recognition of the Irish Republic, in November 1920, Lynch continued his work as secretary of FOIF, while his animus for de Valera grew.

Before his death in 1950, Lynch wrote extensively about his life and experiences in the republican movement. A lengthy manuscript prepared for Ireland's Bureau of Military History included a "Supplementary Statement" about Easter Week, recounting his day-by-day remembrances of what occurred from his perspective. Rich in detail and specificity, Lynch chronicled his involvement and points out errors he had discovered in books about the Rising and its leaders. Describing his final duty at the GPO—trying to prevent bombs from going off accidentally after the building was vacated—he recalls (with his emphasis): "To my astonishment there was *not a man left in that room in which the garrison had been assembled—the evacuation had been completed while I was engaged in the task of averting the danger of a premature explosion.* (This is a fact worth remembering in view of the controversy as to who was 'the last man to leave the GPO'—which was a matter of no consequence as I view it.)"[3]

Lynch's personal modesty might explain why he was reluctant to turn his reminiscences into an autobiography or memoir. Like Devoy with his *Recollections of an Irish Rebel*, publication of Lynch's *The IRB and the 1916 Insurrection* occurred posthumously, in 1957, and the book included a foreword and two chapters on his "American phase" by Florence O'Donoghue. Early on, Lynch expressed the emotional attraction of the land to which he immigrated in March 1896: "Though U.S. citizenship was acquired by me shortly after the minimum term of five years elapsed, I can say that on first sight of the Statue of Liberty I felt myself to be a good American."[4] For Lynch and others who fought during the Rising, the United States meant freedom from British rule and breathing the fresh air of independence. In that environment, he could pursue Ireland's cause from a distance until he felt compelled to return to take up the fight.

In one of the chapters that rounds out and amplifies Lynch's recollections, O'Donoghue (a historian, an IRA intelligence officer during the War for Independence, and a major in the Irish Army) makes a crucial point, particularly as it pertains to the involvement of Americans on behalf of Ireland following the Rising. He writes:

> The aid given to the many phases of the Irish struggle for freedom by men and women of Irish birth or extraction residing in the United States has, for over one hundred years, been a significant factor influencing the ebb and flow of the movement at home. There never was a period in which that aid was so valuable, and so necessary, as in the years from 1913 to 1921.[5]

O'Donoghue went on to say that the support came from Americans who had no doubts about their principal allegiance. Instead of a hyphen that might connote division, or at least duality, these people carried, in effect, a plus sign, adding a genuine concern for an independent Ireland to their thinking and action. In O'Donoghue's explanation, assistance was provided "by American citizens whose first loyalty is to the United States. On no other basis could they publicly agitate for Irish liberty, on no other basis could they create and maintain great nationwide organizations, on no other basis could they enlist the sympathy and good will of their fellow citizens."[6]

American values and principles animated and informed the agitation that advanced the objective of Irish liberty. Financially, prior to the Rising, the Redmondite United Irish League of America and the republican Clan na Gael served as conduits to subsidize political activity in Ireland. The clan's clandestine shipments of money bankrolled expenses to help stage the Rising, and in full public view, Americans contributed assistance to the Irish after the bloodshed and carnage occurred. For instance, the FOIF established the Irish Relief Fund shortly after the last executions. According to O'Donoghue in the Lynch book, "350,000 dollars were sent to Ireland for the relief of distress amongst the dependants of those who had been killed, wounded or taken prisoner after the Rising."[7]

The Irish Relief Fund began the post-Rising support to Ireland, which subsequently evolved into substantial aid from Americans as the cause of Irish independence gained broader mainstream acceptance, both throughout Ireland and in the States. Two events in late 1918 proved particularly influential in focusing U.S. attention on the possibilities for helping the Irish bring an end to British governance. With the armistice on November 11, the Great War ended—and ethnic loyalties no longer needed to be deliberately subordinated to the larger American purpose, which included wartime's all-for-one cooperation with fellow ally Great Britain. In addition, the success of Sinn Féin's candidates in the general election that December put Irish republicanism front and center for the American Irish and likeminded supporters. (Sinn Féin won 73 constituencies, the Irish Unionists 22, and the Irish Parliamentary Party just 6, a drop in 68 seats from the previous election.)

At the third Irish race convention, which was held in Philadelphia in February 1919, the FOIF endorsed what was called "the Irish Victory Fund," raising over a million dollars in eight months. Among other benefactions of this largesse, the fund launched the American Commission on Irish Independence, which dispatched three representatives to the Paris Peace Conference.[8] Though Woodrow Wilson met with the trio in France, he prevented them from making their case during the multi-country formal proceedings at the conference, as discussed in chapter 3. Wilson's refusal to do anything formally to advance Irish independence served to embolden Irish Americans and other sympathizers in the cause to work harder on their own. When de Valera arrived in America in mid-1919 to campaign for recognition of an Irish republic and to sell bonds to help finance the government of Dáil Éireann, he drew large, cheering crowds and remarkably raised over $5 million in bond certificates, according to one accounting.[9]

During the eighteen months de Valera barnstormed across the United States, the War for Independence was being waged in Ireland against the British, and fighting continued into 1921. As happened when the Rising occurred, humanitarian concern prompted people in the States to take up collections—in this case under the auspices of the American Committee for Relief in Ireland. Over $5 million in contributions assisted the disabled, the orphaned, those in "famine areas," and others trying to cope during the war. The Irish White Cross administered the funds, and in its published report, which appeared in 1922 as a short book with a full accounting of funds and contextual testimonials, the full impact of the American generosity becomes clear. From the total of 1,374,795 British pounds reported as income, 1,273,246 pounds (or the equivalent of just more than $5 million) were provided by the American Committee for Relief in Ireland and "direct" gifts from the United States. Other countries sent less than 10 percent of what the Irish White Cross received at the time.[10]

Through his high-profile, "presidential" campaign of personal appearances to rally support, de Valera kept Ireland at the forefront of American attention.

However, other Irish men and women came to the United States on political or cultural visits, adding to the interest in a country enduring persistent upheaval. In late January 1920, for instance, W. B. Yeats arrived in New York for a four-month tour of lectures and poetry readings. In the second volume of *W. B. Yeats: A Life*, R. F. Foster remarks:

> WBY's American visit coincided with a new turn in the Irish crisis, as Lloyd George sent over mercenary troops and the Sinn Féin publicity machine intensified its efforts. De Valera was also touring America, and President Wilson was being pressed hard by Irish-American activists. As on previous occasions, WBY spoke more forthrightly to American journalists than to interviewers in Britain or Ireland; as soon as he arrived on 24 January, he announced that Ireland was now "a country of oppression," stifled by censorship, and called for "some form of self-government."

Nonetheless, according to Foster, Yeats also stressed that Ulster should not be "coerced any more than the remainder of the country; there should be some way to permit both to work out their destiny."[11]

Though reluctant to discuss certain subjects, Yeats "spoke more forthrightly" on U.S. soil and couldn't avoid the Rising or what it unleashed at some of his appearances. Later in 1920, he finally published "Easter 1916," a poem which he had started to compose on May 11, 1916, the day before the last two executions, and completed on September 25, 1916. Twelve days after he began writing the poem, he sent a letter to John Quinn, a friend and prominent New York attorney, which included this assessment: "This Irish business has been a great grief. We have lost the ablest and most fine-natured of our young men. A world seems to have been swept away. I keep going over the past in my mind and wondering if I could have done anything to turn those young men in some other direction." At the end of the letter (the original is in the New York Public Library and a label on the envelope reads "Opened by Censor"), Yeats wrote: "I am planning a group of poems on the Dublin rising but cannot write till I get into the country."[12]

The New Statesman, based in London, printed "Easter, 1916" (with the haunting refrain "A terrible beauty is born") in its October 23 issue. In the United States, the November number of *The Dial* carried ten poems by Yeats, including "Easter 1916" (the comma between "Easter" and "1916" does not appear in this version), "Sixteen Dead Men," "The Rose Tree," and

"On a Political Prisoner"—each, in its way, a response to the Rising and its participants. In effect, "Easter, 1916" (or "Easter 1916"—you see the title rendered both ways in books and collections today) came out simultaneously in the United Kingdom and the United States; however, *The Dial* provided its readership with a more comprehensive appraisal of 1916 by Ireland's most eminent poet and person of letters. Though cagey for personal and political reasons to express his complex and ambiguous reactions, Yeats decided after four years to give them their widest first airing in a literary magazine with editorial offices in New York City. Is it possible that Yeats's time in the United States, which allowed for more candid personal expression, helped to embolden him to publish these poems later the same year? This sequence of poems about 1916 subsequently appeared in the collection *Michael Robartes and the Dancer* (1921), which was published in Ireland by the Cuala Press, with Yeats being awarded the Nobel Prize for Literature in 1923.

The Rising, the War of Independence, the American Commission on Irish Independence, and individual figures, such as de Valera and Yeats, kept Ireland on the public's mind in the United States, and concern for what was happening some three thousand miles away extended beyond raising money. The War of Independence, for instance, resulted in the establishment of the American Commission on the Conditions in Ireland, a committee of 150 public figures, intellectuals, and religious leaders (such as Jane Addams, W. E. B. Du Bois, William Randolph Hearst, and William Allen White) who conducted hearings with witnesses from Ireland to learn firsthand the situation there. The preface to the 1,105-page volume, which brought together the evidence and statements the commission collected, explains its objective in matter-of-fact prose:

> The American people have a right to know the truth about what is happening in Ireland. That concern is not a matter of idle curiosity. We are bound by ties of kinship and race, by a common culture and language, to the participants in this struggle. Even though we wish, we can not sit unmoved at civil war between peoples whose blood tinctures more than half of our population. The fact that the relatives and loved ones of our fellow citizens are being terrorized, imprisoned without trial, even murdered, and their property violently destroyed, brings this conflict home to our very door. Even though we would ignore the Irish question, the Irish question will not ignore us.[13]

At the end of the preface, the report's transcriber and annotator, Albert Coyle, pointed out "this inquiry was not an official undertaking of the United States Government."[14] Throughout the revolutionary years, from the Rising in 1916 until the creation of the Irish Free State in 1922, the executive branch of government in Washington did little to advance Irish independence. In *The Irish in America*, Carl Wittke observes that early in Wilson's presidency the impression started to form that he was "at heart a Britisher masquerading in American colors,"[15] a perception that grew stronger through World War I and in the years following. Wilson's successor, the Republican Warren G. Harding, also saw Ireland as an internal matter for Britain to settle without U.S. involvement.[16]

While the United States—formally through the Wilson and, to a lesser extent, the Harding administrations—pursued a policy of avoidance for the sake of maintaining the status quo of Ireland within the United Kingdom, Americans, including certain members of Congress and millions among the American Irish, were much more activist, providing continuous encouragement and support for the dawning of a new day, with independence from Britain the ultimate prize. This distinction between official and unofficial forms of democratic action or participation is critical to understand and underscores a key conclusion of this book. The "exiled children" and the people who sympathized with them (in other words, the governed) worked around the White House and State Department (the government) of successive administrations to do whatever they could to enlighten other Americans to the merit of their cause. Over time, with this bottom-up rather than top-down exertion of influence, the cause of Irish independence became a mainstream objective, as the circle of support kept widening. Still, formal U.S. recognition of the Irish Free State didn't occur until June 28, 1924 (more than two years after the signing of the Anglo-Irish Treaty), and an American Legation wasn't established in Dublin for over three more years—on July 27, 1927.[17]

In this respect, the U.S. press, especially large-city newspapers, played a significant role in keeping the American citizenry informed about Ireland and the turmoil there. The conflict provoked substantial news coverage, and to be sure, a sizable percentage of the urban readership could claim a blood connection to the stories. One historian credited "public opinion in America and in Britain" with demanding an end to the bloodshed during the War of Independence—it's telling that America is mentioned first. The treaty that followed the truce spelled out the dominion status for the twenty-six counties outside Ulster and their "freedom to achieve freedom."[18]

To a noteworthy degree, journalism helped shape that "public opinion in America"; the crystallization process began with the extensive coverage that chronicled the Rising and its aftermath in 1916. Moreover, the Wilsonian rhetoric of self-determination for small countries and a postwar world of his idealistic design rang increasingly hollow for those backing an independent Ireland. In his last speech supporting the League of Nations before he fell ill, Wilson told an audience in Pueblo, Colorado, on September 25, 1919, that opponents of the treaty were creating propaganda marked with a disloyalty stemming from divided allegiances. It was combative phrasing combined with talk of peace, as Wilson resorted to his favorite metaphor for reproach of Americans who (from his perspective) weren't completely loyal as U.S. citizens. He argued: "I want to say—I cannot say it too often—any man who carries a hyphen about with him carries a dagger that he is ready to plunge into the vitals of this republic whenever he gets the chance." As though that line weren't provocative enough for Irish Americans or German Americans, Wilson sharpened his attack on duality:

> If I can catch any man with a hyphen in this great contest, I will know that I have caught an enemy of the republic. My fellow citizens, it is only certain bodies of foreign sympathies, certain bodies of sympathy with foreign nations that are organized against this great document, which the American representatives have brought back from Paris.[19]

The virulence of his language had the effect of rallying a substantial portion of the American Irish to oppose the treaty—and to withhold support for the 1920 Democratic ticket of James Cox for president and Franklin D. Roosevelt for vice president. Both northerners, Cox (of Ohio) and Roosevelt (of New York) carried only eleven Southern states, losing the popular vote to Warren Harding and Calvin Coolidge, at 60.3 percent to 34.2 percent. The urban political machines, with their millions of hyphenated voters, remained bruised by Wilson's words, policies, and failures to act.

However, more than four decades later, another president, with a familial self-regard for his own ethnic identity, put the contributions of earlier Americans into the proper perspective, with authority and eloquence. In June 1963, when John Kennedy became the first White House incumbent to visit Ireland, a republic for just fourteen years, and shortly after the solemn ceremony at Arbour Hill, he traveled to Leinster House and told the Oireachtas of Ireland:

> No people ever believed more deeply in the cause of Irish freedom than the people of the United States. And no country contributed more to building my own than your sons and daughters. They came to our shores in a mixture of hope and agony, and I would not underrate the difficulties of their course once they arrived in the United States. They left behind hearts, fields, and a nation yearning to be free. It is no wonder that James Joyce described the Atlantic as a bowl of bitter tears. And an earlier poet wrote, "They are going, going, going and we cannot bid them stay."[20]

Political rhetoric always runs the risk of veering into sycophantic blarney. In this case, though, the historical record supports the stateliness ("No people," "no country") of the statement. Proudly American and Irish, Kennedy put into words what Arbour Hill represented in the struggle for Irish independence. He also applauded "the people of the United States" for their direct involvement in the cause nearly a half-century earlier. Kennedy looked back further, too, and celebrated the immigrant forebears, such as his own great grandparents, for helping in the development of America. To a certain extent, Kennedy's words echoed what Roger Casement had said in 1916, after he received his death sentence. Casement acknowledged "the generous expressions of sympathy" and "the abiding inspiration" that the American people— rather than the U.S. government—provided for him, as he summarized his efforts to advance Irish nationalism.

Moreover, but without naming Woodrow Wilson in his address, Kennedy refuted, if not repudiated, that former president's cynical approach to Ireland. The concept of "self-determination" now assuredly applied to the republic that Kennedy was visiting, and as far as he was concerned, more than "self-determination" deserved recognition: "No larger nation did more to spark the cause of independence in America, indeed, around the world."[21] The relationship between Ireland and independence grew even stronger as Kennedy focused on the cold war struggle between democracy and communism, with several small, iron curtain countries currently looking to what the Irish had accomplished a few decades earlier: "every new nation knows that Ireland was the first of the small nations in the twentieth century to win its struggle for independence, and that the Irish have traditionally sent their doctors and technicians and soldiers and priests to help other lands to keep their liberty alive."[22]

If all the references to freedom, independence, and liberty were not sufficient to make amends for Wilson's refusal to confront the Irish Question in a deliberate and sustained manner, Kennedy then revealed a willingness to see the past with nationalist eyes and to view Ireland as existing independently, rather than as part of the United Kingdom: "For knowing the meaning of foreign domination, Ireland is the example and inspiration to those enduring endless years of oppression."[23] Kennedy's speech, given with the former rebel commandant and now president Éamon de Valera sitting in the Oireachtas, listening to every word, was both a validation of the collaborative, two-nation effort he celebrated and a valediction to an earlier time. By 1963, Ireland had forged its way and could now serve as a model for men and women elsewhere in the world with similar aspirations.

The Easter Rising and the events that flowed from it set people in motion, with a commitment (in Kennedy's words) to "the cause of Irish freedom" and the cessation of "foreign domination." What earlier generations in America had accomplished for themselves, for their heirs, and for their immigrant successors animated men and women thousands of miles away to achieve a similar destiny for Ireland. And, as the "exiled children" matured and found their place in the New World, they neither forgot nor abandoned the island with their ancestral roots. The inspiration of America, symbolized most strikingly for Diarmuid Lynch and countless others by the Statue of Liberty, served as much more than a beacon to welcome immigrants to America. It also helped light the way across the Atlantic to an Ireland that eventually became an independent and free republic.

Acknowledgments

Writing this book required research expeditions through microfilm, archives, personal papers, and library stacks in the United States, Ireland, and Great Britain. The first reconnaissance mission took place in 2006 and the last in 2014. Thanks to a research fellowship from the John Hume Institute for Global Irish Studies at University College Dublin in 2009, I had the chance to explore in a sustained way the holdings of the National Library of Ireland, the National Archives of Ireland, the UCD Archives, and other repositories of papers and artifacts in Ireland.

Three years later, a semester's assignment at the University of Notre Dame's London Centre allowed me to spend valuable time at the British Library and the National Archives at Kew, besides making trips to consult papers at Oxford and Cambridge. Later that year, research travels to the Library of Congress, the Georgetown University Library's Special Collections, and the New York Public Library proved valuable, especially in understanding Woodrow Wilson, Joyce Kilmer, and John Devoy more completely.

Books about the Rising abound and continue to roll off the presses—both popular and academic—with what seems seasonal, if not monthly, regularity. Most accounts, however, make only passing reference, if any reference at all, to American involvement or reaction. A few scholarly appraisals—such as Charles Callan Tansill's *America and the Fight for Irish Freedom 1866–1922* (1957) or Francis M. Carroll's *American Opinion and the Irish Question 1910–23* (1978); and individual essays, notably Owen Dudley Edwards's "American Aspects of the Rising" in *1916: The Easter Rising* (1968)—tell a portion of the story. In most cases, though, these studies appeared decades ago and aren't readily available today, except in well-stocked research libraries.

With the centenary commemoration in 2016, a single volume examining America's influence, role, and involvement proved irresistible to someone intrigued at the possibility of combining nearly a half-century of work in

159

American Studies with a more recent interest in Irish Studies. By examining the subject from this dual perspective, I could see that historically, politically, and symbolically, the Easter Rising of 1916 invites comparison (as I suggested earlier) to America's Fourth of July, with its Declaration of Independence in 1776, and to the Battle of the Alamo in Texas during early 1836. (That each of these events occurred in a year ending in "6" we entrust to numerologists to contemplate and to decipher.)

Students of Irish history know about "the wild geese," the name given to the thousands of men who migrated from Ireland to continental Europe during the seventeenth and eighteenth centuries to fight in the armies of France, Italy, and Spain rather than support the English Crown. From time to time, writers engage in wild-goose chases, with some producing (if you will) red herrings.

For example, in several American sources, it is reported as fact that P. H. Pearse was named for the American revolutionary hero and orator Patrick Henry, who famously ended a speech in 1775 by saying: "I know not what course others may take; but as for me, give me liberty or give me death!" In *The Imagination of an Insurrection*, William Irwin Thompson makes that connection, as does Malachy McCourt in *Malachy McCourt's History of Ireland*, who calls it "a prescient gesture." Alas, it is just not true.

All one has to do is consult Pearse's own autobiographical account of his boyhood, in which he says that he was named for his great uncle (Patrick) and his father's youngest brother, Henry. So much for that Irish-American canard.

This book began as a paper for spoken delivery and kept growing in response to other lecture invitations or seminar presentations. I'm grateful beyond these few words for the suggestions from patient listeners who attended the Byrne Perry Summer School in Gorey, County Wexford (2006); the R. I. Best Memorial Lecture at the National Library of Ireland (2009); the conference of the Newspaper and Periodical History Forum of Ireland (2009); the Irish Diaspora Forum of UCD's Hume Institute that met in London (2009); the Hibernian Lecture, sponsored by the Cushwa Center for American Catholicism at the University of Notre Dame (2011); the "1916: What It Means" conference Notre Dame organized at the Royal Irish Academy in Dublin (2012); the conference on "Roger Casement (1864–1916): The Glocal Imperative" in Tralee, County Kerry (2013); and several other less formal talks and discussions at both University College Dublin and Notre Dame since 2008. Each occasion to discuss Easter 1916 and America became both a chance to look back or take stock of the continuing research and a starting point for developing sections of this book. Portions of it (in vastly different forms) have already appeared in *Irish Communications Review* (volume 12, 2010) and *History Ireland* (volume 21, no. 3, May/June 2013) or have been made available on the Internet through UCD's Scholarcast series (number 27, released in 2012).

Acknowledgments of a personal nature—more accurately, deep bows of thank-you—could fill a small volume unto itself. The 2009 fellowship at UCD's Hume Institute, then under the able direction of Brian Jackson, proved critically important in launching the sustained, uninterrupted research for this book. Padraic Conway, UCD's Vice President for University Relations at that time, was instrumental in securing the fellowship. That Padraic is no longer stimulating thought and provoking laughter on this earth is an enduring sadness for anyone who knew him.

Rev. Timothy R. Scully, C.S.C., Hackett Family Director of the Institute for Educational Initiatives and Professor of Political Science at the University of Notre Dame, was instrumental in launching my interest and involvement in Irish Studies, when he suggested the possibility of teaching in Dublin for the spring semester of 2000 as the first Naughton Fellow to UCD.

A research leave, awarded by Notre Dame for the academic year 2012–2013, enabled me to write a draft of the manuscript, and travel awards in 2014 from two scholarly enterprises at Notre Dame, the Cushwa Center for the Study of American Catholicism and the Keough-Naughton Institute for Irish Studies, supported the research to select the pictures and illustrations that appear in the book. In addition, grants from the University's Institute for Scholarship in the Liberal Arts provided funds for a research assistant, Colleen Minta, to hunt down many useful sources and, later, to acquire several illustrations as well as prepare the volume's index.

At Notre Dame, where I have been a faculty member since 1980, I am sincerely grateful to Provost Thomas Burish; Dean John McGreevy of the College of Arts and Letters; Professor Chris Fox, Director of the Keough-Naughton Institute for Irish Studies; Dr. Kevin Whelan, Director of Notre Dame's Dublin Centre; Professor Kathleen Sprows Cummings, Director of the Cushwa Center for the Study of American Catholicism; Professor Thomas V. Merluzzi, Director of the Institute for Scholarship in the Liberal Arts; and Aedín Clements, the Irish Studies Librarian for Notre Dame's Hesburgh Library, who suggested possible titles with characteristic generosity. In the

Department of American Studies and the John W. Gallivan Program in Journalism, Ethics & Democracy at Notre Dame, Katie Schlotfeldt and Mary Jo Young handled their work as administrative assistants with such professionalism that it wasn't necessary to worry very much about quotidian office concerns as this book was being written. American Studies student assistant Sarah Morris located several photos and assisted in the preparation of the bibliography. At Notre Dame, I also profited greatly from conversations about 1916 with several professors: Patrick Griffin, Declan Kiberd, Bríona Nic Dhiarmada, and Brian Ó Conchubhair.

Over in Dublin, several professionals associated with the National Library of Ireland—notably Ciara Kerrigan and Mary Broderick—helped in myriad ways as the project developed, and the entire staff of the NLI deserves a Yank's appreciative acknowledgment. Daire Keogh, currently President of St. Patrick's College and Cregan Professor of Modern Irish History at Dublin City University, invited me to compose a paper on American journalistic coverage of the Rising in 2006, the 90th anniversary year, and that planted the first seeds that developed over the next decade.

Felix M. Larkin, former chairman of the Newspaper and Periodical History Forum of Ireland, provided numerous research references of considerable value as this book took shape. Moreover, I learned much, usually at most pleasant Dublin lunches, by talking with Cathal Goan, Cathal Mac Coille, and Ed Mulhall.

In addition, Anne Kilmer Hillis and Miriam Kilmer provided invaluable background about their grandfather, Joyce Kilmer, which enriched my understanding of him and his writing. Many other generous people in Ireland and in America, really too numerous to mention by name, offered their assistance along the way. Without them and those who are cited, you wouldn't be holding this book in your hands or reading these words. A large, transatlantic thank-you to them for making what is here possible—and this author profoundly indebted.

At the Oxford University Press, Timothy Bent, the Executive Editor of Trade History in New York, made wise suggestions for improving the manuscript each step of the way. It was a genuine pleasure to work with Tim once again, as well as Editorial Assistant Alyssa O'Connell and everyone else at OUP. Copy editor Carole Berglie provided stylistic and punctuational reactions with an unblinking professionalism that improved the manuscript throughout.

As it happened, a few hours after typing the concluding pages of the first draft of the epilogue into the computer, I started to experience some physical discomfort of mysterious origin. A late-night trip to the emergency room of a local hospital was the first adventure on the way to a quadruple heart bypass and nearly two weeks in intensive care prior to a lengthy recovery. Then, a little over a year later and while making some final changes and additions to the manuscript, more chest distress resulted in another surgery involving what the cardiologist calls "the fuel lines"—and a couple more unwanted (and, frankly, unpleasant) incarcerations in the hospital.

This book is dedicated to my wife, Judy, who—with unwavering good cheer and love—has put up with an obsessive wordsmith and, more recently, a cardiac case. Difficult duty for anyone, to be sure.

Appendix
Irish Girl Rebel Tells of Dublin Fighting

Moira Regan, Now Here, Served in Post Office, the Headquarters
of the Irish Republic, and Carried Dispatches for the Leaders

By Joyce Kilmer

New York Times Magazine

August 20, 1916, pages 54–55

Moira Regan is a slight, gray-eyed girl. There is a charming flavor of County
Wexford in her manner and in her voice. But back of her gray eyes and charming manner there is a depth of tragic experience. For Moira Regan has worked
night and day in a beleaguered fort, has breathed air redolent with gunpow-
der, and heard the groans of men torn by shot and shell. She has seen her
friends led away to death, their bodies to be thrown into a pit of quicklime.
Moira Regan took part in the uprising in Dublin last Easter week, and did
active service in the Post Office, which was the headquarters of the forces of
the Irish Republic. She is now living in New York.

She tells of her experiences quietly, without gesture and without emotion.
But her voice is vibrant with restrained passion when she tells of the deaths of
Padraic Pearse, Joseph Plunkett, Thomas MacDonagh, and James Connolly,
and there is a strange fire in her gray eyes when she speaks of the April evening when for the first time she saw the flag of the Irish Republic floating on
its staff at the head of O'Connell Street.

Here is Moira Regan's story. It is more than the narrative of an eyewitness—
it is the narrative of a friend of and fellow-worker with Plunkett and Pearse
and MacDonagh—of one who shared with them the hopes, ambitions, perils,
and pains of their brief but great adventure.

"At 6 o'clock on the evening of Easter Monday I went down O'Connell Street
to the Post Office," she said. "But that was not my real entrance into the affairs
of the uprising. You see, I belonged to an organization called Cumann na

Mban—the Council of Women. We had been mobilized at noon on Monday near the Broad Stone Station, being told that we'd be needed for bandaging and other Red Cross work.

"But late in the afternoon we got word from the Commandant that we might disperse, since there would not be any street fighting that day, and so our services would not be needed. The place where we were mobilized is three or four blocks from the Post Office, and we could hear the shooting clearly. There were various rumors about—we were told that the Castle had been taken, and Student's Green and other points of vantage. And at last, as I said, we were told that there would be no street fighting, and that we were to go away from the Broad Stone Station and do what good we could.

"When I got to the Post Office that evening I found that the windows were barricaded with bags of sand, and at each of them were two men with rifles. The front office had been made the headquarters of the staff, and there I saw James Connolly, who was in charge of the Dublin division; Padriac Pearse, Willie Pearse, O'Rahilly, Plunkett, Shane MacDiarmid [Seán Mac Diarmada], Tom Clarke, and others sitting at tables writing out orders and receiving messengers.

"On my way to the Post Office I met a friend of mine who was carrying a message. He asked me had I been inside, and when I told him I had not, he got James Connolly to let me in.

"I didn't stay at the Post Office then, but made arrangements to return later. From the Post Office I went to Stephen's Green. The Republican army held the square. The men were busy making barricades and commandeering motor cars. They got a good many cars from British officers coming in from the Fairy House races.

"The Republican army had taken possession of a great many of the public houses. This fact was made much of by the English, who spread broadcast the report that the rebels had taken possession of all the drinking places in Dublin and were lying about the streets dead drunk. As a matter of fact, the rebels did no drinking at all. They took possession of the public houses because in Dublin these usually are large buildings in commanding positions at the corners of the streets. Therefore the public houses were places of strategic importance, especially desirable as forts.

"That night there was not much sleeping done at our house or at any other house in Dublin, I suppose. All night long we could hear the rifles cracking—scattered shots for the most part, and now and then a regular fusillade.

"On Tuesday I went again to the Post Office to find out where certain people, including my brother, should go in order to join up with the Republican forces. I found things quiet at headquarters, little going on except the regular executive work. Tuesday afternoon my brother took up his position in the Post Office, and my sister and I went there, too, and were set at work in the kitchen. There we found about ten English soldiers at work—that is, they wore the English uniform, but they were Irishmen. They did not seem at all sorry that they had been captured, and peeled potatoes and washed dishes uncomplainingly. The officers were imprisoned in another room.

"The rebels had captured many important buildings. They had possession of several big houses on O'Connell Street near the Post Office. They had taken the Imperial Hotel, which belongs to Murphy, Dublin's great capitalist, and had turned it into a hospital. We found the kitchen well supplied with food. We made big sandwiches of beef and cheese, and portioned out milk and beef tea. There were enough provisions to last for three weeks.

"About fifteen girls were at work in the kitchen. Some of them were members of the Cumann na Mban, and others were relatives or friends of the Republican army which James Connolly commanded. Some of the girls were not more than sixteen years old.

"We worked nearly all Tuesday night, getting perhaps an hour's sleep on mattresses on the floor. The men were shooting from the windows of the Post Office, and the soldiers were shooting at us, but not one of our men was injured. We expected that the Inniskillings would move on Dublin from the north, but no attack was made that night.

"On Wednesday I was sent out on an errand to the north side of the city. O'Rahilly was in charge of the prisoners, and he was very eager that the letters of the prisoners should be taken to their families. He gave me the letter of one of the English officers to take to his wife, who lived out beyond Drumcondra. It was a good long walk, and I can tell you that I blessed that English officer and his wife before I delivered that letter!

"As I went on my way, I noticed a great crowd of English soldiers marching down on the Post Office from the north. The first of them were only two blocks away from the Post Office, and the soldiers extended as far north as we went—that is, as far as Drumcondra. But nobody interfered with us—all those days the people walked freely around the streets of Dublin without being interfered with.

"As we walked back, we saw that the British troops were setting up machine guns near the Post Office. We heard the cracking of rifles and other sounds which indicated that a real siege was beginning. At Henry Street, near the Post Office, we were warned not to cross over, because a gunboat on the river was shelling Kelly's house—a big place at the corner of the quay. So we turned back and stayed that night with friends on the north side of the town. Our home was on the south side.

"There was heavy firing all night. The firing was especially severe at the Four Courts and down near Ring's End [Ringsend] and Fairview. The streets were crowded with British soldiers; a whole division landed from Kingstown.

"That was Wednesday night. On Thursday we thought we'd have another try at the Post Office. By devious ways we succeeded, after a long time, in reaching it and getting in. We found the men in splendid form, and everything seemed to be going well. But the rebels were already hopelessly outnumbered. The Sherwood Foresters had begun to arrive Tuesday night, and on Wednesday and Thursday other regiments came to reinforce them. Now, a division in the British Army consists of 25,000 men, so you can see that the British were taking the rising seriously enough.

"The British soldiers brought with them all their equipment as if they were prepared for a long war. They had field guns and field kitchens, and everything else. Most of them came in by Boland's Mills, where de Valera was in command. They suffered several reverses, and many of them were shot down.

"The chief aim of the British was, first of all, to cut off the Post Office. So on Thursday messengers came to Pearse and Connolly, reporting that the machine guns and other equipment were being trained on the Post Office. But the men were quite ready for this and were exceedingly cheerful. Indeed, the Post Office was the one place in Dublin that week where no one could help feeling cheerful. I didn't stay there long on Thursday morning, as I was sent out to take some messages to the south side. I had my own trouble getting through the ranks of soldiers surrounding the Post Office, and when I eventually delivered my messages I could not get back. The Post Office was now completely cut off.

"Thursday evening, Friday, and Saturday I heard many wild rumors, one insistent report being that the Post Office was burned down. As a matter of fact, the Post Office was set on fire Friday morning by means of an incendiary bomb which landed on top of the door. All the other houses held by the rebels had been burned to the ground, and the people who had been in them had gone to the Post Office, where there were now at least 400 men.

"The Post Office burned all day Friday, and late in the afternoon it was decided that it must be abandoned. First Father Flanagan, who had been there all the time, and the girls and a British officer—a Surgeon Lieutenant, who had been doing Red Cross work, were sent to Jervis Street Hospital through an underground passage. Then all the able-bodied men and James Connolly (who had broken his shin) tried to force their way out of the Post Office, to get to Four Courts, where the rebels were still holding out. They made three charges. In the first charge O'Rahilly was killed. In the second many of the men were wounded. In the third the rebels succeeded in reaching a house in Moor Lane [Moore Street] back of the Post Office. There they stayed all night. They had only a little food and their ammunition was almost exhausted. So on Saturday they saw that further resistance was useless, and that they ought to surrender, in order to prevent further slaughter.

"There were three girls with the men. They had chosen to attend Commandant Connolly when the other girls were sent away. One was now sent out with a white flag to parley with the British officers. At first she received nothing but insults, but eventually she was taken to Tom Clarke's shop, where the Brigadier General was stationed. Tom Clarke was a great rebel leader, one of the headquarters staff, so it was one of the ironies of fate that the General conducted his negotiations for the surrender of the rebels in his shop.

"Well, the Brigadier General told this girl to bring Padraic Pearse to him. Pearse came to him in Clarke's shop and surrendered. Pearse made the remark that he did not suppose it would be necessary for all his men to come and surrender.

"'But how,' said the General, 'can I be sure that all your men will lay down their arms?'

"'I will send an order to them,' said Pearse. And he called to him Miss Farrell, the girl who had been sent to the General, and asked her would she take his message to his men. She said she would, and so she took the note that he gave her to the rebel soldiers that were left alive, and they laid down their arms.

"There are a few things," said Moria Regan, "that I'd like every one in America to know about this rising, and about the way in which the British officers and soldiers acted. When the rebels surrendered they were at first treated with great courtesy. The British officers complimented them on the bold stand they had made, and said they wished they had men like them in the British Army. But after they had surrendered they were treated in the worst possible way. They were cursed and insulted, marched to the Rotunda Gardens, and made to spend the night there in the wet grass. They were not given a morsel of food.

"The man chiefly picked out for insult was Tom Clarke. He was very shamefully treated—it was a great contrast to the way in which the British officers spoke to him at the time of his surrender.

"The next morning the prisoners were marched to Richmond Barracks on the other side of the city from the Rotunda. One of the prisoners, Sean MacDiarmuid [Mac Diarmada], was very lame, but was obliged to march with the rest. And on the way the crowds of English soldiers in the streets kept shouting, 'Shoot the dogs! What's the use of taking them any further?'

"Now, all the headquarters staff had surrendered. Notice was sent around that a truce had been arranged. The priests had arranged this. Miss Farrell was sent around in a motor car with Pearse's note calling on all the rebels to surrender. Now, most of the fighting stopped, except for sniping from the roofs, and for some heavy fighting at Ring's End [Ringsend], which continued for two days.

"The treatment of the prisoners in the jails was horrible. Many of the men arrested were not at all in sympathy with the Sinn Fein movement. The British arrested every one who had advocated the restoration of the Irish language, or had lectured on Irish literature, or had worked for the cause of Irish manufactures—they arrested every one, indeed, who had been conspicuously associated with anything definitely Irish.

"In one small room eighty-four prisoners were kept for two weeks. For two days they were not permitted to leave the room at all for any purpose. For thirty-seven hours they were without food. Then some dog biscuits were thrown in among them and they were given a bucket of tea. Later they were taken out of the room once a day. All their money was taken from them, but a few of them managed to hide a shilling or so, which they used to buy water of the soldiers.

"After the court-martial they were taken to Kilmainham Jail. There they were put into the criminal cells, without even plank beds. I went to visit one of the leaders, a particular friend of mine, and there was in his cell a blanket and a coverlet—nothing else at all.

"The night before they were to die the prisoners were left to write letters, and some of them were permitted to receive visitors for the first time since their capture. Padraic Pearse was not allowed to see any one. MacDonagh was not allowed to see his wife; he was allowed to see his sister, a nun. The food given them was scanty in quantity and poor in quality. On the morning that he was shot he was given for breakfast a little dry, uncooked cereal, with nothing to put on it.

"The prisoners were shot in the yard of Kilmainham Jail. Then the bodies were taken, in their clothes, outside Dublin to Arbor Hill Barracks and thrown into quicklime in one large trench. In every case the bodies were refused to the relatives of the dead men.

"One thing that would strike you about the conduct of the rebels was the absolute equality of the men and women. The women did first-aid work and cooking, and some of them used their rifles to good advantage. They just did the work that was before them, and they were of the greatest moral aid.

"About eighty women were taken prisoner and thrown into cells in Kilmainham Jail. There were no jail matrons; there was no one in charge of them but soldiers, who took every opportunity to insult them. They were not allowed to leave their cells for any purpose for two days. They were treated just as the men prisoners were treated. The women slept over the yard while the men were shot. They would be awakened in the morning by the sound of the quick march, the brusque command, and the sound of the rifles. One woman imprisoned in Kilmainham Jail was the Countess Plunkett."

Moira Regan was asked what advantages had come to Ireland as a result of this insurrection.

"Well," she replied, "for one thing it has shown England that things in Ireland are not all right—that Ireland is not 'the one bright spot'—that Castle Government in Ireland is a perilous thing. It has made conscription in Ireland impossible. And had it not been for the rising we should have had conscription by now. And Ireland cannot spare any more men. As it is, a great many of the young men of Ireland joined the British Army, being led to do so by Redmond's urging and by the plea that Ireland should fight for Belgium, and that the small nations of the world should stand together. This was Redmond's great recruiting argument. I wonder how he reconciles this with the words he used to Asquith the other day in the House of Commons when he said: 'You betrayed Belgium, now you are betraying Ireland!'

"But the greatest result of the rising, the thing that will justify it even if it were the only good result, is the complete and amazing revival of Irish nationality. We have been asleep—we had been ready to acquiesce in things as they were, to take jobs under the Castle Government and to acquiesce in the unnatural state of affairs. But now we have been awakened to the knowledge that there is a great difference between Ireland and England, that we are really a separate nation. Even the people who were not in sympathy with the rebels feel this now.

"We have been living in a country that had no national life. And suddenly we were shown that we had a national life—that we were a nation, a persecuted and crushed nation, but, nevertheless, a nation.

"You cannot understand the joy of this feeling unless you have lived in a nation whose spirit had been crushed and then suddenly revived. I felt that evening, when I saw the Irish flag floating over the Post Office in O'Connell Street, that this was a thing worth living and dying for. I was absolutely intoxicated and carried away with joy and pride in knowing that I had a nation. This feeling has spread all over Ireland; it has remained and it is growing stronger. We were a province, and now we are a nation; we were British subjects, and now we are Irish. This is what the rising of Easter week has done for Ireland."

Notes

PROLOGUE

1. Emma Lazarus, *The Poems of Emma Lazarus in Two Volumes* (Cambridge, Mass.: Riverside, 1889), 1: 203.
2. For population statistics, see Francis M. Carroll, "America and the 1916 Rising," in *1916: The Long Revolution*, ed. Gabriel Doherty and Dermot Keogh (Cork: Mercier, 2007), 122.
3. "Complimentary Festival in Honor of John Mitchel," *The Sun* (Baltimore), 21 December 1853, 1.
4. Shane Leslie, *The Irish Issue in Its American Aspect: A Contribution to the Settlement of Anglo-American Relations During and After the Great War* (New York: Charles Scribner's Sons, 1917), 183–184.
5. Leslie, *Irish Issue*, 184.
6. Kevin B. Nowlan, "Tom Clarke, Mac Dermott, and the IRB," in *Leaders and Men of the Easter Rising: Dublin 1916*, ed. F. X. Martin OSA (London: Methuen, 1967), 117.
7. See Margaret Macmillan, *The War That Ended Peace: The Road to 1914* (New York: Random House, 2013), 523–525 and 578–579; and David Reynolds, *The Long Shadow: The Legacies of the Great War in the Twentieth Century* (New York: W. W. Norton, 2014), 19–25.
8. Keith Jeffery, *Ireland and the Great War* (Cambridge: Cambridge University Press, 2000), 52.
9. For statistical information about the Rising, see R. F. Foster, *Modern Ireland 1600–1972* (London: Allen Lane, 1988), 483; and George Dangerfield, *The Damnable Question: A History of Anglo-Irish Relations* (Boston: Little, Brown, 1976), 207–208.
10. Conor Cruise O'Brien, foreword, *The Shaping of Modern Ireland*, ed. Conor Cruise O'Brien (London: Routledge & Kegan Paul, 1960), 3.
11. *Weekly Irish Times, 1916 Rebellion Handbook* (1916; Belfast: Mourne River, 1998), 38.

12. Michael Laffan, *The Resurrection of Ireland: The Sinn Féin Party, 1916–1923* (Cambridge: Cambridge University Press, 1999), 54.

13. A. J. P. Taylor, *The First World War: An Illustrated History* (London: Hamish Hamilton, 1963), 110.

14. See Stephen Walker, *Forgotten Soldiers: The Irishmen Shot at Dawn* (Dublin: Gill & Macmillan, 2008).

15. See Felix M. Larkin, "No Longer a Political Side Show: T. R. Harrington and the 'New' *Irish Independent*, 1905–31," in *Independent Newspapers: A History*, ed. Mark O'Brien and Kevin Rafter (Dublin: Four Courts, 2012), 35–36.

16. Eric Hobsbawn, *The Age of Empire 1875–1914* (New York: Pantheon, 1987), 287.

17. Shane Leslie, letter to John Redmond, 15 May 1916, Ms. 15,236/14, Papers of John Redmond, National Library of Ireland, Dublin.

18. Michael J. Ryan, telegram to John Redmond, 15 May 1916, Ms. 15,236/24, Papers of John Redmond, National Library of Ireland, Dublin.

19. See "Mr. John Redmond. Irish Leader Dead. 'A Broken-Hearted Man,'" *Sydney Morning Herald*, 8 March 1918, 7.

20. *Weekly Irish Times, 1916 Rebellion Handbook*, 151.

21. In his probing exegesis *On the Easter Proclamation and Other Declarations*, Liam de Paor explains that the American Founders drafted "the charter of a new political age" with significant reverberations that transcended the time and place of its origin (Dublin: Four Courts, 1997), 16.

22. Tim Pat Coogan, *Michael Collins: A Biography* (1990; London: Arrow, 1991), 53–54.

23. Coogan, *Michael Collins*, 54.

24. Michael Collins, *The Path to Freedom* (1922; Dublin: Mercier, 1995), 55.

25. "Shaw Denounces Shootings," *New York Times*, 11 May 1916, 3.

26. Bernard Shaw, *Prefaces* (London: Constable, 1934), 469.

27. Shaw, *Prefaces*, 470.

28. Shaw, *Prefaces*, 469.

29. "Would Fight for Erin," *Washington Post*, 15 May 1916, 1, 10.

30. J. J. Lee, *Ireland 1912–1985: Politics and Society* (Cambridge: Cambridge University Press, 1989), 29.

31. Maureen Dezell, *Irish America: Coming into Clover* (New York: Doubleday, 2001), 102. According to the Library of Congress, the recording date was 19 July 1916.

CHAPTER 1

1. John O'Connor, *The 1916 Proclamation*, rev. ed. (Dublin: Anvil, 1999), 10.

2. Desmond Ryan, "Stephens, Devoy, Tom Clarke," in *The Shaping of Modern Ireland*, ed. Conor Cruise O'Brien (London: Routledge & Kegan Paul, 1960), 32.

3. Desmond Ryan, *The Phoenix Flame: A Study of Fenianism and John Devoy* (London: Arthur Barker, 1937), 74.

4. Kerby A. Miller, *Emigrants and Exiles: Ireland and the Irish Exodus to North America* (New York: Oxford University Press, 1985), 346.

5. John Rutherford, *The Secret History of the Fenian Conspiracy: Its Origin, Objects, & Ramifications* (London: C. Kegan Paul, 1877), 1: 15. Italics in the original.

6. Philip H. Bagenal, *The American Irish and Their Influence on Irish Politics* (Boston: Roberts Brothers, 1882), 109–110.

7. Quoted by Conor Cruise O'Brien, *States of Ireland* (London: Hutchinson, 1972), 45.

8. See Patrick O'Farrell, *Ireland's English Question: Anglo-Irish Relations 1534–1970* (New York: Schocken, 1971), 109.

9. O'Brien, *States of Ireland*, 45.

10. Thomas N. Brown, *Irish-American Nationalism, 1870–1890* (Philadelphia: J. B. Lippincott, 1966), 37.

11. Brown, *Irish-American Nationalism*, 38.

12. O'Connor, *The 1916 Proclamation*, 10.

13. Quoted in Bagenal, *The American Irish*, 223.

14. Bagenal, *The American Irish*, 223. Italics in the original.

15. William O'Brien and Desmond Ryan, eds., *Devoy's Post Bag* (Dublin: Fallon, 1948), 2: 109.

16. Thomas N. Brown, "The Origins and Character of Irish-American Nationalism," in *The Image of Man*, ed. M. A. Fitzsimons et al. (Notre Dame: University of Notre Dame Press, 1959), 376.

17. Ryan, *Phoenix Flame*, 321.

18. See Seamus de Burca, *The Soldier's Song: The Story of Peadar O Cearnaigh* (Dublin: P. J. Bourke, 1957), especially ch. 8.

19. Quoted in Ruth Dudley Edwards, *James Connolly* (Dublin: Gill & Macmillan, 1981), 50.

20. Miller, *Emigrants and Exiles*, 544.

21. James Connolly, "Harp Strings," *The Harp* 1, no. 12 (December 1908): 2.

22. James Connolly Heron, ed., *The Words of James Connolly* (Cork: Mercier, 1986), 121.

23. Terry Golway, *Irish Rebel: John Devoy and America's Fight for Ireland's Freedom* (New York: St. Martin's, 1998), 193.

24. Sean Cronin, *The McGarrity Papers* (Tralee: Anvil Books, 1972), 34.

25. Ruth Dudley Edwards, *Patrick Pearse: The Triumph of Failure* (1977; Dublin: Irish Academic Press, 2006), 184.

26. Edwards, *Patrick Pearse*, 78–79.

27. Padraic Pearse, *Collected Works of Padraic H. Pearse: Political Writings and Speeches* (Dublin: Maunsel & Roberts, 1922), 71.
28. Pearse, *Collected Works*, 72.
29. Pearse, *Collected Works*, 80.
30. Pearse, *Collected Works*, 86.
31. Ryan, *Phoenix Flame*, 293.
32. Edwards, *Patrick Pearse*, 197.
33. John Devoy, *Recollections of an Irish Rebel* (New York: Charles P. Young, 1929), 332.
34. Devoy, *Recollections*, 332.
35. Pearse, *Collected Works*, 136–137.
36. Devoy, *Recollections*, 332.
37. John Devoy, letter to Joseph McGarrity, 24 August 1915, Maloney Collection of Irish Historical Papers, New York Public Library.
38. See Honor O Brolchain, *Joseph Plunkett* (Dublin: O'Brien, 2012), 323–332.
39. Thomas MacDonagh, letter to Dominick [J. D.] Hackett, 15 March 1909, Ms. 22,934, National Library of Ireland, Dublin.
40. "All Irish Leaders Shot; Disaffection in Dublin," *Los Angeles Times,* 13 May 1916, 12.
41. Kevin Kenny, *The American Irish: A History* (New York: Longman, 2000), 173.
42. Devoy, *Recollections*, 407.
43. Giovanni Costigan, "The Treason of Roger Casement," *American Historical Review* 60 (1955): 297.
44. Devoy, *Recollections*, 403.
45. John Devoy, "Some Facts About Easter Week, 1916," *The Gaelic American,* 23 September 1922, 2. Italics in the original.
46. Devoy, *Recollections*, 432.
47. In his *Asquith: Portrait of a Man and an Era*, Roy Jenkins writes: "On August 3rd Casement was hanged. There can be few other examples of a Cabinet devoting large parts of four separate meetings to considering an individual sentence—and then arriving at the wrong decision. The effect in the United States was as bad as it could have been. In Ireland, Casement became a martyr. And even in England the effects of the case reverberated on for forty years or more" (New York: Chilmark, 1964), 404.
48. Devoy, *Recollections*, 393.
49. *Weekly Irish Times, 1916 Rebellion Handbook* (1916; Belfast: Mourne River, 1998), 157.
50. Devoy, *Recollections*, 457.
51. "Documents Relative to the Sinn Fein Movement," *The Irish Uprising, 1914–21: Papers from the British Parliamentary Archive* (London: Stationery Office, 2000), 34.

52. John Devoy, letter to Joseph McGarrity, 19 April 1916, Maloney Collection of Irish Historical Papers, New York Public Library.

53. John Devoy, letter to Joseph McGarrity, 1 March 1916, Joseph McGarrity Collection, Ms. 17,609 (4), National Library of Ireland, Dublin.

54. John Devoy, letter to Joseph McGarrity, 18 July 1916, Joseph McGarrity Collection, Ms. 17,609 (4), National Library of Ireland, Dublin.

55. "Betrayal of Plot Denied by Lansing," *New York Times,* 28 April 1916, 1.

56. "Irish Organ Attacks President Wilson," *New York Times,* 28 April 1916, 2.

57. "Irishmen Uphold Revolt in Dublin," *New York Times,* 1 May 1916, 2.

58. "Call Executed Men Martyrs to Cause," *New York Times,* 4 May 1916, 2.

59. "Egan Denounces Devoy," *New York Times,* 4 May 1916, 2.

60. "Raid Irish Meeting Here," *New York Times,* 6 May 1916, 4.

61. "Praise Irish, Score England," *Boston Globe,* 8 May 1916, 1, 3.

62. "Says Next Revolt Will Win," *New York Times,* 8 May 1916, 6.

63. "Inside History of the Easter Week Rebellion," *The Gaelic American,* 29 July 1916, 1.

64. "Sir Roger Casement Arraigned in Court," *The Gaelic American,* 20 May 1916, 6.

65. "Lying for England," *The Gaelic American,* 5 August 1916, 3.

66. Devoy, *Recollections,* 439.

67. O'Brien and Ryan, *Devoy's Post Bag,* 2: 503.

68. J. J. Lee, *Ireland 1912–1985: Politics and Society* (Cambridge: Cambridge University Press, 1989), 24.

69. O'Brien and Ryan, *Devoy's Post Bag,* 2: 504.

70. O'Brien and Ryan, *Devoy's Post Bag,* 2: 505.

71. Ryan, "Stephens, Devoy, Tom Clarke," in O'Brien, *Shaping,* 30.

72. Devoy, *Recollections,* 470.

73. "Wilson Bitterly Hates the Irish," editorial, *The Gaelic American,* 7 October 1916, 4.

74. See Golway, *Irish Rebel,* 158.

75. In his *With De Valera in America,* Patrick McCartan writes: "I was making preparations for sailing when de Valera arrived suddenly in New York. . . . He had come as a stowaway. Ship rats had eaten into the bundle of clothes in which he had intended to come ashore" (New York: Brentano, 1932), 137.

76. Golway, *Irish Rebel,* 275.

77. T. Desmond Williams, "John Devoy and Jeremiah O'Donovan Rossa," in *The Fenian Movement,* ed. T. W. Moody (Cork: Mercier, 1978), 96.

78. Quoted in Charles Callan Tansill, *America and the Fight for Irish Freedom 1866–1922: An Old Story Based Upon New Data* (New York: Devin-Adair, 1957), 389.

79. Quoted in Tim Pat Coogan, *De Valera: Long Fellow, Long Shadow* (London: Hutchinson, 1993), 161.

80. Quoted in Golway, *Irish Rebel*, 271.

81. See John Devoy, "John Devoy's Objections," *The Gaelic American,* 14 February 1920, 1.

82. Coogan, *De Valera*, 139.

83. Quoted in Golway, *Irish Rebel*, 282.

84. Quoted in Golway, *Irish Rebel*, 311.

85. Quoted in Golway, *Irish Rebel*, 313–314.

86. Quoted in Golway, *Irish Rebel*, 314.

87. "Mr. John Devoy," *London Times,* 1 October 1928, 19.

88. Terence Dooley, *"The Greatest of the Fenians": John Devoy and Ireland* (Dublin: Wolfhound Press, 2003), 3.

89. de Burca, *Soldier's Song*, 89.

90. de Burca, *Soldier's Song*, 92.

91. "The Late Mr. John Devoy," *Irish Times,* 17 June 1929, 5.

92. Pearse, *Collected Works*, 127.

CHAPTER 2

1. Charles Townshend, *Easter 1916: The Irish Rebellion* (2005; London: Penguin, 2006), 246.

2. "Shaw Declares Revolt Silly—But Honorable," *The World* (New York), 4 May 1916, 1.

3. Joyce Kilmer, *Trees & Other Poems* (Garden City, N.Y.: Doubleday, 1914), 19.

4. Thomas Lask, "Brooks, 40 Years Later, Says New Criticism Was Misunderstood," *New York Times,* 28 May 1979, C11.

5. Cleanth Brooks Jr. and Robert Penn Warren, *Understanding Poetry: An Anthology for College Students* (New York: Henry Holt, 1938), 387.

6. "Trees," *Irish Times,* 1 July 1961, 9.

7. See Robert Hass et al., eds., *American Poetry: The Twentieth Century* (New York: Library of America, 2000), 1: 651.

8. Joyce Kilmer, *Main Street and Other Poems* (New York: George H. Doran, 1917), 78.

9. Joyce Kilmer, "Poets Marched in the Van of Irish Revolt," *New York Times Magazine,* 7 May 1916, 3.

10. Kilmer, "Poets Marched," 3.

11. Kilmer, "Poets Marched," 4.

12. W. B. Yeats, "Man and the Echo," in *The Collected Poems of W. B. Yeats*, ed. Richard J. Finneran, rev. 2nd ed. (New York: Scribner Paperback Poetry, 1996), 345.

13. Kilmer, "Poets Marched," 4.

14. "Dublin Is Still Cut Off," *New York Times,* 28 April 1916, 1.

15. Mary E. Daly, "Less a Commemoration of the Actual Achievements and More a Commemoration of the Hopes of the Men of 1916," in *1916 in 1966: Commemorating the Easter Rising,* ed. Mary E. Daly and Margaret O'Callaghan (Dublin: Royal Irish Academy, 2007), 25.

16. "Fate of Sir Roger Casement," *New York Times,* 26 April 1916, 12.

17. "Casement's Case and Tone's," *New York Times,* 27 April 1916, 12.

18. "Ireland," editorial, *New York Times,* 29 April 1916, 10.

19. "The Irish Folly," editorial, *New York Times,* 2 May 1916, 12.

20. "Fate of the Irish Rebels," editorial, *New York Times,* 4 May 1916, 10.

21. "Premier Asquith Goes to Ireland to Investigate," *New York Times,* 12 May 1916, 1.

22. "Irish Rebels," editorial, *New York Times,* 12 May 1916, 10.

23. Elmer Davis, *History of the New York Times: 1851–1921* (New York: New York Times, 1921), 345.

24. Meyer Berger, *The Story of the New York Times, 1851–1951* (New York: Simon and Schuster, 1951), 211.

25. James Leonard Bates, *Senator Thomas J. Walsh of Montana: Law and Public Affairs, from TR to FDR* (Urbana: University of Illinois Press, 1999), 1.

26. Berger, *The Story,* 210.

27. Berger, *The Story,* 528.

28. "The Outbreak in Ireland," editorial, *Washington Post,* 26 April 1916, 6.

29. "The Irish Uprising," editorial, *Washington Post,* 2 May 1916, 6.

30. "The Irish Revolt," editorial, *Chicago Tribune,* 2 May 1916, 6.

31. "Unnecessary and Inexpedient," editorial, *Chicago Tribune,* 5 May 1916, 6.

32. "Irish Executions," editorial, *Washington Post,* 7 May 1916, 4.

33. Jay P. Dolan, *The Irish Americans: A History* (New York: Bloomsbury, 2008), 201.

34. "Poets Mourn Sinn Fein Dead," *New York Tribune,* 29 June 1916, 11.

35. "Memorial to Irish Poets," *New York Times,* 29 June 1916, 9.

36. Joyce Kilmer, "Easter Week," in *Main Street and Other Poems* (New York: George H. Doran, 1917), 66–67.

37. Augustine Martin, "To Make a Right Rose Tree: Reflections on the Poetry of 1916," *Studies* 55, no. 217 (1966): 45.

38. John Jerome Rooney, letter to Joyce Kilmer, 31 March 1917, Joyce Kilmer Papers, Georgetown University Library Special Collections Research Center, Washington, D.C.

39. Joyce Kilmer, "Apology," in Kilmer, *Main Street,* 32.

40. Joyce Kilmer, *Poems, Essays and Letters in Two Volumes,* ed. Robert Cortes Holliday (New York: George H. Doran, 1918), 2: 196.

41. Kilmer, *Poems, Essays*, 2: 196.

42. Robert Cortes Holliday, "Memoir," in Kilmer, *Poems, Essays*, 1: 18.

43. Kenton Kilmer, *Memories of My Father, Joyce Kilmer* (New Brunswick, N.J.: Joyce Kilmer Centennial Commission, 1993), 103.

44. K. Kilmer, *Memories*, 104.

45. K. Kilmer, *Memories*, 104.

46. Miriam A. Kilmer, "Joyce Kilmer: Frequently Asked Questions," at risingdove .com/Kilmer/FAQ.asp, 2014.

47. Holliday, "Memoir," in Kilmer, *Poems, Essays*, 1: 53.

48. Joyce Kilmer, "Lionel Johnson, Ernest Dowson, Aubrey Beardsley," in *The Circus and Other Essays and Fugitive Pieces*, ed. Robert Cortes Holliday (New York: George H. Doran, 1921), 250.

49. Joyce Kilmer, "Irish Girl Rebel Tells of Dublin Fighting," *New York Times Magazine*, 20 August 1916, 4.

50. Kilmer, "Irish Girl Rebel," 5.

51. Kilmer, "Irish Girl Rebel," 5.

52. John Quinn, "Roger Casement, Martyr," *New York Times Magazine*, 13 August 1916, 4.

53. "Press Censorship Records 1916–1919," box 3, folder 128, National Archives of Ireland, Dublin. In *The Pity of War*, Niall Ferguson reports: "In 1916 alone the Press Bureau, assisted by the secret service department MI7 (a) [the censorship subsection], scrutinized over 38,000 articles, 25,000 photographs, and no fewer than 300,000 private telegrams. Metternich would have been envious" (London: Allen Lane, 1998), 221.

54. "How the Irish Press Is Gagged," *The Gaelic American*, 8 July 1916, 5.

55. "Press Censorship Records 1916–1919," box 1, folder 30, National Archives of Ireland, Dublin.

56. "Press Censorship Records," box 1, folder 30.

57. "Press Censorship Records," box 1, folder 30.

58. "Press Censorship Records," box 1, folder 30.

59. "Press Censorship Records," box 1, folder 30.

60. "Military Tightens Grip on Ireland," *New York Times*, 22 August 1916, 4.

61. "Vanities of Martyrdom," editorial, *New York Times*, 30 June 1916, 10.

62. Roy J. Harris Jr., *Pulitzer's Gold: Behind the Prize for Public Service Journalism* (Columbia: University of Missouri Press, 2007), 111.

63. Harris, *Pulitzer's Gold*, 384.

64. "Meaningless, Therefore Important?" *New York Times*, 29 April 1916, 10.

65. "The Irish Outbreak," editorial, *The Nation*, 4 May 1916, 471.

66. "The Irish Executions," editorial, *The Nation*, 11 May 1916, 509–510.

67. William Dean Howells, letter, *The Nation*, 18 May 1916, 541.

68. Henry W. Nevinson, "Sir Roger Casement and Sinn Fein," *Atlantic Monthly*, August 1916, 242.

69. Nevinson, "Sir Roger Casement," 243.

70. Holliday, "Memoir," in Kilmer, *Poems, Essays*, 1: 76.

71. Joyce Kilmer, "Irish-American Opinion on the Home Rule Deadlock," Joyce Kilmer Papers, box 3, folder 18, Georgetown University Library Special Collections Research Center, Washington, D.C.

72. Kilmer, "Irish-American Opinion," box 3, folder 18.

73. Holliday, "Memoir," in Kilmer, *Poems, Essays*, 1: 78–79.

74. Kilmer, *Poems, Essays*, 2: 136–137.

75. Kilmer, *Poems, Essays*, 2: 141.

76. Kilmer, *Poems, Essays*, 1: 112.

77. Quoted in "Joyce Kilmer," *The Literary Digest*, 7 September 1918, 32.

78. Quoted in "Joyce Kilmer," *The Literary Digest*, 32.

79. "English Tribute to Joyce Kilmer," *New York Times*, 27 October 1918, 43.

80. "Publisher's Note," in Joyce Kilmer, *Trees and Other Poems* (London: Duckworth, 1941), 11.

81. See the sheet music: "When the Sixty-Ninth Comes Back" (New York: M. Witmark & Sons, 1919).

82. Francis P. Duffy, *Father Duffy's Story: A Tale of Humor and Heroism, Of Life and Death with the Fighting Sixty-Ninth* (Garden City, N.Y.: Garden City Publishing, 1919), viii.

83. Joyce Kilmer, "Historical Appendix," in Duffy, *Father Duffy's Story*, 339.

84. Duffy, *Father Duffy's Story*, 97.

CHAPTER 3

1. Quoted in Joseph P. Tumulty, *Woodrow Wilson as I Know Him* (Garden City, N.Y.: Doubleday, Page, 1921), 476.

2. Arthur S. Link, ed., *The Papers of Woodrow Wilson* (Princeton, N.J.: Princeton University Press, 1971), 11: 439.

3. Link, *Papers*, 19: 103.

4. Link, *Papers*, 24: 251.

5. Link, *Papers*, 25: 400.

6. Link, *Papers*, 25: 400–401.

7. Link, *Papers*, 25: 401.

8. Link, *Papers*, 30: 35–36.

9. U.S. Bureau of the Census, *Thirteenth Census of the United States: Taken in the Year 1910* (Abstract of the Census) (Washington, D.C.: Government Printing Office, 1913), 194–195.

10. Arthur S. Link, *Wilson: The Road to the White House* (Princeton, N.J.: Princeton University Press, 1947), 32.

11. Sigmund Freud and William C. Bullitt, *Thomas Woodrow Wilson: A Psychological Study* (1967; New Brunswick, N.J.: Transaction, 1999), 107.

12. Freud and Bullitt, *Thomas Woodrow Wilson*, 108.

13. Edmund Morris, *Colonel Roosevelt* (New York: Random House, 2010), 419.

14. Morris, *Colonel Roosevelt*, 420.

15. Count Bernstorff, *My Three Years in America* (London: Skeffington & Son, 1920), 24.

16. A. Scott Berg, *Wilson* (New York: G. P. Putnam, 2013), 5.

17. Link, *Papers*, 37: 57.

18. Link, *Papers*, 37: 115.

19. Link, *Papers*, 37: 116.

20. Link, *Papers*, 37: 168.

21. Link, *Papers*, 37: 467.

22. Bernadette Whelan, *United States Foreign Policy and Ireland: From Empire to Independence, 1913–29* (Dublin: Four Courts, 2006), 95.

23. F. Cunliffe-Owen, "Silent Ambassador, Sir Cecil Spring-Rice, Has Consistently Discouraged Frequent Attempts to Launch Pro-British Propaganda," *New York Herald*, 25 June 1916, Papers of Sir Cecil Spring Rice, CASRI 8/5, "Press Cuttings," file 3, Churchill College, University of Cambridge.

24. Stephen Gwynn, ed., *The Letters and Friendships of Sir Cecil Spring Rice* (Boston: Houghton Mifflin, 1929), 2: 331.

25. Gwynn, *Letters and Friendships*, 2: 335–336.

26. Gwynn, *Letters and Friendships*, 2: 338.

27. Cecil Spring Rice, despatch to Edward Gray, 1 May 1916, FO 371/2797, National Archives, Kew.

28. Cecil Spring Rice, telegram, 1 August 1916, FO 371/2798, National Archives, Kew.

29. Angus Mitchell, *Roger Casement* (Dublin: O'Brien, 2013), 335.

30. "American Press Résumé," 25 May 1916, WO 395/43, National Archives, Kew.

31. Gwynn, *Letters and Friendships*, 2: 309.

32. Gwynn, *Letters and Friendships*, 2: 341.

33. Ray Stannard Baker, *Woodrow Wilson: Life and Letters* (Garden City, N.Y.: Doubleday, Doran, 1937), 6: 353.

34. Link, *Papers*, 38: 132–133.

35. Link, *Papers*, 38: 286.

36. Link, *Papers*, 38: 289.

37. Link, *Papers*, 38: 317.

38. Joseph McGarrity, "Memorandum on 1916," Ms. 17,550, Joseph McGarrity Papers, National Library of Ireland, Dublin.

39. Woodrow Wilson, letter to Joseph Tumulty, 2 May 1916, file 3085, Woodrow Wilson Papers, Library of Congress, Washington, D.C.

40. Link, *Papers*, 37: 353.

41. Link, *Papers*, 37: 446. Italics in original letter from Doyle.

42. Link, *Papers*, 14: 184.

43. "Lynch Alive; British Get Request of President," *San Francisco Chronicle,* 20 May 1916, 3.

44. Woodrow Wilson Papers, 28 June 1916, file 3152, Library of Congress, Washington, D.C.

45. Robert P. Troy, letter to Woodrow Wilson, 11 July 1916, file 3152, Woodrow Wilson Papers, Library of Congress, Washington, D.C.

46. "Knights of St. Patrick Appeal for Casement," *San Francisco Chronicle,* 22 July 1916, 8.

47. Francis M. Carroll, *American Opinion and the Irish Question 1910–23* (Dublin: Gill & Macmillan, 1978), 72.

48. Joseph Tumulty, letter to Frank L. Polk, 9 June 1916, file 3152, Woodrow Wilson Papers, Library of Congress, Washington, D.C.

49. Link, *Papers*, 42: 24–25.

50. Gwynn, *Letters and Friendships*, 2: 392–393.

51. Link, *Papers*, 42: 93.

52. Link, *Papers*, 42: 223.

53. Link, *Papers*, 45: 560.

54. Link, *Papers*, 45: 560–561.

55. E. David Cronon, ed., *The Cabinet Diaries of Josephus Daniels: 1913–1921* (Lincoln: University of Nebraska Press, 1963), 265.

56. Hanna Sheehy-Skeffington, *Impressions of Sinn Féin in America* (Dublin: Davis, 1919), 27.

57. Sheehy-Skeffington, *Impressions*, 27.

58. Sheehy-Skeffington, *Impressions*, 29.

59. William O'Brien and Desmond Ryan, eds., *Devoy's Post Bag: 1871–1928* (Dublin: Fallon, 1948), 2: 519–520.

60. Link, *Papers*, 45: 537.

61. Link, *Papers*, 46: 321.

62. Fearghal McGarry, *The Rising: Ireland: Easter 1916* (Oxford: Oxford University Press, 2010), 10.

63. Robert Lansing, *The Peace Negotiations: A Personal Narrative* (Boston: Houghton Mifflin, 1921), 97–98.

64. Link, *Papers*, 46: 249.

65. Link, *Papers*, 48: 64.

66. Link, *Papers*, 48: 466.
67. Link, *Papers*, 48: 471–472.
68. Godfrey Hodgson, in *Woodrow Wilson's Right Hand: The Life of Colonel Edward M. House* (New Haven: Yale University Press, 2006), writes that House's influence was "arguably greater than any single adviser has ever had over an American president" (9). A more comprehensive treatment of the House–Wilson relationship is Charles E. Neu's *Colonel House: A Biography of Woodrow Wilson's Silent Partner* (New York: Oxford University Press, 2014).
69. In *Right Hand*, Hodgson quotes Wilson as saying of House: "He is my independent self. His thoughts and mine are one" (6).
70. Link, *Papers*, 49: 275.
71. Link, *Papers*, 49: 275–276.
72. Link, *Papers*, 51: 382.
73. Link, *Papers*, 53: 299.
74. Link, *Papers*, 53: 306.
75. Link, *Papers*, 54: 333. (House Joint Resolution 357 was introduced on 3 December 1918.)
76. Link, *Papers*, 54: 381.
77. Link, *Papers*, 55: 242–243.
78. Link, *Papers*, 55: 348.
79. Link, *Papers*, 55: 363–364.
80. "Wilson Won't Meet Cohalan with Irish," *New York Times,* 5 March 1919, 2.
81. Link, *Papers*, 55: 422.
82. Link, *Papers*, 55: 411–412.
83. Link, *Papers*, 55: 443.
84. Link, *Papers*, 56: 79.
85. Link, *Papers*, 56: 438.
86. David Lloyd George, *Memoirs of the Peace Conference* (New Haven: Yale University Press, 1939), 1: 147.
87. Lloyd George, *Memoirs*, 1: 139.
88. Lloyd George, *Memoirs*, 1: 145.
89. Lloyd George, *Memoirs*, 1: 149.
90. Link, *Papers*, 59: 368. The viewpoint of the American Commission for Irish Independence can be seen in the article " 'Up the Republic!'—Ireland Demands Freedom" by Edward F. Dunne, *Collier's*, 19 July 1919, 9, 24–28.
91. Link, *Papers*, 59: 604.
92. Link, *Papers*, 59: 646.
93. Link, *Papers*, 60: 298.
94. Link, *Papers*, 60: 385.
95. Link, *Papers*, 60: 386.
96. Link, *Papers*, 60: 387.

97. Link, *Papers*, 60: 387.

98. "Ireland's Appeal to President Wilson," Irish Large Books, item 85, National Library of Ireland, Dublin.

99. Jan Willem Schulte Nordholt, *Woodrow Wilson: A Life for World Peace*, trans. Herbert H. Rowen (Berkeley: University of California Press, 1991), 132.

100. Link, *Road*, 34.

101. Link, *Papers*, 61: 9.

102. Link, *Papers*, 61: 243.

103. Link, *Papers*, 61: 291.

104. Tumulty, *Wilson*, 392.

105. Tumulty, *Wilson*, 397.

106. Tumulty, *Wilson*, 407.

107. Hodgson, *Right Hand*, 245.

108. *Congressional Record*, 12 August 1919, 58: 3784.

109. Kevin Kenny, *The American Irish: A History* (New York: Longman, 2000), 197.

110. H. G. Wells, *The Shape of Things to Come* (1933; New York: Macmillan, 1936), 82–83.

111. See John Milton Cooper Jr., *Breaking the Heart of the World: Woodrow Wilson and the Fight for the League of Nations* (Cambridge: Cambridge University Press, 2001); and Gene Smith, *When the Cheering Stopped: The Last Years of Woodrow Wilson* (New York: Morrow, 1964).

112. See John Milton Cooper Jr., *Woodrow Wilson: A Biography* (2009; New York: Vintage, 2011), 565–567, 588.

113. Link, *Papers*, 67: 44.

114. Link, *Papers*, 67: 44.

115. Link, *Papers*, 67: 45.

116. Link, *Papers*, 59: 34.

117. Winston S. Churchill, *The World Crisis: 1911–1918* (1931; New York: Free Press, 2005), 695.

CHAPTER 4

1. See http://www.ucd.ie/archives/html/collections/devalera-eamon.htm.

2. Éamon de Valera, P 150/524, Papers of Eamon de Valera, Archives, University College Dublin. For the official text of de Valera's complete statement about his reprieve, see "Reprieve of Eamon de Valera," in Diarmaid Ferriter, *Judging Dev: A Reassessment of the Life and Legacy of Eamon de Valera* (Dublin: Royal Irish Academy, 2007), 49.

3. Birth certificate of "Edward de Valera," P 150/528, Papers of Eamon de Valera, Archives, University College Dublin.

4. Tim Pat Coogan, *De Valera: Long Fellow, Long Shadow* (London: Hutchinson, 1993), 9.

5. See David T. Dwane, *Early Life of Eamonn de Valera* (Dublin: Talbot, 1922); and David T. Dwane, *Early Life of Eamon de Valera* (Dublin: Talbot, 1927).

6. Charles Townshend, *Easter 1916: The Irish Rebellion* (2005; London: Penguin, 2006), 283.

7. Eamon de Valera, P 150/524, Papers of Eamon de Valera, Archives, University College Dublin.

8. León Ó Broin, *W. E. Wylie and the Irish Revolution 1916–1921* (Dublin: Gill & Macmillan, 1989), 32.

9. Ó Broin, *Wylie*, 33.

10. Ó Broin, *Wylie*, 34.

11. See three separate American newspaper articles, P 150/528, Papers of Eamon de Valera, Archives, University College Dublin.

12. "American Led Irish Rebels," *Boston Globe*, 9 July 1916, 4.

13. "American," *Boston Globe*, 4.

14. "American," *Boston Globe*, 4.

15. Senator James Wadsworth, letter to Rev. Thomas J. Wheelwright, 18 July 1916, P 150/528, Papers of Eamon de Valera, Archives, University College Dublin.

16. Eamon de Valera, P 150/524, Papers of Eamon de Valera, Archives, University College Dublin.

17. Eamon de Valera, P 150/524, Papers of Eamon de Valera, Archives, University College Dublin.

18. Eamon de Valera, P 150/524, Papers of Eamon de Valera, Archives, University College Dublin.

19. Eamon de Valera, P 150/524, Papers of Eamon de Valera, Archives, University College Dublin.

20. Eamon de Valera, P 150/524, Papers of Eamon de Valera, Archives, University College Dublin.

21. Earl of Longford and Thomas P. O'Neill, *Eamon de Valera* (London: Hutchinson, 1970), 50.

22. Owen Dudley Edwards, "American Aspects of the Rising," in *1916: The Easter Rising*, ed. Owen Dudley Edwards and Fergus Pyle (London: MacGibbon and Lee, 1968), 162.

23. Francis M. Carroll, *American Opinion and the Irish Question 1910–23* (Dublin: Gill & Macmillan, 1978), 63.

24. Owen Dudley Edwards, *Eamon de Valera* (Cardiff: GPC Books, 1987), 58.

25. John Dillon, letter to H. H. Asquith, 9 May 1916, 43/p. 64, Papers of Herbert Henry Asquith, Bodleian Library, University of Oxford.

26. General John Maxwell, telegram to H. H. Asquith, 9 May 1916, 43/p. 11, Papers of Herbert Henry Asquith, Bodleian Library, University of Oxford.

27. General John Maxwell, telegram to H. H. Asquith, 10 May 1916, 43/p. 18, Papers of Herbert Henry Asquith, Bodleian Library, University of Oxford.

28. Eamon de Valera, letter, 4 May 1916, National Museum of Ireland.

29. Neil Jordan, *Michael Collins: Film Diary and Screenplay* (London: Vintage, 1996), 74.

30. J. F. Moylan, letter to Edward Bell, 12 August 1916, HO 144/10309, National Archives, Kew.

31. "De Valera Comes Here to Get Help for Sinn Feiners," *New York Times,* 24 June 1919, 1, 4.

32. Patrick McCartan, *With De Valera in America* (New York: Brentano, 1932), 138.

33. McCartan, *With De Valera*, 147.

34. Dave Hannigan, *De Valera in America: The Rebel President's 1919 Campaign* (Dublin: O'Brien, 2008), 17.

35. George Dangerfield, *The Damnable Question: A History of Anglo-Irish Relations* (Boston: Little, Brown, 1976), 210.

36. Dwane, *Early Life of Eamonn de Valera*, 4.

37. Dwane, *Early Life of Eamonn de Valera*, 4–5.

38. Dwane, *Early Life of Eamonn de Valera*, 48.

39. Michael Doorley, *Irish-American Diaspora Nationalism: The Friends of Irish Freedom 1916–1935* (Dublin: Four Courts, 2005), 134–135.

40. David Rankin Barbee, "De Valera's Rise to Presidency Is Thrilling Drama," *Washington Post,* 13 March 1932, 13.

41. Barbee, "De Valera's Rise," 19.

42. Joseph A. Sexton, "The Irish Enigma," *Washington Post Magazine,* 14 August 1932, 1.

43. Francis Hackett, "Eamonn De Valera," *Saturday Evening Post,* 28 May 1932, 5.

44. Hackett, "De Valera," 4.

45. "Prime Minister of Freedom," *Time,* 25 March 1940, 32.

46. Seán Ó Faoláin, *The Life Story of Eamon de Valera* (Dublin: Talbot, 1933), 9.

47. Ó Faoláin, *Life Story*, 40–41.

48. Denis Gwynn, *De Valera* (London: Jarrolds, 1933), 41.

49. Gwynn, *De Valera*, 21.

50. Desmond Ryan, *Unique Dictator: A Study of Eamon de Valera* (London: Arthur Barker, 1936), 65–66.

51. Dorothy Macardle, *The Irish Republic: A Documented Chronicle of the Anglo-Irish Conflict and the Partitioning of Ireland, with a Detailed Account of the Period 1916–1923* (1937; Dublin: Wolfhound, 1999), 186.

52. T. Ryle Dwyer, *De Valera: The Man & The Myths* (Dublin: Poolbeg, 1991), 325.

53. Dwyer, *De Valera*, 134.

54. See the Joseph McGarrity Collection in the Falvey Memorial Library of Villanova University, which has extensive newspaper holdings, including the *Irish Press.*

55. Eamon de Valera, "Broadcast Speech to America on Lincoln's Birthday," 12 February 1933, *Recent Speeches and Broadcasts* (Dublin: Talbot, 1933), 57.

56. M. J. MacManus, *Eamon de Valera: A Biography* (1944; Dublin: Talbot, 1957 [additional matter]), 47.

57. R. M. F., "Eire's Man of Destiny," *Christian Science Monitor,* 17 June 1944, 18.

58. See Coogan, *De Valera,* 144–145.

59. "Legendary Irishman: Eamon de Valera," *New York Times,* 8 March 1957, 6.

60. Charles Callan Tansill, *America and the Fight for Irish Freedom 1866–1922: An Old Story Based Upon New Data* (New York: Devin-Adair, 1957), 202.

61. Seán T. O'Kelly, "Memoirs of Seán T.: Shadow of Death Hangs Over All," *Irish Press,* 15 July 1961, 9.

62. Kenneth P. O'Donnell and David F. Powers with Joe McCarthy, *"Johnny, We Hardly Knew Ye"* (Boston: Little, Brown, 1970), 367–368.

63. Patrick Murray, "Obsessive Historian: Eamon de Valera and the Policing of His Reputation," *Proceedings of the Royal Irish Academy* 101C, no. 2 (2001): 39.

64. "Toasts of the President [Lyndon B. Johnson] and President de Valera," 27 May 1964, The American Presidency Project, at http://www.presidency.ucsb.edu/ws/ ?pid=26272.

65. "Eamon de Valera Oral History Interview—9/15/1966," John F. Kennedy Library, 4.

66. Karl E. Meyer, "Easter Rising Showed All Colonials the Way," *Washington Post,* 10 April 1966, E4.

67. "De Valera, Ireland Rebel and Leader, Dies at 92," Associated Press, *Los Angeles Times,* 30 August 1975, A1.

68. Patrick O'Donovan, "De Valera, the Irish de Gaulle," *The Observer,* 31 August 1975, 8.

69. "A Maker of Ireland," editorial, *New York Times,* 30 August 1975, 18.

70. Albin Krebs, "Eamon de Valera, 92, Dies; Lifelong Fighter for Irish," *New York Times,* 30 August 1975, 1, 24.

71. Michael McInerny, "Eamon de Valera: 1882–1975," *Irish Times,* 30 August 1975, A1.

72. Ronan Fanning, "De Valera, Éamon ('Dev')," in *Dictionary of Irish Biography,* ed. James McGuire and James Quinn (Cambridge: Cambridge University Press, 2009), 3: 194.

73. Thomas Bartlett, *Ireland: A History* (Cambridge: Cambridge University Press, 2010), 393.

74. Seán Enright, *Easter Rising 1916: The Trials* (Sallins, Ireland: Merrion, 2014), 202.

75. Enright, *The Trials,* 202.

76. Enright, *The Trials*, 202.

77. Martin Gilbert, *First World War* (London: Weidenfeld and Nicolson, 1994), 242–243.

78. Morgan Llywelyn, *1916* (New York: Forge, 1998), 420.

79. Terry Eagleton, *The Truth About the Irish* (Dublin: New Island, 1999), 64.

80. Senia Pašeta, *Modern Ireland: A Very Short Introduction* (Oxford: Oxford University Press, 2003), 80.

81. Doorley, *Irish-American Diaspora Nationalism*, 74.

82. Joseph McCullough, *A Pocket History of Ireland* (Dublin: Gill & Macmillan, 2010), 192.

83. Fergal Keane, "Introduction," in Neil Hegarty, *Story of Ireland* (London: BBC Books, 2011), xvi.

84. Ronan Fanning, *Fatal Path: British Government and Irish Revolution 1910–1922* (London: Faber and Faber, 2013), 141.

85. J. J. Lee, *Ireland 1912–1985: Politics and Society* (Cambridge: Cambridge University Press, 1989), 331.

EPILOGUE

1. See Eileen McGough, *Diarmuid Lynch: A Forgotten Irish Patriot* (Cork: Mercier, 2013).

2. "Lynch's Life Spared on President's Plea," *New York Times*, 21 May 1916, 1.

3. Diarmuid Lynch, "The I.R.B.: Some Recollections and Comments," Document W.S. 4, Bureau of Military History, Defence Forces Ireland, 8.

4. Diarmuid Lynch, *The I.R.B. and the 1916 Insurrection* (Cork: Mercier, 1957), 5.

5. Florence O'Donoghue, in Diarmuid Lynch, *The I.R.B. and the 1916 Insurrection* (Cork: Mercier, 1957), 187.

6. O'Donoghue, in Lynch, *The I.R.B.*, 188.

7. O'Donoghue, in Lynch, *The I.R.B.*, 189.

8. See F. M. Carroll, ed., *The American Commission on Irish Independence 1919: The Diary, Correspondence and Report* (Dublin: Irish Manuscripts Commission, 1985).

9. See Tim Pat Coogan, *De Valera: Long Fellow, Long Shadow* (London: Hutchinson, 1993), 158–159.

10. W. J. Williams, *Report of the Irish White Cross to 31st August, 1922* (New York: American Committee for Relief in Ireland, 1922), 13–14.

11. R. F. Foster, *W. B. Yeats: A Life 2* (Oxford: Oxford University Press, 2003), 2: 164–165.

12. W. B. Yeats, letter to John Quinn, 23 May 1916, John Quinn Memorial Collection, box 54/sec. 1, New York Public Library.

13. Albert Coyle, *Evidence on Conditions in Ireland: Comprising the Complete Testimony, Affidavits and Exhibits Presented Before the American Commission on Conditions in Ireland* (Washington, D.C.: Bliss Building, 1921), ix.

14. Coyle, *Evidence*, x.

15. Carl Wittke, *The Irish in America* (Baton Rouge: Louisiana State University Press, 1956), 275.

16. Bernadette Whelan, *United States Foreign Policy and Ireland: From Empire to Independence 1913–29* (Dublin: Four Courts, 2006), 241.

17. Office of the Historian, U.S. Department of State, "A Guide to the United States' History of Recognition, Diplomatic, and Consular Relations, By Country, Since 1776: Ireland," at http://history.state.gov/countries/Ireland.

18. Donal McCartney, "From Parnell to Pearse: 1891–1921," in *The Course of Irish History*, ed. T. W. Moody and F. X. Martin, 4th ed. (Lanham, Md.: Roberts Rinehart, 2001), 258.

19. Arthur S. Link, ed., *The Papers of Woodrow Wilson* (Princeton, N.J.: Princeton University Press, 1990), 63: 501.

20. Papers of John F. Kennedy, President's Office Files, Speech Files, Address to Irish Parliament, Dublin, 28 June 1963, 2–3.

21. Papers of John F. Kennedy, Address, 4.

22. Papers of John F. Kennedy, Address, 5.

23. Papers of John F. Kennedy, Address, 5.

Sources and Selected Bibliography

From the text itself and the endnotes, a reader becomes well aware of the reliance on newspaper or magazine articles and the documents of principal figures throughout this book. The journalism cited provides both immediacy of the time and a gauge for measuring the changes in public opinion after the Easter Rising and the executions. The archival discoveries reveal new or contextual information, helping to take someone closer to the people involved in relevant events during this period.

Access to ProQuest Historical Newspapers, publications on microfilm, and vigorous usage of the services of Interlibrary Loan made Hesburgh Libraries of the University of Notre Dame indispensable to assembling much of the journalistic-related research. Manuscript documents and official papers were unearthed at numerous institutions far distant from the Notre Dame campus in northern Indiana—including the National Library of Ireland (Dublin), the National Archives of Ireland (Dublin), the University College Dublin Archives, the Trinity College Library (Dublin), the National Archives (Kew), the British Library (London), the Bodleian Library (University of Oxford), the Churchill Archives Centre (Churchill College, University of Cambridge), the Library of Congress (Washington, D.C.), the New York Public Library, and the Georgetown University Library Special Collections Center (Washington, D.C.).

The following books also contributed to a more sophisticated understanding of key individuals and actions of a century (or longer) ago:

Ambrose, Jay, ed. *The Fenian Anthology*. Cork: Mercier, 2008.

Augusteijn, Joost. *Patrick Pearse: The Making of a Revolutionary*. Houndmills, Basinstore, Hampshire: Palgrave Macmillan, 2010.

Bagenal, Philip H. *The American Irish and Their Influence on Irish Politics*. Boston: Roberts Brothers, 1882.

Baker, Ray Stannard. *Woodrow Wilson: Life and Letters*. 8 vols. Garden City, N.Y.: Doubleday, 1927–1939.

Bartlett, Thomas. *Ireland: A History*. Cambridge: Cambridge University Press, 2010.

Barton, Brian. *From Behind a Closed Door: Secret Court Martial Records of the 1916 Easter Rising.* Belfast: Blackstaff, 2002.

Bates, James Leonard. *Senator Thomas J. Walsh of Montana: Law and Public Affairs, from TR to FDR.* Urbana: University of Illinois Press, 1999.

Berg, A. Scott. *Wilson.* New York: G. P. Putnam, 2013.

Berger, Meyer. *The Story of the New York Times, 1851–1951.* New York: Simon and Schuster, 1951.

Bernstorff, Count. *My Three Years in America.* London: Skeffington & Son, 1920.

Bew, Paul. *Ireland: The Politics of Enmity 1789–2006.* Oxford: Oxford University Press, 2007.

Bromage, Mary C. *De Valera and the March of a Nation.* London: Hutchinson, 1956.

Brooks Jr., Cleanth, and Robert Penn Warren, eds. *Understanding Poetry: An Anthology for College Students.* New York: Henry Holt, 1938.

Brown, Thomas N. *Irish-American Nationalism, 1870–1890.* Philadelphia: J. B. Lippincott, 1966.

Carroll, F. M., ed. *The American Commission on Irish Independence 1919: The Diary, Correspondence and Report.* Dublin: Irish Manuscripts Commission, 1985.

Carroll, Francis M. *American Opinion and the Irish Question 1910–23.* Dublin: Gill & Macmillan, 1978.

Caulfield, Max. *The Easter Rebellion.* Dublin: Gill & Macmillan, 1995.

Churchill, Winston S. *The World Crisis: 1911–1918.* 1931. New York: Free Press, 2005.

Coates, Tim, ed. *The Irish Uprising, 1914–21: Papers from the British Parliamentary Archive.* London: Stationery Office, 2000.

Collins, Michael. *The Path to Freedom.* 1922. Dublin: Mercier, 1995.

Colum, Padraic, and Edward J. O'Brien, eds. *Poems of the Irish Revolutionary Brotherhood.* Boston: Small, Maynard, 1916.

Coogan, Tim Pat. *De Valera: Long Fellow, Long Shadow.* London: Hutchinson, 1993.

Coogan, Tim Pat. *Ireland in the Twentieth Century.* London: Hutchinson, 2003.

Coogan, Tim Pat. *Michael Collins: A Biography.* London: Arrow Books, 1991.

Coogan, Tim Pat. *1916: The Easter Rising.* London: Cassell, 2001.

Cooper, John Milton Jr. *Breaking the Heart of the World: Woodrow Wilson and the Fight for the League of Nations.* Cambridge: Cambridge University Press, 2001.

Cooper, John Milton. *Woodrow Wilson: A Biography.* 2009. New York: Vintage, 2011.

Costello, Francis. *The Irish Revolution and Its Aftermath, 1916–1923: Years of Revolt.* Dublin: Irish Academic Press, 2003.

Coyle, Albert, ed. *Evidence on Conditions in Ireland: Comprising the Complete Testimony, Affidavits and Exhibits Presented Before the American Commission on Conditions in Ireland.* Washington, D.C.: Bliss Building, 1921.

Cronin, Sean. *The McGarrity Papers.* Tralee: Anvil Books, 1972.

Cronon, E. David, ed. *The Cabinet Diaries of Josephus Daniels: 1913–1921.* Lincoln: University of Nebraska Press, 1963.

Crowley, Brian. *Patrick Pearse: A Life in Pictures*. Cork: Mercier, 2013.

Daly, Mary E., and Margaret O'Callaghan, eds. *1916 in 1966: Commemorating the Easter Rising*. Dublin: Royal Irish Academy, 2007.

Dangerfield, George. *The Damnable Question: A History of Anglo-Irish Relations*. Boston: Little, Brown, 1976.

Davis, Elmer. *History of the New York Times 1851–1921*. New York: New York Times, 1921.

de Burca, Seamus. *The Soldier's Song: The Story of Peadar O Cearnaigh*. Dublin: P. J. Bourke, 1957.

de Paor, Liam. *On the Easter Proclamation and Other Declarations*. Dublin: Four Courts, 1997.

de Valera, Eamon. *Recent Speeches and Broadcasts*. Dublin: Talbot, 1933.

de Valera, Terry. *A Memoir*. Dublin: Currach, 2004.

Devoy, John. *Recollections of an Irish Rebel*. New York: Charles P. Young, 1929.

Dezell, Maureen. *Irish America: Coming into Clover*. New York: Doubleday, 2001.

Doherty, Gabriel, and Dermot Keogh, eds. *1916: The Long Revolution*. Cork: Mercier, 2007.

Doherty, Gabriel, and Dermot Keogh, eds. *De Valera's Irelands*. Dublin: Mercier, 2003.

Dolan, Jay P. *The Irish Americans: A History*. New York: Bloomsbury, 2008.

Dooley, Terence. *"The Greatest of the Fenians": John Devoy and Ireland*. Dublin: Wolfhound, 2003.

Doorley, Michael. *Irish-American Diaspora Nationalism: The Friends of Irish Freedom 1916–1935*. Dublin: Four Courts, 2005.

Duff, Charles. *Six Days to Shake an Empire: Events and Factors Behind the Irish Rebellion of 1916*. South Brunswick, N.J.: A. S. Barnes, 1967.

Duffy, Francis P. *Father Duffy's Story: A Tale of Humor and Heroism, Of Life and Death with the Fighting Sixty-Ninth*. Garden City, N.Y.: Garden City Publishing, 1919.

Dwane, David T. *Early Life of Eamonn de Valera*. Dublin: Talbot, 1922, 1927.

Dwyer, T. Ryle. *De Valera: The Man & the Myths*. Dublin: Poolbeg, 1991.

Dwyer, T. Ryle. *De Valera's Darkest Hour: In Search of National Independence, 1919–1932*. Dublin: Mercier, 1982.

Eagleton, Terry. *The Truth About the Irish*. Dublin: New Island, 1999.

Edwards, Owen Dudley, and Fergus Pyle, eds. *1916: The Easter Rising*. London: MacGibbon and Lee, 1968.

Edwards, Owen Dudley. *Eamon de Valera*. Cardiff: GPC, 1987.

Edwards, Ruth Dudley. *James Connolly*. Dublin: Gill & Macmillan, 1981.

Edwards, Ruth Dudley. *Patrick Pearse: The Triumph of Failure*. 1977. Dublin: Irish Academic Press, 2006.

Enright, Seán. *Easter Rising 1916: The Trials*. Sallins, Ireland: Merrion, 2014.

Fanning, Ronan. *Fatal Path: British Government and Irish Revolution 1910–1922*. London: Faber and Faber, 2013.

Ferguson, Niall. *The Pity of War*. London: Allen Lane, 1998.

Ferriter, Diarmaid. *Judging Dev: A Reassessment of the Life and Legacy of Eamon de Valera*. Dublin: Royal Irish Academy, 2007.

FitzHenry, Edna C., ed. *Nineteen-Sixteen: An Anthology*. Dublin: Browne and Nolan, 1935.

Fitzpatrick, David. *Harry Boland's Irish Revolution*. Cork: Cork University Press, 2003.

Fitzsimons, M. A., Thomas T. McAvoy, and Frank O'Malley, eds. *The Image of Man: A Review of Politics Reader*. Notre Dame, Ind.: University of Notre Dame Press, 1959.

Foster, R. F. *Modern Ireland 1600–1972*. London: Allen Lane, 1988.

Foster, R. F. *Vivid Faces: The Revolutionary Generation in Ireland 1890–1923*. London: Allen Lane, 2014.

Foster, R. F. *W. B. Yeats: A Life*. 2 vols. Oxford: Oxford University Press, 1997–2003.

Foy, Michael, and Brian Barton. *The Easter Rising*. Stroud, U.K.: Sutton, 1999.

Freud, Sigmund, and William C. Bullitt. *Thomas Woodrow Wilson: A Psychological Study*. 1967. New Brunswick, N.J.: Transaction, 1999.

Gaffney, T. St. John. *Breaking the Silence: England, Ireland, Wilson and the War*. New York: Horace Liveright, 1930.

Gilbert, Martin. *First World War*. London: Weidenfeld and Nicolson, 1994.

Golway, Terry. *Irish Rebel: John Devoy and America's Fight for Ireland's Freedom*. New York: St. Martin's, 1998.

Gwynn, Denis. *De Valera*. London: Jarrolds, 1933.

Gwynn, Stephen, ed. *The Letters and Friendships of Sir Cecil Spring Rice*. 2 vols. Boston: Houghton Mifflin, 1929.

Hannigan, Dave. *De Valera in America: The Rebel President's 1919 Campaign*. Dublin: O'Brien, 2008.

Harris, Roy J. Jr. *Pulitzer's Gold: Behind the Prize for Public Service Journalism*. Columbia: University of Missouri Press, 2007.

Hartley, Stephen. *The Irish Question as a Problem in British Foreign Policy, 1914–18*. New York: St. Martin's, 1987.

Hegarty, Neil. *Story of Ireland*. London: BBC Books, 2011.

Hegarty, Shane, and Fintan O'Toole. *The Irish Times Book of the 1916 Rising*. Dublin: Gill & Macmillan, 2006.

Heron, James Connolly, ed. *The Words of James Connolly*. Cork: Mercier, 1986.

Hobsbawn, Eric. *The Age of Empire 1875–1914*. New York: Pantheon, 1987.

Hodgson, Godfrey. *Woodrow Wilson's Right Hand: The Life of Colonel Edward M. House*. New Haven: Yale University Press, 2006.

Horgan, John J. *Parnell to Pearse: Some Recollections and Reflections*. 1948. Dublin: University College Dublin Press, 2009.

Ireland, Tom. *Ireland: Past and Present*. New York: G. P. Putnam, 1942.

Jeffery, Keith. *Ireland and the Great War*. Cambridge: Cambridge University Press, 2000.

Jenkins, Roy. *Asquith: Portrait of a Man and an Era*. New York: Chilmark, 1964.

Johnston, Kevin. *Home or Away: The Great War and the Irish Revolution*. Dublin: Gill & Macmillan, 2010.

Jordan, Neil. *Michael Collins: Film Diary and Screenplay*. London: Vintage, 1996.

Joy, Maurice, ed. *The Irish Rebellion of 1916 and Its Martyrs: Erin's Tragic Easter*. New York: Devin-Adair, 1916.

Kee, Robert. *The Green Flag: A History of Irish Nationalism*. London: Weidenfeld and Nicolson, 1972.

Kenny, Kevin. *The American Irish: A History*. New York: Longman, 2000.

Killeen, Richard. *A Short History of the 1916 Rising*. Dublin: Gill & Macmillan, 2009.

Kilmer, Joyce. *Main Street and Other Poems*. New York: George H. Doran, 1917.

Kilmer, Joyce. *Poems, Essays and Letters in Two Volumes*. Edited by Robert Cortes Holliday. 2 vols. New York: George H. Doran, 1918.

Kilmer, Joyce. *The Circus and Other Essays and Fugitive Pieces*. Edited by Robert Cortes Holliday. New York: George H. Doran, 1921.

Kilmer, Joyce. *Trees & Other Poems*. Garden City, N.Y.: Doubleday, 1914.

Kilmer, Joyce. *Trees and Other Poems*. London: Duckworth, 1941.

Kilmer, Joyce, ed. *Dreams and Images: An Anthology of Catholics Poets*. New York: Boni and Liveright, 1917.

Kilmer, Kenton. *Memories of My Father, Joyce Kilmer*. New Brunswick, N.J.: Joyce Kilmer Centennial Commission, 1993.

Kissane, Bill. *The Politics of the Irish Civil War*. Oxford: Oxford University Press, 2005.

Laffan, Michael. *The Resurrection of Ireland: The Sinn Féin Party, 1916–1923*. Cambridge: Cambridge University Press, 1999.

Lansing, Robert. *The Peace Negotiations: A Personal Narrative*. Boston: Houghton Mifflin, 1921.

Lee, J. J. *Ireland 1912–1985: Politics and Society*. Cambridge: Cambridge University Press, 1989.

Lee, J. J., and Marion R. Casey, eds. *Making the Irish American: History and Heritage of the Irish in the United States*. New York: New York University Press, 2006.

Lee, Joseph. *The Modernisation of Irish Society, 1848–1918*. Dublin: Gill & Macmillan, 1973.

Le Roux, Louis N. *Tom Clarke and the Irish Freedom Movement*. Dublin: Talbot, 1936.

Leslie, Shane. *American Wonderland: Memories of Four Tours in the United States of America*. London: M. Joseph, 1936.

Leslie, Shane. *The Irish Issue in Its American Aspect: A Contribution to the Settlement of Anglo-American Relations During and After the Great War*. New York: Charles Scribner's Sons, 1917.

Link, Arthur S. *Wilson: The Road to the White House*. Princeton, N.J.: Princeton University Press, 1947.

Link, Arthur S., ed. *The Papers of Woodrow Wilson*. 69 vols. Princeton, N.J.: Princeton University Press, 1966–1994.

Lloyd George, David. *Memoirs of the Peace Conference*. 2 vols. New Haven: Yale University Press, 1939.

Llywelyn, Morgan. *1916*. New York: Forge, 1998.

Longford, Earl of, and Thomas P. O'Neill. *Eamon de Valera*. London: Hutchinson, 1970.

Lynch, Diarmuid. *The I.R.B. and the 1916 Insurrection*. Cork: Mercier, 1957.

Macardle, Dorothy. *The Irish Republic: A Documented Chronicle of the Anglo-Irish Conflict and the Partitioning of Ireland, with a Detailed Account of the Period 1916–1923*. 1937. Dublin: Wolfhound, 1999.

MacKenzie, F. A. *The Irish Rebellion: What Happened and Why*. London: C. Arthur Pearson, 1916.

MacManus, M. J. *Eamon de Valera: A Biography*. 1944. Dublin: Talbot, 1957.

Macmillan, Margaret. *Paris 1919: Six Months That Changed the World*. 2001. New York: Random House, 2003.

Macmillan, Margaret. *The War That Ended Peace: The Road to 1914*. New York: Random House, 2013.

Martin, F. X., ed. *Leaders and Men of the Easter Rising: Dublin 1916*. London: Methuen, 1967.

McCaffrey, Lawrence J. *Textures of Irish America*. Syracuse: Syracuse University Press, 1992.

McCaffrey, Lawrence J. *The Irish Diaspora in America*. Bloomington: Indiana University Press, 1976.

McCartan, Patrick. *With De Valera in America*. New York: Brentano, 1932.

McCourt, Malachy. *Malachy McCourt's History of Ireland*. Philadelphia: Running Press, 2004.

McCullough, Joseph. *A Pocket History of Ireland*. Dublin: Gill & Macmillan, 2010.

McGarry, Fearghal. *The Rising: Ireland: Easter 1916*. Oxford: Oxford University Press, 2010.

McGough, Eileen. *Diarmuid Lynch: A Forgotten Irish Patriot*. Cork: Mercier, 2013.

McGuire, James, and James Quinn, eds. *Dictionary of Irish Biography*. 9 vols. Cambridge: Cambridge University Press, 2009.

McMahon, Sean. *Rebel Ireland: From Easter Rising to Civil War*. Cork: Mercier, 2001.

Miller, Kerby A. *Emigrants and Exiles: Ireland and the Irish Exodus to North America*. New York: Oxford University Press, 1985.

Mitchell, Angus. *Roger Casement*. Dublin: O'Brien, 2013.

Moody, T. W., and F. X. Martin, eds. *The Course of Irish History*. 4th ed. Lanham, Md.: Roberts Rinehart, 2001.

Moody, T. W., ed. *The Fenian Movement*. Cork: Mercier, 1978.

Morris, Edmund. *Colonel Roosevelt*. New York: Random House, 2010.

Neu, Charles E. *Colonel House: A Biography of Woodrow Wilson's Silent Partner.* New York: Oxford University Press, 2014.

Nordholt, Jan Willem Schulte. *Woodrow Wilson: A Life for World Peace.* Translated by Herbert H. Rowen. Berkeley: University of California Press, 1991.

O'Brien, Conor Cruise. *States of Ireland.* London: Hutchinson, 1972.

O'Brien, Conor Cruise, ed. *The Shaping of Modern Ireland.* London: Routledge & Kegan Paul, 1960.

O'Brien, Mark, and Kevin Rafter, eds. *Independent Newspapers: A History.* Dublin: Four Courts, 2012.

O'Brien, William, and Desmond Ryan, eds. *Devoy's Post Bag: 1871–1928.* 2 vols. Dublin: Fallon, 1948.

Ó Broin, León. *Revolutionary Underground: The Story of the Irish Republican Brotherhood 1858–1924.* Dublin: Gill & Macmillan, 1976.

Ó Broin, León. *W. E. Wylie and the Irish Revolution 1916–1921.* Dublin: Gill & Macmillan, 1989.

O Brolchain, Honor. *Joseph Plunkett.* Dublin: O'Brien, 2012.

Ó Buachalla, Séamas, ed. *The Letters of P. H. Pearse.* Atlantic Highlands, N.J.: Humanities Press, 1980.

Ó Conchubhair, Brian, ed. *Dublin's Fighting Story 1916–21.* Cork: Mercier, 2009.

O'Connor, John. *The 1916 Proclamation.* Rev. ed. Dublin: Anvil, 1999.

O'Doherty, Katherine. *Assignment: America; De Valera's Mission to the United States.* New York: De Tanko, 1957.

O'Donnell, Kenneth P., and David F. Powers with Joe McCarthy, *"Johnny, We Hardly Knew Ye."* Boston: Little, Brown, 1970.

Ó Dubhghaill, M., ed. *Insurrection Fires at Eastertide: A Golden Jubilee Anthology of the Easter Rising.* Cork: Mercier, 1966.

Ó Faoláin, Seán. *The Life Story of Eamon de Valera.* Dublin: Talbot, 1933.

O'Farrell, Patrick. *Ireland's English Question: Anglo-Irish Relations 1534–1970.* New York: Schocken, 1971.

O'Leary, John. *Recollections of Fenians and Fenianism.* 2 vols. London: Downey, 1896.

Ó Siocháin, Séamas. *Roger Casement: Imperialist, Rebel, Revolutionary.* Dublin: Lilliput, 2008.

Parks, Edd Winfield, and Aileen Wells Parks. *Thomas MacDonagh: The Man, the Patriot, the Writer.* Athens: University of Georgia Press, 1967.

Pašeta, Senia. *Modern Ireland: A Very Short Introduction.* Oxford: Oxford University Press, 2003.

Pearse, Mary Brigid, ed. *The Home-Life of Pádraig Pearse: As Told by Himself, His Family, and Friends.* Dublin: Brown and Nolan, 1934.

Pearse, Padraic. *Collected Works of Padraic H. Pearse: Political Writings and Speeches.* Dublin and London: Maunsel & Roberts, 1922.

Redmond-Howard, L. G. *Six Days of the Irish Republic: A Narrative and Critical Account of the Latest Phase of Irish Politics*. Boston: John W. Luce, 1916.

Reynolds, David. *The Long Shadow: The Legacies of the Great War in the Twentieth Century*. New York: W. W. Norton, 2014.

Rutherford, John. *The Secret History of the Fenian Conspiracy: Its Origin, Objects, & Ramifications*. 2 vols. London: C. Kegan Paul, 1877.

Ryan, Desmond. *The Phoenix Flame: A Study of Fenianism and John Devoy*. London: Arthur Barker, 1937.

Ryan, Desmond. *Unique Dictator: A Study of Eamon de Valera*. London: Arthur Barker, 1936.

Shaw, Bernard. *Prefaces*. London: Constable, 1934.

Sheehy-Skeffington, Hanna. *Impressions of Sinn Féin in America*. Dublin: Davis, 1919.

Smith, Gene. *When the Cheering Stopped: The Last Years of Woodrow Wilson*. New York: Morrow, 1964.

Steffan, Jack. *The Long Fellow: The Story of the Great Irish Patriot EAMON DE VALERA*. New York: Macmillan, 1966.

Stephens, James. *The Insurrection in Dublin*. Dublin: Maunsel, 1916.

Tansill, Charles Callan. *America and the Fight for Irish Freedom 1866–1922: An Old Story Based Upon New Data*. New York: Devin-Adair, 1957.

Taylor, A. J. P. *The First World War: An Illustrated History*. London: Hamish Hamilton, 1963.

Thompson, William Irwin. *The Imagination of an Insurrection, Dublin, Easter 1916: A Study of an Ideological Movement*. New York: Oxford University Press, 1967.

Townshend, Charles. *Easter 1916: The Irish Rebellion*. 2005. London: Penguin, 2006.

Tubridy, Ryan. *JFK in Ireland: Four Days That Changed a President*. London: Collins, 2010.

Tuchman, Barbara. *The Proud Tower: A Portrait of the World Before the War, 1890–1914*. New York: Macmillan, 1966.

Tumulty, Joseph P. *Woodrow Wilson as I Know Him*. Garden City, N.Y.: Doubleday, Page, 1921.

Walker, Stephen. *Forgotten Soldiers: The Irishmen Shot at Dawn*. Dublin: Gill & Macmillan, 2008.

Walsh, Maurice. *The News from Ireland: Foreign Correspondents and the Irish Revolution*. London: I. B. Tauris, 2008.

Ward, Alan J. *The Easter Rising: Revolution and Irish Nationalism*. Arlington Heights, Ill.: AHM, 1980.

Webber, Christopher L. *Give Me Liberty: Speakers and Speeches That Have Shaped America*. New York: Pegasus, 2014.

Weekly Irish Times. 1916 Rebellion Handbook. 1916. Belfast: Mourne River, 1998.

Wells, H. G. *The Shape of Things to Come*. 1933. New York: Macmillan, 1936.

Wells, Warre B., and N. Marlowe. *A History of the Irish Rebellion of 1916.* Dublin: Maunsel, 1916.

Whelan, Bernadette. *United States Foreign Policy and Ireland: From Empire to Independence, 1913–29.* Dublin: Four Courts, 2006.

Williams, W. J. *Report of the Irish White Cross to 31st August, 1922.* New York: American Committee for Relief in Ireland, 1922.

Wills, Clair. *Dublin 1916: The Siege of the GPO.* London: Profile, 2009.

Wittke, Carl. *The Irish in America.* Baton Rouge: Louisiana State University Press, 1956.

Yeats, W. B. *The Collected Poems of W. B. Yeats.* Edited by Richard J. Finneran. Rev. 2nd ed. New York: Scribner, 1996.

Index

Photos featured in the gallery are marked with "G."